Chicago Public Library

REFERENCE

Form 178 rev. 1-94

Women and Property
in China, 960–1949

Law, Society, and Culture in China

EDITORS

Philip C. C. Huang and Kathryn Bernhardt

ADVISORY BOARD

William P. Alford, William T. Rowe, Hugh Scogin, Jr.
Jonathan Spence, Alexander Woodside

The opening of archives on legal case records and judicial administration in China has made possible a new examination of past assumptions about the Chinese justice system. Scholars can now ask where actual legal practice deviated from official and popular conceptualizations and depictions. In the process, they can arrive at a new understanding not only of the legal system, but of state-society relations and the nature of the Chinese social-political system as a whole.

Studies of Chinese justice also permit the joining together of social and cultural history. Historians of society and economy, on the one hand, and of mentalities and culture, on the other, have long tended to go their separate ways. Law, however, is a sphere of life in which the two are inseparable. Legal case records contain evidence for both practice and representation. A study of law can tell us about the interconnections between actions and attitudes in ways that segmented studies of each cannot.

This series comprises major new studies by the editors themselves, as well as other contributions from a new generation of scholarship, grounded both in the archives and in new theoretical approaches.

Women and Property in China, 960–1949

Kathryn Bernhardt

STANFORD UNIVERSITY PRESS, STANFORD, CALIFORNIA

Stanford University Press
Stanford, California
© 1999 by the Board of Trustees of the
Leland Stanford Junior University

Portions of Chapter 1 previously appeared
in *Modern China* 21 (3: 269–309) and
are reprinted here by permission of
Sage Publications.

Printed in the United States of America

CIP data appear at the end of the book

Acknowledgments

Writing a book has got to be the most solitary and lonely of pursuits, but I have been fortunate to have had an exceptionally hospitable and supportive environment in which to write this one. Philip Huang, my colleague and husband, has provided intellectual companionship from beginning to end. I have benefited immensely from his own work on civil justice in China, and I treasure the hours we spent discussing our respective topics. Our shared interest has made the writing of this book all the more enjoyable and rewarding.

I have also been fortunate to have worked with a number of graduate students at UCLA, both past and present, whose interests are also in the fields of Chinese legal history and/or Chinese women's history. These include Yasuhiko Karasawa, Margaret Kuo, Lu Zhongqi, Jennifer Neighbors, Bradly Reed, Matthew Sommer, David Wakefield, Alison Yeung, and Zhou Guangyuan. I have learned a tremendous amount from them. I have also benefited greatly from the gathering of Chinese legal historians from home and abroad at the conferences Philip Huang and I convened under our Luce Foundation grant for "Local Archives and Court Records: Social Change and the Law in Qing and Republican China."

Numerous people read parts or all of the manuscript at different stages and offered both criticism and encouragement. Philip Huang, especially, read and commented on each draft of each chapter, and through our discussions, helped me clarify and refine my thinking. Two anonymous readers for Stanford University Press reviewed the manuscript with unusual care, suggesting ways for improvement on points both large and small. I am also grateful for the helpful comments I received from Joseph Esherick, Robert Hymes, Hal Kahn, Margaret Kuo, Fuma Susumu, Matthew Sommer, Shiga Shūzō, and Hugh Scogin. A special thanks also to Bettine Birge and Shinno Reiko for helping me keep current on Japanese scholarship on the Song, and to Karen Fukushima, Lu Zhongqi, and Jennifer MacFarlane for providing valuable research assistance.

This book would not have been possible without court case records. I owe a special debt of gratitude to the archivists at the Second Historical Archives (Nanjing), the Sichuan Provincial Archives, and the Beijing Municipal Archives for making their collections available. Grants from the Luce Foundation and the Committee on Scholarly Communication with China (CSCC) funded trips to China and the reproduction of materials. Financial support for the writing of this book was provided by the National Endowment for the Humanities and the University of California President's Research Program.

Finally, I would like to express my thanks to Muriel Bell and Stacey Lynn of Stanford University Press for their professional handling of the manuscript, and to Barbara Mnookin, once again, for her superb copyediting.

K.B.
February 1999

Contents

Tables

Women and Property
in China, 960–1949

Introduction

Past scholarship has presented a static picture of property inheritance in China, mainly because it has taken as its primary focus men, whose rights in fact changed little over the centuries. When our focus shifts to women, however, a very different and dynamic picture of property rights emerges. Women's rights to property changed substantially from the Song through the Qing and even more dramatically in the twentieth century under the Republican Civil Code. It is through an examination of those transformations in women's claims that we can best discern the larger changes taking place in property rights as a whole. This book is thus at once a study of women's rights to property specifically and a study of property rights in general.

It is also a study that would not be complete without treating both the imperial period and the Republican period. Imperial and Republican inheritance laws were based on radically different concepts of property, the full implications of which cannot be truly appreciated when each period is studied separately. When the two are examined in conjunction, however, each serves to illuminate the other: the distinctive characteristics of the property logic of each period become clear only when studied against the property logic of the other.

The Issues

As is well known, inheritance in imperial China was governed by the principles and practices of household division: equal division among sons of the father's property. Women, it is generally assumed, had no inheritance rights. At most, an unmarried daughter would be provided with a dowry, if the family could afford one, and a widowed mother would be provided with old-age maintenance, but neither had the right to an independent share of the property.

As is also well known, household division was accompanied by the principles and practices of patrilineal succession: a man had to be succeeded by a son for ritual as well as for property purposes. If he did not have a son of his own, he had to adopt one to carry on his line and to continue the ancestral sacrifices. Patrilineal succession, it is generally assumed, reinforced household division. They were but two aspects of the same phenomenon—inheritance by sons only.

This understanding of household division and patrilineal succession has given rise to a static picture of the inheritance regime of late imperial China, and understandably so. So long as attention is fastened on fathers and sons, one would indeed be hard put to find evidence of significant change from the Song through the Qing, for their rights in fact changed little.

But as this book will demonstrate, the conventional picture leaves out large parts of the story and distorts important parts of the remainder. And it does so because it fails to consider property from the point of view of women in their different capacities as daughters, wives, and concubines. Seen in that light, household division and patrilineal succession are revealed as separate processes with different implications for property inheritance. The principles and practices of household division came into play when a man had birth sons, and those of patrilineal succession when he did not. Moreover, the rules of succession changed in important ways in the Ming and Qing.

Of the two, household division was the much more common form of inheritance in imperial China, although patrilineal succession was by no means insignificant. Something on the order of one family out of every five did not have sons who survived to adulthood.[1] Thus, inheritance in as many as a fifth of families in imperial times took the form not of household division, but of patrilineal succession.

1. Only an adult son could be his father's patrilineal heir. As Ted Telford found in his study of 41 lineage groups in Tongcheng county, Anhui, from 1520 to 1661, 17 percent of married men had no sons who survived to adulthood (1995: 62, 79). Liu Ts'ui-jung reports a similar rate, 17 to 24 percent, among five lineages in central and South China from the fourteenth through the nineteenth centuries (1995: 105, 107). All together, of the 23,029 married men in their two studies, 19 percent (4,348) did not have birth heirs.

For a woman, patrilineal succession mattered even more because of her membership in two separate families, her natal and her marital, during the course of her life. As a daughter, a woman stood about a 6 to 12 percent chance of being born into a family with no surviving sons.[2] And as a wife, she stood roughly a 20 percent chance of being married to a man who had no birth heirs. Thus as many as one woman in three was either a daughter without brothers or a wife without sons (or both), and likely to be involved in patrilineal succession sometime in her life.

Equally important, litigation over inheritance in imperial times was overwhelmingly over patrilineal succession, not household division. The reasons for the discrepancy will be examined later. Suffice it to note here that in the collection of 430 Song to Qing inheritance cases on which this study draws, lawsuits over the adoption of an heir for a sonless man outnumbered those over household division by four to one. That disproportionately high incidence of succession suits is also reflected in the relative attention accorded to each process in the Qing code: household division is covered in just four brief statutes and substatutes totaling a little over 200 characters, compared with 11 laws totaling some 1,100 characters on succession. Patrilineal succession was thus constituted as a legal problem in a way that household division was not.

To anticipate our story, the entry point for the analysis of the late imperial period centers on situations in which the inheritance claims of women have to be considered in their own right, because of the absence of brothers in the case of daughters and the absence of the husband and sons in the case of sonless widows. It is these women, as daughters and wives in the absence of men, who bring out in sharpest relief the different implications of patrilineal succession.

Seen from their points of view, property rights turn out to have been very far from static in imperial China, as conventional wisdom would have it. The first big change came in the early Ming, with the adoption of the legal requirement that all sonless families establish a lineage nephew to be the patrilineal heir to the father, or, in the terms of this book, the adoption of "mandatory nephew succession." That development cost women dearly, seriously dimin-

2. Available fertility and mortality data suggest that married men in the Ming and Qing periods had on average three to four children who survived to adulthood (J. Lee et al. 1995: 173–80; Liu Ts'ui-jung 1995: 99–100; Telford 1995: 67). By genetic chance alone (and assuming for simplicity's sake a sex rate of 100 and not 105), we would expect 12.5 percent of those with three children and 6.25 percent of those with four to have all daughters.

ishing the property claims of both daughters and widows in the ensuing years.

For a daughter, the adoption of mandatory nephew succession in the early Ming meant a virtual loss of any right to inherit in the absence of brothers.[3] Simply put, whereas in the Song a daughter was legally entitled to inherit the family property should her parents die without any sons, whether biological or adopted, under the rule of nephew succession, the claims of nephews took precedence over her claims. A daughter's likelihood of inheriting property by default was very remote.

For a widow, the new rule meant, if not a total loss, at least a severe contraction in her inheritance rights. Where once she stood to inherit all of her husband's property in the absence of sons, she now had merely custodial powers over it, responsible for preserving it for her husband's heir, one that she herself was now legally obligated to adopt. Moreover, initially under the rules of mandatory nephew succession, she had no choice but to adopt the lineage nephew most closely related to her husband.

In time, however, in a change driven in great measure by the growing power of the chaste widow ideal, that requirement was dropped. As is well known, the Ming and Qing saw the rise and solidification of the cult of female chastity. For a widow, the insistence that she not remarry after her husband's death turned out, somewhat surprisingly, to be empowering, at least as far as inheritance was concerned. In legal practice, Ming and Qing judges, acting out of the conviction that a chaste widow deserved the heir of her choice, consistently allowed the widow to reject her husband's closest nephew. Then, in the mid-Qing, the state adopted formal legislation granting her the right to choose freely from among all of the lineage nephews. That expansion in the range of a widowed wife's custodial powers within the nephew succession regime was

3. My use of the term "rights" to describe women's property claims in the imperial period is based on the analysis of magisterial adjudication in Philip Huang's 1996 book, *Civil Justice in China: Representation and Practice in the Qing*. There he demonstrates that, though the Qing state did not have an abstract conception of rights in the Western sense of absolute rights protected by law and independent of the will of the ruler, the Qing code nevertheless contained numerous stipulations that local magistrates consistently used to uphold legitimate property and contractual claims from infringement by others. Conversely, as he also demonstrates, litigants sought recourse to the courts to safeguard their property. The practical consequence of the legal system was therefore the protection of legitimate claims, and to that extent, one can speak of the existence of "rights" (see especially Huang's chap. 4). For the imperial period, I use "rights" in this sense of rights in practice.

the second big change to come in women's property and inheritance rights in the late imperial period.

The custodial rights of widowed concubines over property also expanded as a result of the growth of the chaste widow ideal. For a concubine, as we shall see, widow chastity proved to be the great equalizer, erasing the status distinction that had previously prevented her from sharing any of the wife's claims on her husband's property. By the Qing, a woman's status as a wife or a concubine came to matter less than whether she was a chaste widow. A concubine came to be entitled to the same rights accorded to any chaste widow, including custodial powers over her deceased husband's property and the right to adopt the heir of her choice.

When we turn our attention to the transition from imperial to Republican law, we find patrilineal succession as a crucial point of change between the old and the new. In the early Republican period, although the Qing laws on mandatory nephew succession remained in force on paper, the interim Supreme Court, or Daliyuan, chose to interpret them in such a way as to grant widowed wives complete autonomy in the selection of an heir, even if she chose to go outside of her husband's lineage nephews. In so doing, it effectively overturned the basic principle of nephew succession. That was an important change, introduced within the conceptual frame of the old system.

The old system and its concepts were finally overturned by the Republican Civil Code of 1929–30. Adopting a single new inheritance regime based on the Western concept of individual property, the code removed patrilineal succession from any relevance to inheritance. It did not mandate the appointment of a male heir for a deceased sonless man, nor did it recognize the property claims of patrilineal kin. At the same time, in keeping with its emphasis on gender equality, the code granted women the same inheritance rights as men in principle.

The full implications of those changes in the laws can best be understood through an examination of legal practice as revealed in court case records. The new code was, after all, superimposed on a society long accustomed to operating by household division and patrilineal succession. And it was in the courtroom where the new legal principles came into direct conflict with ages-old established social practices. The result was a complex picture, neither one of simple radical change suggested by the letter of the laws nor one of simple continuity suggested by the powerful persistence of old

practices. Rather, contestations between the new and the old manifested themselves at specific points of tension, with varied implications for women in their different capacities. For all the lawmakers' good intentions, women lost old powers even as they gained
new ones.

Source Materials

To understand the changes in property rights over time, we must
look beyond the codes themselves and study the law in action
through court case records. For the imperial period, the successive
dynastic codes, by themselves, offer little evidence of change. At
most, they reveal subtle revisions of wording and the addition of
new substatutes whose implications are not readily apparent. For
the Republican period, attention on the civil code alone can all too
easily lead to an exaggerated picture of change and a neglect of the
practical effects of some Western-derived principles.

For court cases from the imperial period, the book draws on three
different types of materials. The first is the original archival records
for 68 inheritance-related cases of the Qing period. Those records
contain all manner of documentation generated during litigation,
notably plaints, counterplaints, magistrate instructions, and court
judgments, and involve five different jurisdictions: Qufu county,
Shandong, from the 1710's to the 1890's; Baxian county, Sichuan,
from the 1760's to the 1850's; Baodi county, Shuntian prefecture,
from the 1830's to the 1900's; Danshui subprefecture and Xinzhu
county, Taiwan, from the 1840's to the 1890's; and Taihu subprefecture, Jiangsu, in the 1870's.

In addition, I have drawn on published collections of original
court decisions. Some of these works incorporate the judgments of
numerous officials (the best-known of this sort being the *Collection
of Lucid Decisions by Celebrated Judges* [Minggong shupan qing-
mingji] of the Song period). Others present a single official's judicial
rulings. These latter collections, usually put out by the officials
themselves right after the expiration of a term in office, consist at
most of verbatim reproductions of instructions (*pici*) and judgments
(*tangduan*), and provide only partial documentation of court cases.
Without the litigants' plaints for the essential background, it is often difficult to get a complete picture of any particular case. But for
my purposes, that disadvantage is more than balanced by the fact
that the authors, with eventual publication in mind and out of a de-

sire to showcase their own legal acumen and moral wisdom, tended to write longer and more detailed rulings than was normally the case. They also tended to offer lengthy explanations for their decisions and extended commentary on laws, again something normally not found in the archival documents.

Finally, I have relied on narrative accounts of lawsuits set out in the diaries and autobiographies of local officials. Composed in a storytelling fashion, a typical account begins with the nature and cause of the dispute, continues to the official's interrogation of the litigants, and ends with his resolution of the suit. Interspersed throughout the narrative are the author's personal reflections on the case and the applicable laws. Like the published judicial rulings, these accounts are invariably one-sided and self-glorifying, but they too permit us to see how officials themselves read and understood the law.

For the Republican period, the book relies principally on the original archival court records for 370 inheritance cases. Of that number, 96 are appeals cases heard by the Daliyuan, China's highest court in the 1910's and 1920's, and 134 are appeals cases heard by the Capital Superior Court (*Jingshi gaodeng shenpanting*) located in Beijing, also in the 1910's and 1920's. The remaining 140 sets of records cover cases originating at the Capital District Court (*Jingshi difang shenpanting*) and its successor, the Beijing District Court (*Beijing difang fayuan*), from the 1910's through the 1940's. In roughly half of those cases, the litigants appealed the district court's decision to higher courts, with the result that for some of the more hotly contested disputes the various court judgments alone ran to more than 200 pages.

The Song Baseline

A word, finally, about the Song, with which this book opens. Past scholarship, mainly Japanese, has for a variety of fortuitous reasons come to see the Song as an exception to imperial China, as a period when a daughter enjoyed independent inheritance rights to property under a half-share law that supposedly entitled her to half of what a son got at the time of household division. Even though scholars have accepted this "law" as fact, it seems to me that none has provided a satisfactory explanation for why the Song should have stood apart from the rest of imperial history.

This book begins with a reexamination of the extant evidence and arguments about the Song in order to construct a solid baseline from which to assess the later changes. Readers should be fore-warned that the discussion will, of necessity, be a dense one, given the weight of past scholarship and the need for a close scrutiny of all of the available evidence. That chapter concludes that there was no "half-share law" in the Song and indeed could not have been. In-stead, the principles of patrilineal succession applied, and women enjoyed inheritance rights only by default, in the absence of broth-ers and sons. What set the Song apart from the Ming and Qing was that there was as yet no mandatory nephew succession, with all that that implied for women's inheritance rights.

CHAPTER ONE

The Inheritance Rights of Daughters from the Song Through the Qing

Scholars of Chinese legal and social history have long been intrigued by apparent evidence that daughters had stronger rights to family property during the Southern Song than at any other time in Chinese history before the twentieth century. The evidence comes from the *Collection of Lucid Decisions by Celebrated Judges* (Minggong shupan qingmingji; hereafter referred to as *Qingmingji* and cited as *QMJ*), a collection of 473 Southern Song judgments. Several of the cases suggest that a daughter had the legal right to a set share of property half the size of a son's share at the time of family division, and that she enjoyed a greater claim still if her father's household died out for lack of a male heir.

This point became a matter of heated debate between the modern Japanese legal scholars Niida Noboru and Shiga Shūzō (Niida 1942, 1962; Shiga 1953–55, 1967). At issue were not only the rights of daughters, but what they revealed about the nature of family property and the relationship between property inheritance and patrilineal succession in imperial China.

Niida, following in the tradition of his mentor Nakada Kaoru, contends that family property (*jiachan*) in imperial China was commonly owned by all members of the household, male or female (*kazoku kyōsansei; jiazu gongchanzhi*). It was this co-ownership, not any principle of ritual or lineal succession, that dictated the transmission of property from one generation to the next. In Niida's view, daughters were co-owners (*kyōyūsha; gongyouzhe*) of family property along with sons and enjoyed the same kind of rights to that property, although admittedly not to the same degree.

Niida sees the supposed expansion of daughters' inheritance rights in the Southern Song as a development that proves his central point.

For him, the Southern Song laws were but the most developed expression in Chinese history of a daughter's status as a co-owner of family property. They reflected the absorption into imperial law of local customs in South China after the Song state's move there with the Jin conquest of 1127. His emphasis on local customs in this issue is in keeping with the theme of his life's work: laws generally derive from social practice.

Shiga completely rejects Niida's thesis: the basic unit of ownership of family property was in fact the "father-son unit" (*fushi ittai; fuzi yiti*), not the entire family, and accordingly, property inheritance could be understood only through patrilineal succession. Since sons alone could succeed to the ancestral sacrifices, only they could inherit property. As neither a co-owner of family property nor a ritual successor to the patriline, a daughter could not be an heir. Her only rights were to support as a dependent "beneficiary" (*juekisha; shouyizhe*) as a child and to a dowry when she married.

Shiga sees the Southern Song phenomenon as an aberration that does not disprove his central point. The supposed laws, whatever their origin, did not derive, as Niida would have it, from social practice. Those laws were, at any rate, wholly unique to the Southern Song and as such little more than anomalies from the perspective of Chinese history as a whole. Shiga's argument too is in keeping with the theme of all of his work. He is most interested in uncovering the enduring general principles underlying both social practice and the law in Chinese history and less concerned about specific laws in any particular period or about change over time.

Interest in the *Qingmingji* cases and in the Niida-Shiga debate has been rekindled in recent years with the publication in 1987 of an expanded and widely available edition of the collection. In this renewed debate, some scholars have cast their vote decisively for Niida's argument (Yanagida 1989, 1990; Birge 1992), while others share Shiga's skepticism (Nagata 1991; Itabashi 1993; Takahashi 1995).

Patricia Ebrey has provided an entirely different interpretation of the Southern Song cases. With the decline of aristocratic society and the rise of gentry society, she argues, large brideprices in the Tang gave way to large dowries in the Song as elite men sought to advance their families politically by arranging advantageous marriages for their daughters. The increasing importance of dowries brought about a revision of state law on inheritance in the Song to ensure that orphaned daughters would be properly endowed (Ebrey 1991b).

How one sees the inheritance rights of daughters in the Song necessarily influences the assessment of those rights in later dynasties. None of these three scholars directly addresses the question of how daughters' rights may have changed in the post-Song period, mainly because their interest in the issue is subordinate to other concerns, Shiga and Niida on the nature of family property and the relationship between inheritance and succession, and Ebrey on dowry escalation in the Song. But insofar as Niida and Ebrey in their separate ways see the Southern Song developments as unique, they imply that there was a sharp contraction in daughters' rights in the post-Song period. Shiga, as noted, tends to emphasize continuity rather than change. The precise nature of the post-Song changes thus has yet to be spelled out.

This chapter will examine the relevant Song laws and legal cases on daughters' inheritance rights. Adopting the analytical framework laid out in the Introduction, we will first look at those laws that fall within the patrilineal succession complex, or more specifically, laws on daughters' rights to property when there were no sons. We will then turn to household division and examine the evidence for the right of a daughter to a share half the size of a son's. On the whole, as will be apparent, I find Shiga's view to be the most convincing of the three. But I also find that he shares with Niida and Ebrey certain assumptions about the putative laws and the pertinent *Qingmingji* cases that stand in the way of a clearer understanding of daughters' inheritance rights in the Song and, by extension, the changes they underwent in the post-Song period.

Let me preface my discussion of the main issues by pointing out the limitations of the available materials on daughters' inheritance rights in the Song. To begin with, the Song code (*Song xingtong*) itself is problematical. After it was issued in 963, at the very beginning of the dynasty, it was never formally amended or added to. But a number of its statutes were subsequently overridden by laws that originated (to use the classification of the time) as "edicts, regulations, rules, and specifications" (*chi, ling, ge, shi*), and only some of these can be found in surviving compilations. For the others, we must rely on indirect sources, mainly the *Song huiyao* (Collected Song documents), the *Xu zizhi tongjian* (Continuation of the "Comprehensive Mirror of Aid in Governance"), the legal chapters in the *Songshi* (History of the Song), and the *Qingmingji*.

The main difficulty with the *Qingmingji* is that it does not overlap chronologically with those other sources. Its cases date mainly from the 1220's to the 1260's, beginning roughly where the *Song huiyao*, the most important supplementary source for civil laws, ends. At the same point, the *Xu zizhi tongjian* and the *Songshi* also become increasingly abbreviated. We thus often lack outside sources with which to verify the information on laws contained in the *Qingmingji*.

Patrilineal Succession: Daughters of Extinct Households

The key to understanding changes in daughters' inheritance rights in the Song is state policy on households that had died out for the lack of a male heir. The term "extinct household" (*juehu* or *hujue*) had two meanings in the Tang and Song periods. It meant, on the one hand, the extinction of a patriline. The Tang and Song laws on succession read in part that "those without heirs become extinct households" (*wuhouzhe wei hujue*; Tang: 238). But the term also meant the extinction of a household as a taxable unit. A household with a male head was called a "tax household" (*kehu*); a household headed by a widow with no sons, either natural or adopted, was called a "female household" (*nühu*); and after her death, the household would become an extinct household (Ma Duanlin 1324, 13: 138–39).

From the state's perspective, the extinction of a household had necessarily to involve both the extinction of a male patriline and the extinction of a tax unit. For this reason, the term did not apply to an undivided household of several brothers living together and sharing the ownership of the family property. Even if one of the brothers (and his wife) died without a male heir, the rest of the household remained intact as a tax-paying unit. The state would not consider it to be extinct.

The term thus applied only to a family in which the father had already divided the common property with his brothers and had already set up residence as a separate household. If the father (and the mother) died without a male heir, then his household became extinct in both senses of the word: his patriline had died out and his household had ceased to exist as a taxable unit.

Song Policy on Extinct Household Property

The Tang and the Song shared the same dual-sided definition of extinct household, but they differed in their particular policies on the distribution of its property. Under Tang law, if the deceased father had not made other arrangements in a will, then the property of his extinguished household was to go to his daughters, and if he had no daughters, then to his nearest agnatic male kin (*jinqin*, brothers, nephews, uncles, cousins), and if he had no such kin, then to the state (Niida, comp. 1933: 835–36). Tang law made no distinction between married and unmarried daughters.

In the Song, the policy on the disposition of extinct household property was transformed.[1] Unlike Tang law, Song law differentiated among unmarried, returned (*guizong*), and married daughters.[2] Only unmarried daughters now retained a full right to juehu property; the share of returned daughters was sharply reduced, and that of married daughters even more so. Returned daughters who were the sole surviving members of an extinct household were to receive half of the property and the state was to receive the other half. Married daughters who were the sole survivors were entitled to only a third of the property, with the other two-thirds going to the state. But if they had any unmarried or returned sisters, they were completely cut off, entitled to nothing at all.

Song law also made a novel distinction in regard to appointed heirs. Tang law had conferred on adopted heirs, whether established before or after the death of the parents, the same rights and obligations as natural-born sons. Indeed, so long as there was an heir, even one appointed posthumously, the household would not be considered legally extinct, and its property would not be treated as juehu property.

Song law created the new legal status of the posthumously appointed heir. When a sonless man or, after his death, his widow adopted an heir, the process was called *liji* ("adopting an heir"). But if both died without adopting an heir, the household would become extinct. In this situation, the man's relatives could designate an heir on his behalf posthumously, in a process called *mingji* ("ordering the appointment of an heir").[3]

1. For detailed chronological examinations of the development of extinct household policy in the Song dynasty, see Wei Tianan 1988; Nagata 1991; Yuan Li 1991; and Itabashi 1993.
2. A "returned daughter" was defined as one who had returned to live at her natal home after being expelled from her husband's family or left widowed without a son and without a share of her marital family's property (Song: 198).
3. These meanings of "liji" and "mingji" were specific to Song law. In other dynasties, "liji" referred simply to the establishment of an heir for a sonless man, whether appointed by the man himself, by his widow, or by his agnatic kin; and "mingji" meant "to order [one's son or grandson] to be another man's heir" (Niida, comp. 1933: 234; Wu Kuntian n.d., 67: 16a–19a). Thus, "liji" and "mingji" were not construed as entirely different processes as they were in the Song, but could be part of the same process, with one party as the heir-taker (liji), and the other as the heir-giver (mingji).

Only heirs adopted by parents before their deaths bore the same rights and responsibilities as a natural son, including the right to inherit the family property in its entirety. Those appointed by others after the parents' death had no right to inherit the family estate; they had a right only to juehu property—a right that they had to share with daughters and the state (*QMJ*: 265–68, 287–89). By the 1220's at the latest, a law specifying in great detail the division of extinct household property among a postmortem heir, daughters, and the state was in place. The most a postmortem heir could acquire was one-third.[4] Table 1 shows the entitlements for each.

Tang and Song law on extinct households differed in still another respect. In the Tang, close agnatic male kin could acquire all of the property if an extinct household had no daughters. But they lost this right in a 1015 imperial edict decreeing that the landed property of extinct households was henceforth not to be given to male relatives but was instead to be confiscated and then either sold or rented out by the state (*Song huiyao jigao*: 4812). The only chance any male relative stood of securing juehu property was as an appointed posthumous heir (or the appointment of one of his sons or grandsons, depending on the generational relationship to the deceased). But even then the most he could acquire was a third.

The most important change in the Song was the state's expanded claim on the property of extinct households. Where the Tang state had reserved the right to confiscate juehu property only if there were no daughters and no close male kin, its successor substantially increased its share over time. It did so, first of all, by restricting in absolute terms what daughters and postmortem heirs could receive. By the end of the twelfth century, they could acquire an entire estate only if it was worth less than 500 *guan* (1 guan was nominally 1,000 copper *cash*). Otherwise, they were entitled to just 500 guan of an estate worth 500 to 1,500 guan, and just one-third of any of a higher value, with a cap of 3,000 guan. If the value of the property reached 20,000 guan and above, they were entitled to an additional 2,000 guan, for a total of 5,000 guan. All property above those ceil-

---

4. In the Song, posthumously appointed heirs were not legally entitled to any extinct household property until 1132, when the state decided to give them at least a share. That decision was prompted by a memorial submitted by the judicial commissioner of the Jiangnan Eastern Circuit, who pointed out that such an heir existed in a kind of limbo, not entitled by custom to the property of his original family and not entitled by law to the property of the extinct household. The commissioner recommended that henceforth posthumously appointed heirs (*mingji zhi ren*) be treated the same as married daughters and be accorded one-third of juehu property (*Song huiyao jigao*: 5905).

TABLE I
Distribution of Extinct Household Property
in the Southern Song

Survivors	Daughter(s)' share	Postmortem heir's share	State's share
Daughter(s) only			
Unmarried daughter(s)	Full		
Unmarried and returned daughters	Full		
Returned daughter(s)	1/2		1/2
Married daughter(s)	1/3		2/3
Married with returned and/or unmarried sisters	None		
Daughter(s) and postmortem heir			
Unmarried daughter(s)	3/4	1/4	
Unmarried and returned daughters	4/5	1/5	
Returned daughter(s)	1/2	1/4	1/4
Married daughter(s)	1/3	1/3	1/3
Postmortem heir only		1/3	2/3

SOURCE: *OMJ*: 265–68, 287–89, 315–16.

ings was to go to the state (*Song huiyao jigao*: 5905–6; *Xu zizhi tongjian*: 3922; *QMJ*: 110–11, 287–89). To help put these amounts in perspective, in the early thirteenth century, the conditional sale price of a mu (0.164 acre) of land ranged from nine to 14 guan (*QMJ*: 170, 315).

The Song's right to juehu property did not end with this "cut" off the top. It also staked out a claim to what remained. It eventually extended this claim to include all situations except when there were unmarried daughters. Its portion of the property in other circumstances ranged from one-fourth to two-thirds, depending on the marital status of any daughters and the presence or absence of a postmortem heir (Table 1).

From the state's perspective, the most critical change was the distinction between liji and mingji and the corresponding restriction of the rights of posthumous male heirs. Indeed, limiting their rights of inheritance was crucial to the state's expanded claims. At the same time, that distinction had the coincidental consequence of enlarging daughters' rights at their expense, for daughters in the Tang did not have any claims on the family estate—outside of provisions for their marriages—in the presence of a male heir.

It is important to note that a daughter's right to extinct household property was by no means absolute. Both in the Song and in the Tang, the juehu laws came into effect only when the deceased had not arranged for the disposition of his property in a will. Any bequests in a will would override the laws. This meant, of course, that a daughter could be left a larger share than mandated in law, but it also meant that she could be left a smaller one. In any case, in Song times, she could inherit only as much as the law allowed, because the state placed essentially the same ceilings on the amount of property a man without male posterity could bequeath to people as it placed on juehu property (Xing Tie 1992). Here too the state was staking out a claim to property that lacked a male heir.

Now, what do these specific Song laws about extinct household property tell us generally about daughters' rights of inheritance? Niida argues that as joint owners of family property, daughters, like wives, possessed rights of survivorship (*zonmeishaken*; *cunmingzhe quan*) when the family had no natural or adopted sons (1942: 61, 479; 1962: 383). After the death of her husband (and barring the subsequent adoption of an heir), a widow became the sole surviving owner of the family property. The same held true for a daughter who outlived her parents. What distinguished the different survivorship rights of widows and daughters was when these rights came into effect. They did not differ in kind.

Shiga rejects that view. For him, a widow's right was fundamentally different from a daughter's. In his analysis, outside of the father-son unit, the most important relationship was the husband-wife unit (*fusai ittai*; *fuqi yiti*)—a relationship that allowed the wife, much like a son, to represent her husband after his death. No such bond linked a father and daughter. It was no accident, Shiga maintains, that a sonless household was considered extinct only after the death of both the husband and the wife. A wife could represent her husband, but a daughter, even if unmarried, could not represent her father. Speaking metaphorically, Shiga concludes that with the dying out of the household, family property as an organic entity also died, and what a daughter received was nothing more than the corpse (*zangai*; 1953–55, part 4: 38–46).

Shiga's argument on this score is the more persuasive of the two. What the Song juehu laws show most conclusively is how conditional a daughter's right to family property was. It could be abrogated by the whims of the father in his will and by the policies of the state in ways that a son's or even a widow's could not.

The difference between a widow's right and a daughter's right calls for a stricter definition of terms. Since a widow was entitled to family property only in the absence of any male heirs, whether natural or adopted, her right can best be characterized as inheritance by default (of male heirs). Since a daughter was entitled to family property only in the absence of any male heirs and a widowed mother, she too inherited only by default. Yet, at the same time, her right to do so was dependent on the wishes of her father and existing state policy. Her right can thus best be characterized as *conditional* inheritance by default.

Explaining the Song Policies

How are we to explain the transformation in juehu policy in the Song? Let us take stock, first, of Niida's view. Clearly aware of the escalating claims of the state, he nevertheless locates the primary source of the Song juehu laws in local custom. He contends that the Southern Song legal distinction between liji and mingji and the consequent expansion in the rights of daughters at the expense of postmortem heirs resulted from the incorporation of southern Chinese customs into imperial law (1962: 391).

There is, however, no evidence in the *Qingmingji* cases to suggest a distinction between premortem and postmortem heirs in popular practice. On the contrary, there is evidence that the distinction was imposed by law. For example, in a review of a succession dispute in Jianchang county (Jiangxi) in the 1240's, the official Liu Kezhuang noted that the defendant Tian Tongshi (the birth father of the posthumous heir), "had initially been ignorant of the law and had wanted his son to receive all of Shiguang's [the deceased's] property. . . . Now that he is aware of the law that unmarried daughters are to receive three-fourths and the posthumously designated heir only one-fourth, he is willing for the property to be divided that way" (*QMJ*: 253). Four other cases in the *Qingmingji* document the same point (*QMJ*: 107–8, 110–11, 265–68, 287–89). Social practice was not the source of the distinction.

In a different vein, Ebrey argues that the source of these changes in the juehu laws lay solely in the Song state's desire to ensure adequate dowries for orphaned daughters. To be sure, the finely tuned attention to the different needs of unmarried, returned, and married daughters does suggest that a concern with dowry did indeed play a part in the making of the laws. However, Ebrey's interpretation overlooks the crucial consideration of the state's own expanded share.

Even Shiga shares the assumption that the Song juehu laws were mainly concerned with property inheritance and patrilineal succession, that is, with the extinction of a household as the extinction of a patriline. In so doing, he, like the others, does not consider sufficiently the extinct household from the state's point of view, that is, as a unit of taxation. It was surely no coincidence that the majority of the juehu regulations of the Song came into being as agricultural and tax policies (and are so classified in the sources) and not as inheritance and succession laws. Song policy on extinct households can be fully understood only by taking the state's interests into account.

The state's interest in juehu property was threefold. First, it was vitally concerned that the land continue to be farmed, taxes paid, and labor services rendered. Song law required that the extinction of a household be reported to local officials within three days after the death of the surviving parent (Wei Tianan 1988: 31), or, as one Northern Song official sarcastically put it, even before "the deceased's eyes have fully closed" (*sizhe mu wei ming*; Li Xin n.d., 22: 16b). The fear behind the urgency was that the land would lie fallow or that other families in the village would secretly assume cultivation of it. Either outcome would deprive the state of much-needed taxes and labor services.

A related concern was the state's desire to check the engrossment of land by powerful official and gentry families who, through a combination of legal exemptions and illegal means, were able to evade labor service duties and taxes. The state saw these "aggrandizers" (*jianbing zhi jia*) as responsible for a growing inequality in landownership and the disproportionately heavy tax and service burden borne by the peasantry. As is well known, land engrossment became a particular target of the reformer Wang Anshi's New Policies between 1068 and 1085. It also was of great concern in the early Southern Song, when the state sought to prevent aggrandizers from privately reclaiming the vast stretches of the Huainan region (the area between the Huai and Yangzi rivers) that had been heavily devastated and depopulated during the recent wars (Zhu Jiayuan 1983: 248–54; Wei Tianan 1988: 38). Not surprisingly, as the state's concern about land engrossment grew, the laws on extinct households became more stringent, especially the ones setting ceilings on the amounts of property that daughters and posthumous heirs could receive. In this context, the laws on extinct household property should be seen as part of the Song's attempt to limit the concentration of landownership.

Finally, the Song state also saw juehu property, especially land, as an immediate source of revenue.[5] After its reversion to the state, juehu land, much like abandoned land (*taotian*), was categorized as "official land" (*guantian*), which could be rented out or sold. The sale of juehu property was the preferred method in the Song, with rental a temporary measure in the event that no buyers could be found (Wei Tianan 1988: 35–38).

The Song's reasons for staking such a large claim to juehu property were related to its precarious military situation and the vast increase in the cost of war and defense. Indeed, proceeds from the rental or sale of extinct household property were periodically earmarked for military provisions (*Song huiyao jigao*: 5874). Once the state replaced the Tang's comparatively inexpensive militia system with a professional standing army of some 1.2 million men, it was forced to devote an enormous amount of revenue to its maintenance. Paul Smith has calculated that, in the middle of the eleventh century, defense expenditures consumed 83 percent of the state's annual cash income and 43 percent of its total annual income (cash plus tax payments in kind), thus "surpassing by 35 percent the entire Ming budget of 1502" (1991: 8). The situation became even graver in the next century, after the Song lost half of the country and thus much of its productive base to the Jin in 1127.

All of the above—the concern to maintain agricultural productivity, to curb land aggrandizement, and to fill a dire need for revenue—lay behind the Song state's extinct household policies. But those considerations can only go so far in explaining why it adopted the particular measures it did. After all, other dynasties shared the Song's concern with agricultural productivity and unequal concentration of landownership and at various times found themselves as

---

5. The clearest evidence that the state saw juehu property as a source of revenue comes from denunciations of the laws. The principal complaint was that the government was sacrificing its concern for the people to its desire for more revenue. See, for example, *Song huiyao jigao*: 1316; Li Tao n.d.: 383; and *QMJ*: 282.

woefully short of funds. Yet they did not adopt the same sort of policies. Indeed, such policies would have been virtually impossible in
the Ming and Qing. What exactly made them possible in the Song?

Two factors in particular enabled the Song to adopt the policies
that it did. The first was the state's claim to absolute ownership of
all land in the realm. The laws on extinct households were, after all,
first formulated within the context of the equal field system of the
Tang, and in that system, the state claimed ownership of all land
and exercised the attendant right to parcel it out as it saw fit. Land
allotted to individuals (*koufentian*) was to revert to the state for
redistribution as soon as the person had died. Land in perpetuity
(*shiyetian*) was to be passed down from household head to household head. If there was no such person, then the household was to
be declared extinct and its land in perpetuity was also to revert to
the state for redistribution (*Tang huiyao*: juan 83).

Much of Song law, based as it was on Tang law, continued in this
tradition, even as the state was being forced to confront the reality
of private property. The property of extinct households "belonged"
first and foremost to the state and, that being the case, it was up to
the state to determine if and how it was to be distributed. It was for
that reason that the juehu regulations spoke in terms of "giving"
(*gei* or *yu*) the property to daughters, postmortem heirs, and/or close
male relatives. They did not use the language of property inheritance (*chengshou* or *chengfen*).

Second, the Song's juehu policies were formulated in a legal culture where mandatory (nephew) succession had not yet taken firm
root. Shiga dismisses those policies as anomalous exceptions to
what he sees as the enduring principle that every man should have
an heir, whether natural or adopted, and that the heir (or heirs in the
case of birth sons) was entitled to the property in its entirety. In so
arguing, Shiga assumes that this principle was every bit as deeply
entrenched in Tang and Song law as it was in Ming and Qing law.
As a result, he cannot but see the Song policies, especially their dis-
criminatory treatment of posthumously appointed heirs, as an anomalous exception to his general rule. I would suggest that far from being a mere anomaly, those extinct household policies were actually
consistent with the state's overall posture on succession. What the
policies demonstrate, above all, is that mandatory succession had
not yet become part of state law.

Tang and Song law, in fact, nowhere mandated the appointment of an heir for a sonless man. Judges in the *Qingmingji* cases speak of the need to establish an heir for a sonless man always as a moral obligation (*yi*), never as a legal one (e.g., *QMJ*: 208, 215). The Tang and Song codes permitted a man to adopt a successor from among the male agnates of the proper generation in his own lineage (*tong-zong*) during his lifetime if he so chose, as could his widow after his death (Tang: 237; Song: 192–93), but this was not legally required. Neither was it legally required for agnatic kin to appoint a successor after the death of both the husband and the wife.

In this, Tang and Song law was informed by the descent-line system described in the Classics, in which mandatory succession was by no means the established rule. The classical ideal, which purportedly depicted the kinship organization of the Zhou feudal aristocracy, distinguished between the great descent line (*dazong*) and lesser descent lines (*xiaozong*) in a single descent group (*zong*).

The great line began with the eldest son of the lineage's primogenitor and descended from eldest son to eldest son down through the generations. The heir to that line succeeded to the primogenitor's government office, titles, and land grants, as well as to leadership of the entire group, responsible for the welfare of its members. He also succeeded to the position of officiant at the ritual sacrifices offered to all of the lineage's forebears, no matter how remote. The lesser lines all descended from the younger son(s) of the primogenitor, with new collateral lines being formed in each generation. Unlike the great line, which had limitless generational depth, a lesser line was restricted to five generations, a boundary set by the mourning relationships. The heir to a lesser line was entitled to offer sacrifices only to the preceding four generations (from his father to his great-great-grandfather).

In this system, only the continuation of the great descent line need be assured. It was, after all, that line that held the entire group together politically, socially, economically, and ritually. Should it die out, the lineage would lose its benefices from the state, its position among the feudal aristocracy, its social and economic coherency, as well as its ability to sacrifice to its more remote ancestors. Thus the ritual classics mandated that, should the current heir to the great descent line die without sons, a younger son of a lesser descent line had to be appointed as his successor. At the same time, the classics mandated that a lesser line facing extinction should just be left to perish, its ritual duties to deceased members to be assumed by the heir to the great descent line. The classical ideal thus prescribed mandatory succession only for eldest sons in the great descent line.[6]

It should also be pointed out that in the classical ideal, ancestral rites were the prerogative of the privileged few and not the obligation of all. Or, as the Book of Rites explained, "the rites do not extend down to the commoners; the punishments do not extend up to the great officers" (*li buxia shuren, xing bushang daifu*). How commoners conducted their affairs did not fall within the state's purview.

While neither the Tang nor the Song government subscribed to the classical ideal in all of its particulars, its influence can nevertheless be seen in certain of their laws relating to succession. In the first place, in both dynasties, ancestral rites remained a privilege of rank. Only those men with official status could offer sacrifices to their ancestors, with the number of generations so honored and the type of structure in which the ceremonies were to take place carefully calibrated to one's position in the nine-rank system (see Ebrey 1991a: 47–61 passim). Moreover, succession to ranks and titles and succession to ancestral rites remained intimately linked. Although an official position itself was not inheritable in the Tang and the Song, it nevertheless brought with it certain perquisites that were— titles of nobility (*fengjue*), property associated with those titles (*shifeng*), and the special *yin* privilege of the civil service examination system. The order of succession to those and the order of succession to ancestral rites were one and the same.

In the Tang and the Song, the state's principal concern was the selection of the appropriate heir (*lidi*) from a man's male offspring to be his successor to state benefices and to the ancestral sacrifices. The eldest son was to have priority over his younger brothers, and the sons of wives (*diqi*) priority over the sons of concubines. If one established an heir in violation of this order (*lidi weifa*), the punishment was one year of penal servitude. The Tang and Song codes also provided that if a man's wife had passed the age of 50 sui without having produced a son, then he would be permitted to establish his eldest son of a concubine as heir (Tang: 238; Song: 193).

What the Tang and the Song were not so vitally concerned with

6. For general information on the history of the classical descent line ideal, see Ebrey 1984a, 1991a; and Chow 1994. For specific information on the appointment of heirs in the classical system, see Cai Xin n.d.; Ji Dakui n.d.; Qin Huitian n.d.; Wang Wan n.d.; and Zhu Shi n.d.

was the appointment of an heir for a man who had no male offspring of his own (*liji* or *lisi*). In this as well, the influence of the classical ideal can be seen. Although neither dynasty attempted to enforce the great-line/lesser-line distinction of antiquity, considering its basis in the inheritability of office to be ill-suited to the times, both nonetheless adhered to the five generations of the lesser descent–line model as the basis for mourning and ancestral rites. That model, as we have seen, came with no particular imperative for a sonless man's relatives to appoint an heir for him should he and his wife die without having done so themselves.

The Tang and early Song governments did not explicitly prohibit postmortem heirs among their officials, but neither did they accord them legal recognition. Codified law excluded posthumously appointed heirs from succession to titles of nobility and other inheritable perquisites of office, the only exception being if the man had died in battle in service to the emperor (Niida, comp. 1933: 305–6, 316; Song: 392–93). It also did not recognize posthumous heirs as the ritual successor to the ancestral sacrifices. If an official did not have any male offspring of his own, or if neither he nor his wife had adopted a son during their lifetimes, his line was to be declared extinct. No allowance was made for its continuation through the establishment of a postmortem heir by his kinsmen. Exceptions could be made only by the Board of Rites, which, if it deemed the circumstances warranted it, would issue a special decree (*tezhao*) to the relatives of the deceased, permitting them to establish a postmortem heir with the same rights and responsibilities as a premortem heir (for examples, see *Song huiyao jigao*: 1315–16). The appointment of a postmortem heir for a deceased official was thus a privilege to be granted by the state.

It was this ambiguous status of the posthumously appointed male heir, in combination with the state's presumptive claims on extinct household property, that gave the Song the latitude to adopt the policies it did. Although Tang law, as we have seen, did permit postmortem heirs to inherit all of their adoptive father's property, it did so not out of any confirmed commitment to the principles of mandatory succession. At any rate, as the fate of postmortem heirs in the Song suggests, their property rights were not so secure that they could not be abrogated by a government intent on ensuring its own fiscal well-being. Its extinct household policies were thus not mere anomalies in a legal culture that otherwise affirmed mandatory succession, as Shiga would have it. Rather they were perfectly consistent with the state's overall posture on succession as it had evolved in the Tang and the Song.

Household Division: Half-Shares for Daughters?

The question of an unmarried daughter's legal right to a set share of family property at the time of household division is the more difficult and the more controversial of the two issues. In contrast to the juehu laws, the evidence for which comes from outside sources as well as from a variety of *Qingmingji* judgments, the evidence for a half-share law comes from just two *Qingmingji* cases of a single official. Also, unlike the juehu laws, which granted daughters property only in the absence of a natural son or a premortem adopted heir, the supposed half-share law granted unmarried daughters property even in their presence. According to the half-share formula, the division between one son and one unmarried daughter would be two-thirds to the son and one-third to the daughter; between one son and two unmarried daughters, one-half to the son and one-fourth to each daughter; between two sons and one unmarried daughter, two-fifths to each son and one-fifth to the daughter; between two sons and two unmarried daughters, one-third to each son and one-sixth to each daughter, and so on.

Niida contends that half-shares for unmarried daughters was a prevalent social practice that then became embodied in state law. Here we will first examine his evidence for a half-share custom and then his evidence for a half-share law.

The Evidence on Social Practice

The only proof Niida provides of half-shares as a widespread custom is a case that was adjudicated by the official Fan Yingling in the 1220's, most likely during his term as either the vice-prefect (*tongpan*) of Fuzhou prefecture (Jiangxi) or the vice-prefect of Qizhou prefecture (Hubei).[7]

Zheng Yingchen had two daughters, Xiaochun and Xiaode, but no successor (*si*). He therefore adopted (*guofang*) a son, Xiaoxian, from another branch of the family. Before his death, Zheng Yingchen drew up a will leaving 130 mu of land and one storehouse (out of his total wealth of 3,000 mu and 10 storehouses) to each of his daughters.

---

7. For his biography, see *Songshi*, 410: 12344–47.

After his death, his adopted son, Xiaoxian, brought suit, claiming that the will was not authentic. When the case reached Fan Yingling, he admonished Xiaoxian for his greediness, pointing out to him that "if the customary practice [*li*] of equal division [*junfen*] in some other prefecture were to be applied to this case, then two daughters and an adopted son [*yangzi*] would each receive one-half of the property" (*ruo yi tajun junfen zhi li chu zhi, ernü yu yangzi ge he shou qi ban*). Instead of stubbornly contesting the will, Xiaoxian should be thankful that no such custom existed in his home prefecture. Fan Yingling then ordered the daughters to be given the property specified in the will (*QMJ*: 290–91).

In Niida's argument, the crucial part of this case is Fan Yingling's reference to a custom elsewhere. Since in that reference the distribution of property works out to one-half for an adopted son and one-half for the two daughters (or one-fourth each), Niida concludes that the general principle of division in the custom was half-shares for daughters.

But an accurate reading of this line must go beyond the specified distribution of property in the second part of the sentence, to also take into account the phrase "equal division" (*junfen*) in the first part. The only possible interpretation, it seems to me, is that the equal division is between an adopted son and *all* daughters. That is to say, whether the deceased had one daughter or three daughters, the total share was just one-half, with the other half going to the adopted son. The lawsuit before Fan Yingling just *happened* to involve two daughters, so that in his hypothetical application of the custom to make his point to Xiaoxian, equal division with them worked out to each daughter receiving the equivalent of half Xiaoxian's share. Half-shares for the two daughters in this sentence was purely coincidental. It was not the principle of division at work.

Niida and I also depart on the interpretation of *tajun* in the reference. He takes it to mean "other prefectures," which would suggest a relatively widespread custom. But "tajun" can mean just one other prefecture or, as I have translated it, some other prefecture.

Niida assumes further that this custom applied not just to daughters and adopted sons but also to daughters and natural sons (1962: 381–82). But that assumption is not borne out by the facts of the case. Fan Yingling gives prominence to Xiaoxian's status as an adopted son throughout his judgment, always referring to him as either a *yangzi* or a *guofang zhi ren*. He also wrote that since the two daughters, Xiaochun and Xiaode, "were born of their father," it would not be proper for them to "receive no benefit at all from the ancestral property [*zuye*] and for all of it to go to the adopted son [*guofang zhi ren*]." There is also nothing in his statement about the social practice in some other place that would suggest he had anything other than adopted sons in mind. It cannot be assumed that this custom pertained also to families with birth sons.

Furthermore, such a custom would have clearly been the exception rather than the rule. In common social practice, all sons, whether natural or adopted, had the right to inherit their father's property in its entirety. In this case, the adopted son, Xiaoxian, fully expected to inherit all of his adoptive father's property, begrudging his sisters even the small bequests in the will. All other relevant *Qingmingji* cases on succession and inheritance demonstrate the same point: in popular practice, sons, adopted or not, had full rights to succeed to the property; daughters were customarily entitled at most to dowries, the amount of which was left to the discretion of the father and, if he had left no will, to the sons themselves (e.g., *QMJ*: 107–8, 110–11, 141–42, 175–76, 215–17, 217–23, 237–38, 265–68, 287–89, 296–97).

In the end, this case cannot bear the weight of Niida's conclusions. It suggests only the existence of a local practice calling for a 50–50 division of property between an adopted son and all daughters. It does not confirm the existence of a custom according each unmarried daughter a share of property half the size of a son's share.

The Evidence for a Half-Share Law

Niida's evidence for a state law decreeing half-shares for unmarried daughters comes from two cases reviewed by Liu Kezhuang when he served as the judicial commissioner (*tidian xingyu gongshi*) for the Jiangnan Eastern Circuit from 1244 to 1248.[8] The first case concerned the estate of Zhou Bing of Poyang county (Jiangxi). Zhou had a daughter who had married uxorilocally and a son who was born after his death (*yifu zhi nan*). The uxorilocal son-in-law, Li Yinglong, claimed that before Zhou Bing died, he had promised him one-half of his property. The county official (*xianwei*, "county sheriff") who originally heard the case dismissed the son-in-law's claim of one-half, according him three-tenths instead. As his justification

---

8. For his biography, see Lu Xinyuan n.d., 29: 12a–17b. Both cases also appear in Liu Kezhuang's collected works, where he explicitly pins them to that term in office. See Liu Kezhuang n.d.: 1712, 1725, 1726–30. On the role of the judicial commissioner in the appeals process, see McKnight 1992: 233–37.

for doing so, the official cited a famous case from the Xianping reign (998–1003), in which the official Zhang Yong (Zhang Guaiya) determined that the proper division between a son and a uxorilocal son-in-law was seven-tenths and three-tenths. (For the particulars, see Li Tao n.d., 44: 11b.)

When the case reached Judicial Commissioner Liu on appeal, he ruled that the uxorilocal son-in-law did not have any right to the property on his own account, but that "according to the law, when the parents are already both dead and the sons and daughters divide the property, a daughter is to receive one-half of what a son receives" (*zai fa, fumu yi wang, ernü fenchan, nü he de nan zhi ban*). He therefore ordered that the property be divided into three shares, with two going to the posthumous son and one to the daughter (*QMJ*: 277–78; Liu Kezhuang n.d.: 1725).

In the second case, the issue turned on the estate of Vice-Magistrate (*xiancheng*) Tian of Jianchang county (Jiangxi). Although never formally married, Tian had two sons, an adopted son, Shiguang, and a younger natural son, Zhenzhen, born of a concubine, (Tian) Liu Shi.[9] The adopted son, Shiguang, also never married and had no sons. But he did have two young daughters by a maid of the household, Qiuju. The occasion of the lawsuit was the attempt, after the death of both Tian and his adopted son Shiguang, of the vice-magistrate's younger brother, Tian Tongshi, to establish one of his own sons, Shide, as Shiguang's heir. The concubine Liu Shi contested his claim in court on the very sound legal grounds that such a succession would violate the proper order, since Shide and Shiguang, as cousins, belonged to the same generation.

In his review of the case, Commissioner Liu decided, first of all, to permit the succession of Shide on the testimony of the lineage head that there was no suitable candidate of the proper generation. He then ruled that Vice-Magistrate Tian's property was to be divided into two equal shares, with one-half going to the natural son, Zhenzhen. Finally, having sanctioned Shide as Shiguang's post-mortem heir, he went on to apply the laws on extinct households, granting Shide one-fourth of the other half and the two (unmarried) daughters three-fourths.

---

9. In imperial China, a married woman, whether a wife or concubine, was usually referred to by her husband's last name, followed by her father's last name, and then the honorific *shi*. To avoid confusion between wives and concubines, I will render a wife's name into English as Mrs. X (née Y), but will keep a concubine's name in the original.

The case, however, did not end there. For Liu Shi rather belatedly informed the court that she too had two young daughters, both the children of Vice-Magistrate Tian. Taking this new fact into consideration, Commissioner Liu wrote:

In my previous decision, I was unaware that Liu Shi also has two daughters. Since these two daughters are the vice-magistrate's natural daughters [*qinnü*], if [Shiguang] were still alive, he would divide the property equally with Zhenzhen, and the two daughters would each receive one-half of what a son receives (*ernü ge he de nan zhi ban*).

Commissioner Liu went on to note that in this formula, Vice-Magistrate Tian's property would be divided into thirds, with a third going to Shiguang's daughters and Shide, a third to Zhenzhen, and a third to Liu Shi's two daughters (one-sixth apiece, or a half-share each).

In the end, for reasons that are not all that clear, Commissioner Liu decided not to divide the property strictly by this formula, although half-shares for daughters did figure into his ruling. He first divided the property into two equal shares, one going to the concubine Liu Shi's three children, and the other going to the maid Qiuju's two daughters and the postmortem heir, Shide. To determine the distribution of the second share, he then again applied the law on extinct households, but with some adjustment to provide Shide with the wherewithal to see to his adoptive father's funeral. To determine the distribution of the first share, the commissioner applied the half-share formula, granting the natural son, Zhenzhen, one-half and each daughter one-fourth (*QMJ*: 251–57; Liu Kezhuang n.d.: 1726–30).

Discussion of the Liu cases. On the face of it, the evidence does seem unequivocal. Commissioner Liu Kezhuang did indeed seem to have a specific law in mind during his adjudication of these two cases. He also did indeed seem to believe that this law required him to grant each daughter a share half the size of a son's share.

Before we turn to Liu Kezhuang's specific references to a half-share law in more detail, it would be helpful to step back and evaluate a supposed half-share law in the context of the times. If there truly was such a law, I argue, it would have had to be a highly anomalous one at best.

Liu Kezhuang's references to a half-share law first have to be weighed against all evidence to the contrary. No other official in the *Qingmingji*, many of whose cases also date from the 1240's and after, cited a half-share law explicitly or decreed a property division that suggests they were following any such law implicitly. In fact, these other cases, plus all outside sources, point overwhelmingly to the opposite conclusion: equal division among sons, with at most dowry provisions for unmarried daughters, was the custom and the law in the Song, just as it was in all other periods of imperial Chinese history.

Liu's references also have to be weighed against a contemporary case from Tongcheng county (Hubei), which cites an entirely different law about an unmarried daughter's right to property at the time of household division. The case concerned the disposition of property among three married daughters, one unmarried daughter, and the adopted son of the only son. The presiding official wrote that the "established law" (*dingfa*) prescribed that "in the division of property, unmarried sons are to be given marriage expenses [*pincai*], unmarried or returned sisters and daughters [of marriageable age] are to be given dowries [*jiazi*], and those [sisters and daughters] who have not yet reached marriageable age are to be given some property [*caichan*], the value of which cannot exceed the value of the dowry." The deceased father's property, the judge concluded, was to go to the son's adopted heir. The unmarried daughter, who had already attained the marriageable age of 13 sui, was entitled only to a dowry (*QMJ*: 215–17). Clearly, the legal basis for the judge's ruling here was not half-shares for unmarried daughters.

A half-share law, moreover, would have been utterly inconsistent with the laws on extinct households and wills. As discussed above, an heir established before the death of both parents had the same rights to family property as a birth son. Only in the case of a postmortem heir did the regulations on daughters' shares come into play. The numerous *Qingmingji* cases in which this law was applied provide ample testimony that it was by no means a dead letter in the late Southern Song. The problem is how to reconcile that law, which entitled a premortem adopted heir to all of the property even in the presence of unmarried daughters, with a law that purportedly entitled unmarried daughters to half-shares even in the presence of a premortem adopted heir.

A similar sort of conflict would arise with the ceilings imposed on bequeathed property and extinct household property. As we have seen, Song law set strict limits on how much an heirless man could bequeath to daughters and others. These ceilings came to be attached to the juehu laws, thus restricting the amounts that daughters, posthumously appointed heirs, and others could receive of extinct household property. How do we square these ceilings with a half-share law, through which a daughter could acquire property in excess of the legal limit?

As we have also seen, a daughter's right to the property of an extinct household was not absolute. The precise apportionment spelled out in the regulations applied only when the deceased had not left a will providing for some other disposition of his property. Since a daughter's claim to family property was conditional even in the absence of a male heir, it is difficult to see how she could at the same time have an absolute right to a half-share of the family estate even in the presence of a natural or a premortem adopted son.

We need also to consider carefully the implications of daughters' half-shares for both individual families and the state. If each unmarried daughter, as Niida and others suppose, was entitled to half a son's share, the bulk of the property could, depending on the family's composition, be given to daughters and through their marriages be forever lost to their father's patriline. For example, if the daughters in a family outnumbered sons by a ratio of two to one, they would together receive half of the family property at the time of division. If they outnumbered sons by a higher ratio, they would receive more than half the estate. The effect of this imbalance would only multiply down through the generations with future household divisions.

Conceivably, for elite families, the impact of a half-share law might not have been so great. After all, as Ebrey shows, they had already become accustomed to bestowing large endowments on their daughters in the hope of forging politically expedient marriage alliances. Moreover, since these families' financial resources encompassed more than just land, they had the option of giving a daughter her half-share in money or other movable goods, or both, thereby keeping the land more or less intact for transmission down the patriline. For peasant families, however, which usually had no resources other than land and which lacked the political incentives operative among the elite, a legal imperative to provide unmarried daughters with half-shares of the family estate could have (again depending on the composition of the family) a devastating impact on the livelihood of the immediate generation, not to mention future ones.

Finally, and not least, such a law would have worked against the state's own best fiscal interests. As in other dynasties, the Song's land-tax and labor-service systems depended on a certain congruence between the location of the property and the residence of its owner to work effectively. The more distant the property from the person, the more difficult it was to coordinate the registration of households and property and the assessment and collection of taxes and services. Song officials complained generally of the ways in which geographically dispersed landownership confounded the state-imposed community-based mechanisms for assessment and collection (McKnight 1971), and specifically of the difficulty of keeping track of wealth transmitted through dowry (*Song huiyao jigao*: 6342).

Any half-share law would only have aggravated the problem. Since marriage was principally exogamous, an unmarried daughter's rights to her half-share of the family property would leave the village with her as dowry upon her marriage into a family in another village. As prescribed in law, the responsibility for the payment of the taxes and services on that property would transfer to the head of her marital household (Ma Duanlin 1324, 13: 138–39; *QMJ*: 607). Thus the land itself and the taxpaying household would be located in different villages. Multiplied countless times, this separation would result in a widespread divergence between the residence of taxable households and the location of their property—a nightmarish situation for state tax collection.

Given the possible consequences of a half-share law, the Southern Song would have had to have a very compelling reason for promulgating it. Niida's explanation that the Song state absorbed local custom after its move south is not very convincing. It depends, first, on establishing that a social practice of half-shares to daughters did indeed exist in the territory of the Southern Song. But not only is his reading of the proof he offers on this score highly questionable; he cannot support it with even one of the other some 70 *Qingmingji* cases on patrilineal succession or household division.

But even if this custom did exist, Niida would still have to explain why the Song state supposedly saw fit to make it into law. As it happens, he does not supply any specific rationale, instead presenting the process as little more than one of passive absorption. But that of course does not explain why the state would turn this particular custom into law when it so resolutely held the line against other local customs, such as different-surname adoption, same-generation succession, uxorilocal son-in-law inheritance, to name just a few.

Patricia Ebrey, in her dowry explanation, at least furnishes a specific reason for the promulgation of the law: to protect orphaned daughters from unscrupulous brothers, uncles, and others, and to ensure that they were provided with the dowries that were so vital in the Song to contracting decent marriages. She differs from Niida also on when the half-share law came into effect, seeing it as applied only with the division of a household after the death of the parents (i.e., orphaned daughters), not, as Niida contends, whenever a household divided.[10]

Yet Ebrey's argument also falls short in the end. In the first place, it conflicts with the ample evidence she herself presents of grave official concern over the escalation in dowries and the rise of mercenary marriage. With the Song's officials so deploring the practice of large dowries, why would the state adopt a law that would only encourage the trend? More important, her conclusion that the half-share law applied only to orphaned daughters rests on the assumption that in his presentation of the law, Liu Kezhuang was deliberately drawing a distinction between household division before and after the death of the parents.

But was Liu Kezhuang really making a distinction, or merely describing the conditions under which family partition was legally permissible and therefore presumably practiced? Unlike the Ming and Qing legal codes, which incorporated a substatute permitting premortem household division if the parents or parent so desired it (*Da Ming huidian* 1587, 19: 20b–21a; Qing: 087-01), Song law (and before it Tang) took a very strict position on the matter. Although there is some evidence to suggest that the state was beginning to moderate its tough stance in the late twelfth and early thirteenth centuries, the officials in the *Qingmingji* cases generally assumed that the division of family property would take place only after the death of both parents.[11] Liu Kezhuang was no exception. He was not drawing a distinction between premortem and postmortem house-

10. Takahashi Yoshirō (1995) has recently advanced an argument similar to Ebrey's, the primary difference turning on when the supposed half-share law was to be applied. In Takahashi's view, unmarried orphaned daughters were entitled to half-shares only when their brothers were minors and thus unable to support their sisters or provide for their dowries. In Ebrey's, unmarried orphaned daughters were entitled to half-shares regardless of the age of their brothers.

11. One judge even went so far as to order a mother and her three sons to reunite their household and property, even though all parties had divided willingly in the first place (*QMJ*: 278–79). The Song state abhorred family partition before the death of the parents not only for ideological reasons, but also for very practical reasons. In the Song's labor service system, households were categorized into five grades on the basis of total wealth. Households would divide before the death of the parents as a

hold division, for in his legal universe premortem division simply did not exist. In this respect, Ebrey's argument, like Niida's, rests on a shaky foundation.

A half-share law, then, was implausible, even within the context of the Southern Song. There is absolutely no evidence for it outside of Liu Kezhuang's two cases. It would have been completely inconsistent with the body of existing laws on daughters' inheritance rights. It would not have been in the best interests of peasant families, let alone in the best interests of the state. And the state would not have had any compelling reason to promulgate it in the first place.

Explaining the Liu Kezhuang anomaly. How, then, do we explain Liu Kezhuang's two references? To begin with, it seems clear enough that he was not quoting any law verbatim, for the language he used differed from normal legal usage in two important respects. Consider his statement "according to the law, when the parents are already both dead and the sons and daughters divide the property, a daughter is to receive one-half of what a son receives" (*zai fa, fumu yi wang, ernü fenchan, nü he de nan zhi ban*). No known Song law used "sons and daughters" (*ernü*) in reference to the division of family property; all used "brothers" (*xiongdi*) or "sons and grandsons" (*zisun*) instead. The phrase was in fact exceedingly uncommon even in ordinary legal discourse, as evidenced by other cases in the *Qingmingji*. What is more, Song law, as we have seen, drew a very precise distinction among daughters based on marital status. A half-share law for unmarried daughters, one would expect, would have done so also. But Liu used "daughter" (*nü*) instead of "unmarried daughter" (*zaishinü*). For this reason, too, we must take it that he was merely paraphrasing.

What law, in that case, might Liu Kezhuang have been paraphrasing? It could be he had taken note of some idiosyncratic law and thought it applied to the two cases before him. Law was, after all, exceptionally fluid throughout the Song with the endless stream of edicts from emperors and regulations from the various ministries. Moreover, any previous law, no matter how old, was held to be still in force unless specifically revoked or replaced, and any imperial

---

way to lower their grade and hence their liability (*Song huiyao jigao*: 6248; Zhao Yashu 1969: 143). The moderation of the Song's position came in an 1192 law that allowed parents to give a son a portion of the family estate and to let him live separately (*QMJ*: 371–72).

decision, even on a single individual case, automatically became
law unless explicitly specified otherwise (McKnight 1987). The situation was even more chaotic in the thirteenth century, for the pe-
riodic compilations that helped to keep matters under control were
increasingly few and far between (Shen Jiaben n.d.: 1013–30). Conceivably, out of the vast body of edicts and regulations, Liu Kezhuang
came across one that he interpreted and used as he did.

But a much more likely explanation is that Liu was paraphrasing
a law cited by the official Hu Ying in a case he adjudicated during
his tenure as the supervisor of relief granaries (*tiju changping*) for Hunan in the early 1240's (*QMJ*: 280–82).[12] As we shall see below, that
law—*zaishinü yi zi cheng fu fen fa gei ban*—can be read in different
ways.

There are several reasons to suppose that Liu Kezhuang did indeed have this law in mind. In his judgment on the uxorilocal son-
in-law case, for instance, he specifically referred to his legal authority as a *tiaoling* ("regulation"), rulings that were usually issued by
the various ministries.[13] Hu Ying referred to the law he cited as a
tiao, as in *zhaotiao* ("in accordance with the *tiao*"), and tiao used in
this way was usually a shorthand reference in the *Qingmingji* for
tiaoling (e.g., *QMJ*: 253, 266–67, 289).

There is also an important chronological correspondence. Liu
himself never applied any half-share regulation earlier in his career
as the magistrate of Jianyang county (Fujian) in the 1220's, even
when it would have been appropriate for him to do so (*QMJ*: 353–
56). This suggests that the regulation he cited in his two cases was
a relatively recent one that came into being sometime between his
term as a magistrate in the 1220's and his term as a judicial commissioner from 1244 to 1248. As noted, the judgment in which Hu
Ying cited this regulation dates from the early 1240's.

Most important, this regulation can be read to mean that each
unmarried daughter was to receive a share half the size of a son's
share. The phrase "zaishinü" can be taken as singular—"an unmarried daughter"—just as the "zi" in "zi cheng fu fen" can be either

12. For Hu's biography, see *Songshi*, 416: 12478–79. The case bears no date, but
other evidence in the *Qingmingji* makes clear that he served as the supervisor of relief granaries for Hunan in the early 1240's (*QMJ*: 97–98, 124–26, 322–24).

13. Because he used "regulation" (*tiaoling*) instead of the word "statute" (*lütiao*),
he clearly did not have in mind the statute in the Song (and Tang) code specifying
that at the time of family division, each unmarried sister and daughter was to receive
for marriage expenses one-half of what a son received for the same purpose (Song:
197; Niida, comp. 1933: 245–46).

"son" or "sons." The phrase "zi cheng fu fen" was often used by officials in the *Qingmingji* cases to mean simply "son(s) inherit their father's property" (e.g., *QMJ*: 175, 268). Implicit in this usage was the principle of equal division among sons. Finally, the "half" (*ban*) in the regulation would explain where exactly Liu Kezhuang came up with the idea of half-shares (and not third-shares, quarter-shares, and so on) for daughters, since, as we have seen, it cannot be found in normal customary practice.

The regulation that Hu Ying cited thus could be translated literally as "an unmarried daughter, in accordance with the law that son(s) inherit equally their father's property, is to be given half" or, more grammatically, as "an unmarried daughter is to be given half of what a son receives in accordance with the law that son(s) inherit equally their father's property."

Liu Kezhuang's own description of the way the supposed half-share law was to be applied further suggests that he actually had this regulation in mind. In his judgment on the Vice-Magistrate Tian case, he wrote: "Since these two daughters are the vice-magistrate's natural daughters [*qinnü*], if [Shiguang] were still alive, he would divide the property equally with Zhenzhen, and the two daughters would each receive one-half of what a son receives." According to Liu Kezhuang, the vice-magistrate's property was first to be divided equally between the two brothers, Shiguang and Zhenzhen. Here he was applying "the law that son(s) inherit equally their father's property" (*yi zi cheng fu fen fa*). Having arrived at what a son's share would be, each daughter was then to be granted half of it. Here he was applying "each daughter . . . is to receive half" (*zaishinü . . . gei ban*).

The problem, of course, is that Liu's way of calculating a half-share for each daughter just does not work. If each got a share equal to half of each son's share (one-half), she would get one-fourth. This would seem to make the sum of the four children's shares—$1/2 + 1/2 + 1/4 + 1/4$—nonsensical. In fact, a son's share cannot be computed before a daughter's share, since what a daughter received would affect what a son could receive. The shares of sons and daughters had to be calculated simultaneously.

What all this suggests is that the regulation should actually be read differently. To break it down again, let us read the "zaishinü" as plural instead of singular—"unmarried daughters" instead of "an unmarried daughter." The phrase "yi zi cheng fu fen fa" can be read "according to the law that son(s) inherit their father's *share*." This law (*fa*) comes directly from the statute in both the Tang and the Song code on family division: "Whenever real estate [*tianzhai*] and other property is to be divided, it shall be divided equally among brothers. . . . If a brother has died, his son(s) shall inherit his share [*zi cheng fu fen*]" (Song: 197; Niida, comp. 1933: 245–46. My translation follows Jing Junjian 1994: 53). The "zi cheng fu fen" here means literally "son(s) inherit their father's share [of undivided family property]."

The phrase "zi cheng fu fen" can thus be read in two different ways, depending upon the context. Liu Kezhuang's interpretation that "son(s) inherit equally their father's property" applied to a household with only one couple in the senior generation. Upon the death of the man, his sons were to inherit his property in equal shares. The households in Liu's two cases were of this sort. But the actual passage in the code that "son(s) inherit their father's share [of undivided family property]" applied only to an undivided household in which two or more brothers (and their wives) made up the senior generation and owned property in common. Upon the death of one of the brothers, his sons were to succeed to his share of that property.

The final phrase, "gei ban," identifies the regulation as a law on extinct households. Since the state saw juehu property as something it "owned," which it then distributed to others, it used the language of "giving" (*gei* or *yu*) in its laws rather than the language of inheritance. As a juehu law, this regulation called for one-half of the property to be given to unmarried daughters, the implication being that the state was to retain the other half.

Putting it all together, the regulation should be read: "Unmarried daughter(s) are to be given one-half of what son(s) would have received [had there been son(s)] in accordance with the law that son(s) inherit their father's share [of undivided family property]"; or, in other words, unmarried daughters were to be given one-half of their father's share of undivided family property in the absence of sons or an adopted heir.

This reading is exactly how Hu Ying himself understood and applied the regulation in the lawsuit before him. In that case, Zeng Ergu of Shaoyang county (Hunan) had brought suit against one or several of her uncles for illegally appropriating her deceased father's property. Hu Ying, explicitly referring to the circumstances as the extinction of a household, ruled in her favor. He ordered that she receive one-half of her father's share of the as yet undivided family estate according to the regulation "zaishinü yi zi cheng fu fen fa gei ban." He further noted that the regulation called for the other half to revert to the state.[14]

This case makes clear that, contrary to Liu Kezhuang's reading, the regulation Hu cited, like the other juehu laws, came into effect only when the father lacked a natural or adopted son to carry on his line and to inherit his property, which in this case consisted of his share in the undivided estate he held with his brothers. The regulation did not grant an unmarried daughter any rights to her father's share of an undivided estate in the presence of a male heir.

The Hu case also makes clear that, again contrary to Liu's reading, the regulation did not call for a half-share for *each* unmarried daughter. A single daughter in a sonless family would have been entitled to 50 percent of the father's share of an undivided estate, with the other 50 percent going to the state, just as in this case. If there were two daughters, then conceivably each could receive 50 percent and the state nothing. But what about three or more daughters? Each could not possibly receive half of what a son or sons would have been entitled to (100 percent). Half-shares for daughters was thus not the principle of division in this juehu regulation. Rather, like the other juehu laws, it spoke not about what each daughter was to receive individually, but about what all daughters were to receive collectively—one-half of what son(s) would have received of their father's share of undivided property.

The regulation Hu Ying cited was clearly a latter-day supplement to the earlier juehu laws. It was intended to cover a situation that those laws did not, and by doing so, expand both the definition of what constituted juehu property and the state's claim to it.[15] Those earlier juehu laws, as explained above, applied only to a household

14. *QMJ*: 280–82. Rather than confiscating the other half of the share, however, Hu Ying ordered that it be divided equally between Zeng Ergu's two uncles—no doubt for the sake of restoring family harmony. He also ruled that, in addition to the half portion of her father's share of the undivided property, she was to receive all of her father's privately acquired property in accordance with the juehu regulations. Private property (*sichan*) in an undivided family consisted of official salaries, wives' dowries, and any land or businesses acquired without using common family funds. On the distinction between private and family property, see Niida 1942: 455–59; Shiga 1967: 507–11; and Ebrey 1984b: 198–200.

15. One inspiration for the state's expanded claim may have been the law specifying the order of inheritance to property that came with titles of nobility (*shifeng*). The *Tang liudian* (Tang administrative code) stipulated that if the holder had no sons and no surviving widow, then his unmarried daughters together were to receive one-half of the property. That proportion was not to be increased no matter how many daughters a man might have (cited in Niida 1942: 526–27).

in which the father's property was his alone and not property that he still owned with any brother(s). Upon the death of the heirless father and mother, the household would became extinct in both meanings of the word: the father's patriline would die out, as would his household as a tax unit. In those circumstances, the juehu laws discussed in the first part of this chapter would take effect. Unmarried daughters would be entitled to all of their father's property up to the legal limit if no heir was appointed posthumously. Otherwise, they would receive three-fourths and the heir one-fourth.

Those laws did not apply to an undivided household in which brothers owned the property together. The death of an heirless brother and his wife did not constitute extinction, for the rest of the household remained as a taxpaying unit. As stipulated in the Song code of 963 (following Tang law), when the household did undergo division, the man's share was to be absorbed into the general pot for distribution among his surviving brothers and their sons (Song: 197). Daughters were not entitled to receive it, nor did the state lay claim to it, for again it did not define the situation as the extinction of a household.

With the promulgation of the regulation cited by Hu Ying, however, the state staked out such a claim in the late Southern Song. A deceased brother's share of undivided family property was now defined as potential juehu property, which, at the time of household division, would be divided equally between unmarried daughters and the state. For unmarried daughters, of course, the regulation represented an expansion in their rights to property. But, as with the other juehu laws, that expansion came only coincidentally with the extension of the state's claim.

Thus, the key to Liu Kezhuang's two anomalous cases almost certainly lies in the extinct household laws of the Song. All evidence points to the likelihood that the source of his authority was the regulation promulgated in the late Southern Song on the disposition of a father's share of undivided property. And that regulation, far from entitling daughters to shares along with sons during household division, applied merely when the father died without a male heir to receive his property. It had nothing to do with a daughter's claims during household division, but was instead part of the Song's corpus of legislation on patrilineal succession.

Liu Kezhuang and the Qingmingji. If, as I claim, there was not any half-share law, why did the compiler(s) of the *Qingmingji* see fit to include Liu Kezhuang's two cases in the collection in the first place? Would not their very inclusion suggest that there was nothing questionable about them?

Part of the answer is that the *Qingmingji* was a private collection, not an imperially sponsored work. The Song edition, preface 1261, was compiled by a scholar known only by the pseudonym Manting Zengsun, and the much larger Ming edition, preface 1569, by a scholar named Zhang Siwei (Chen Zhichao 1987: 650–52). Since, as with other such private compilations, the purpose was to entertain as much as it was to educate, fidelity to the law was not the sole consideration behind the selection of cases. In fact, the *Qingmingji* contains all manner of decisions that did not conform to written law.

More important, in both the Song and the Ming edition, Liu Kezhuang's case concerning the uxorilocal son-in-law appears under the title "A son-in-law must not claim one-half of the property of his wife's family" (*nüxu buying zhongfen qijia caichan*). The compilers thus did not present the case as an illustration of the practical application of some half-share law. Rather, they made a deliberate decision to highlight the issue of a uxorilocal son-in-law's property rights and downplay Liu Kezhuang's reference to half-shares for daughters.

As tellingly, the Ming edition of the *Qingmingji* does not contain Liu's other case at all, and the Song edition does not contain the relevant part about half-shares for daughters (Chen Zhichao 1987: 649; *QMJ*: 254). It includes only the first half of the dispute under the title "Posthumous heirs can acquire only one-fourth of the property" (*jijue zisun zhi de caichan sifen zhi yi*), stopping right at the point of Commissioner Liu's discovery of the existence of Vice-Magistrate Tian's two daughters and his application of a supposed half-share formula. (The full text appears only in the 1987 Zhonghua shuju edition of the *Qingmingji*, which draws on Liu Kezhuang's collected writings to complete the case; *QMJ*: 254.) The Song compiler's decision not to relate the entire case strongly suggests that he too found Liu's reference to some half-share law to be very problematical. In short, the way in which the compilers of the *Qingmingji* dealt with Liu Kezhuang's two cases casts even greater doubt on the presumed existence of a half-share law.

Daughters' Inheritance Rights in the Post-Song Period

If we accept that a half-share law did not exist or, at the very least, was a highly anomalous law that had virtually no impact on

legal and social practice, then the changes in the inheritance rights
of daughters in the post-Song period were much less dramatic than
Niida and Ebrey would have us believe. It is simply not the case that
by Song law daughters possessed the legal right to half-shares of the
family estate at the time of household division and then somehow
lost that right in later dynasties. They never had that right in the
first place. In the Song, as in the Yuan, the Ming, and the Qing, a
daughter's rights in the household division complex were limited
to maintenance while she was growing up and a dowry when she
married.

This does not mean that no change at all took place, as Shiga tends
to suggest, for patrilineal succession underwent a major transformation that had significant consequences for daughters' legal claims
on property. After the Song, there was a contraction in the rights of
daughters to inherit by default and at the same time an expansion
in the rights of potential male heirs. These two developments were
closely related, and one cannot be understood without the other.

The post-Song changes were of two types. The first was a series
of changes that represented a reversion to earlier Tang law. The second and the more important was a series of changes that represented change not just from the Song but from the Tang as well.

Neither the legal distinction between pre- and postmortem heirs
nor the legal distinction among daughters based on marital status
lasted long after the fall of the Southern Song. Beginning in the
Yuan, any adopted heir to the patriline, whether appointed before or
after the parents' death, had full rights to the family property. Thus,
daughters of extinct households no longer enjoyed any legal claim
to share in the family property with posthumously established male
successors. At the same time, although Yuan law still distinguished
between unmarried and married daughters and, like Song law, permitted married daughters only one-third of juehu property (*Shen ke
Yuan dianzhang* 1908, 19: 12b–14a), this distinction disappeared in
the Ming. As in the Tang, all natural daughters (*qinnü*) again shared
the same rights to juehu property, regardless of their marital status
(*Da Ming huidian* 1587, 19: 20b; Qing: 088-02; Shiga 1967: 409).

Moreover, post-Song law did not accord unmarried daughters
rights to half their father's share of a family estate in the default of
a male heir. This change too represented a return to earlier Tang
law, in which unmarried daughters of a deceased brother in an undivided household were at most to be provided with marriage funds.

Partly as a result of these changes, the state in the post-Song period pared down its own stake in juehu property. It no longer commanded a share along with posthumous heirs and returned and married daughters, and it no longer placed ceilings on what they could receive. By the Ming and Qing, the state reserved the right to confiscate juehu property only if there were no male heirs and no daughters of whatever marital status. A daughter's right to juehu property thus became less contingent on the will of the state, although it remained as dependent as ever on the will of the father.

There was, finally, a restoration in the Qing of the rights of agnatic male kin to extinct household property. Yuan and Ming law continued to exclude male relatives, stating that officials were to confiscate (*ruguan*) the property outright if there were no male heirs and no surviving daughters (*Shen ke Yuan dianzhang* 1908, 19: 12a–14b; *Da Ming huidian* 1587, 19: 20b; see also Yanagida 1995: 266–73). The Qing initially incorporated this law into its code, but revised it in 1740 to make confiscation no longer compulsory, but merely something that local officials should consider, depending on the circumstances (Qing: 088-02). The reason for the amendment was that "when a person dies and the household becomes extinct, unless there is some crime to be taken into consideration, it is not appropriate to speak of confiscation" (*Qing huidian shili* 1899, 9: 314). The agnatic male kin's recovery of the legal right to juehu property represented another reversion, albeit a rather belated one, to Tang law.

Thus by the mid-eighteenth century, the Tang order of rights to extinct household property had been fully restored—posthumous heirs, then daughters of whatever marital status, and then agnatic male kin. But this surface similarity masks a deeper transformation, and that was the imperial state's recognition of the private ownership of land. Although in theory all land in the realm continued to belong to the emperor, in practice the state came to recognize, and through its laws to protect, private ownership. And its claim on extinct household property changed accordingly. Where in both the Tang and the Song, the state perceived juehu property as something it owned and then "gave" to others, Ming and Qing laws explicitly used the language of inheritance, as, for example, in the Ming "daughters are to *chengfen*" and in the Qing "daughters are to *chengshou*" (*Da Ming huidian* 1587, 19: 20b; Qing: 088-02). The state's retreat from its claim on juehu property became complete in the eighteenth century with its relinquishment of the right of confiscation, except as part of the penalty for crimes committed.

The other big change from both the Tang and the Song was the consolidation in codified law of mandatory nephew succession. Beginning in the early Ming, the appointment of an heir became a legal (as well as a moral) obligation. To accommodate this new legal imperative, the dynastic codes expanded the range of permissible heirs. As a result, the scope of daughter inheritance by default grew narrower and narrower.

Tang and Song law, as we have seen, nowhere specified that heirs had to be appointed for men who lacked birth sons. A sonless man was legally allowed to adopt a successor during his lifetime if he so chose, as could his widow or other kin on his behalf after his death, but that was not legally required. At the same time, no male relative—no matter how closely related to the deceased—had any *legal* claim whatsoever to a succession. The Yuan dynasty followed in this tradition, permitting the appointment of heirs, both premortem and postmortem, but not legally requiring it (*Shen ke Yuan dianzhang* 1908, 17: 19a–24a).

Mandatory nephew succession became the law of the land at the beginning of the Ming dynasty. In the second year of the Hongwu emperor's reign (1369), he issued a number of regulations (*ling*) on the issue. If a sonless man did not make a lineage nephew his heir during his lifetime, the emperor decreed, his widow must (*xu*) do so after his death. If she failed to establish an heir during her lifetime, then the man's surviving relatives must do so after her death (*Da Ming huidian* 1587, 19: 20a–21a).

The early Ming regulations also introduced into law the principle that eligible heirs in the lineage possessed an actual legal claim on the succession and, through it, on the property of the deceased. Those with such a claim were called *yingji zhi ren* (loosely, "the person who ought to succeed") or, in other words, the required heir. As a rule of thumb, the required heir was the lineage nephew most closely related to the deceased as determined by the mourning degrees. The relevant Ming regulation read in part:

> He who is without sons is permitted to have a nephew of the same lineage [*tongzong*] and of the appropriate generation succeed as heir, giving priority first to the sons of his brothers [second degree] and next to the sons of his first cousins [third degree], then the sons of his second cousins [fourth degree], and finally the sons of his third cousins [fifth degree].   (*Da Ming huidian* 1587, 19: 20a–b)

On this principle, a first-order nephew had the superior claim on the succession and the property that came with it because his father had participated in household division with the deceased. A second-order nephew came next because his grandfather had participated in household division with the deceased's father, and so on.

Now, what were the early Ming state's reasons for imposing these new laws? One important concern was no doubt administrative. The Ming's military system of hereditary soldier households (*junhu*) depended on mandatory succession for its very survival.[16] So too did its system of hereditary artisan households (*jianghu*). Given that the rate of heirlessness among married men was close to 20 percent in Ming times (as discussed in the Introduction), had succession not been made compulsory, both systems would have been seriously short of manpower within a few generations. Furthermore, since succession to a military or artisan household was generally an onerous duty to be avoided at all costs, it was necessary to spell out precisely who could be legally compelled to assume the succession—hence the emphasis on the "person who ought to succeed," as well as the clear delineation of the lineage sequence.

More generally, however, mandatory nephew succession was part and parcel of Ming Taizu's campaign to eradicate the moral turpitude into which China, in his view, had sunk under Mongol rule and to reorder society along Neo-Confucian lines. Foremost among his advisers in this endeavor were Song Lian and Liu Ji, members of the Jinhua (Zhejiang) school of Neo-Confucianism, who, in keeping with the intellectual traditions of that school, saw the resurrection of the classical rituals (*li*), as reinterpreted by Zhu Xi, and the legislation of laws (*fa*) as the best way to regulate society. In their formulation, both rites and law were necessary, with law as the principal means by which the rites would be enforced (Langlois 1981; Dardess 1983; Farmer 1995). Since those rites were no longer to be confined to government officials but were to "extend down to the commoners," the emphasis on them, particularly mourning and ancestral rituals, necessarily created a greater insistence on the continuity of patrilines.

Finally, and most fundamentally, the early Ming laws reflected the absorption into codified law of customary expectations and traditions of long standing. As the succession cases in the *Qingmingji* make clear, whatever the written law of the Song, nephew succes-

16. Although the Ming *weisuo* system of self-sufficient military colonies was not effected empire-wide until the 1390's, Zhu Yuanzhang established a colony of hereditary military households in Nanjing even before he founded the new dynasty in 1368 (Wakeman 1985, 1: 33–35).

sion had in fact been a dominant social practice. It was assumed that a sonless man had to have an heir if at all possible. It was also assumed that the most closely related nephews had the superior claim on the succession, and that the chosen heir, whether pre-mortem or postmortem, was entitled to all, and not just part, of the property. In that sense, the Ming regulations represented the con-vergence of codified law and existing practice.

For daughters, the consolidation of mandatory nephew succes-sion meant a contraction in their claims to juehu property. Ming (and then Qing) law explicitly stipulated that in the event a house-hold died out, an heir was to be appointed from among the suitable candidates within the lineage. Only if there was no suitable male could daughters inherit (*Da Ming huidian* 1587, 19: 20b; Qing: 088-02). A daughter's legal rights to extinct household property thus took second place to those of all of her agnatic male cousins out to fourth cousins (*zu xiongdi*).

To work, the new succession law required an enlarged pool of possible heirs. This was accomplished, first of all, by pushing the range of potential candidates out beyond the boundaries of the five degrees of mourning. Where Tang and Song law had restricted legal heirs to male agnates of the proper generational order within the "same lineage" (*tongzong*), as defined by the five degrees of mourn-ing (Tang: 237; Song: 193), Ming and Qing law accepted not only male relatives outside of the five degrees as heirs, but even males who merely bore the same surname as the adopting father (on the assumption that somewhere in the past, however distant, the two families must have been related; *Da Ming huidian* 1587, 19: 20a–b; Qing: 078-01).

Greater latitude was further achieved with the incorporation of a substatute in the Qing code permitting combined succession (*jian-tiao*), whereby an only son could succeed his father as well as one (or more) of his father's brothers (Qing: 078-05). Previously, combined succession, though a common social practice, had been strictly for-bidden because it violated mourning and sacrificial rituals: a man could not be the full-fledged son of two sets of parents simultane-ously. But in 1775, amid escalating legal cases about even more ir-regular types of succession (same-generation succession, different-surname succession, and so on), the state relented and permitted combined succession. It solved the ritual problem by decreeing that if a single heir succeeded both the eldest brother (the main branch, *zhangfang*) and a younger brother (secondary branch, *cifang*), he was to observe the three years' mourning for the eldest brother and his wife, and only the one year's for the other brother and his wife. If a single heir succeeded to two younger brothers, then he was to observe the three years' mourning for his birth parents and only the one year's for his other set of parents (*Qinding libu zeli* 1845, 59: 6b–7b). With combined succession, of course, came the right to inherit the property of both branches.

The effects of these changes on daughters' legal inheritance rights should be obvious. The more necessary and the easier it became to find an heir, the less likely it became for daughters to inherit by default. There was thus in written law a contraction of daughter inheritance by default, most dramatically from the Song, but even from the Tang.

Whether this contraction in law reflected a similar contraction in reality is another question. It probably did not, for the changes outlined above resulted from the incorporation into the codes of various social practices of long standing. Even in the Song, the claims of male cousins to the property of an extinct household customarily took precedence over the claims of daughters, despite the law limiting the rights of heirs appointed posthumously. Similarly, there existed in social practice, if not in law, the clear understanding that the nephew most closely related to the deceased had a superior claim to the succession and the property that went with it. And people in search of an heir had never kept to the kinship boundaries prescribed in the Tang and Song codes. The contraction in daughters' rights in law did not reflect so much a similar contraction in fact as a narrowing of the gap between codified law and customary practice.

The major changes in daughters' inheritance rights from the Song through the Qing thus occurred not in the domain of household division, but in that of patrilineal succession. As this chapter has argued, a law entitling daughters to half-shares of the family property during household division probably did not exist, but even if it did, it was an anomaly, not just, as Shiga contends, in the long sweep of Chinese history, but even in the Southern Song itself.

What was truly exceptional about the Song was the extent of its claim on the property of extinct households. The Song state established more precise regulations on the disposition of juehu property than any other dynasty, and it did so for reasons that had more to do with its own fiscal health than with any concern about succession, inheritance, or dowry. The Song laws had a mixed effect on daughters' inheritance rights, expanding them in certain situations, but contracting them in others.

After the Song, imperial law and popular practice converged with the state's recognition of private ownership of land and its incorporation into law of mandatory nephew succession. As a result, a daughter's right to inherit by default became ever more contingent. Whether she could inherit anything at all came to depend not just on the absence of brothers, but on the absence of lineage nephews as well.

CHAPTER TWO

The Inheritance Rights of Widows
from the Song Through the Qing

Outside of their role as daughters, women came into contact with issues of property most frequently as widows. Widows' rights to property went through complex historical change after the Song. The first major transformation came with the adoption of mandatory nephew succession in the early Ming. And the second, driven by the chaste widow ideal, occurred within the mandatory nephew succession regime itself, culminating in mid-Qing legislation that permitted a widow to reject an heir not of her liking.

That story of dynamic change within the domain of patrilineal succession is best told with reference to the work of Shiga Shūzō, whose scholarship has so dominated the field on late imperial family law.[1] At the heart of his analysis of a widow's property claims is his concept of the husband-wife unit, which he defines as "a rule whereby during the husband's lifetime the wife's personality is absorbed in the husband's, whereas after the latter's death his personality is represented by his wife" (1978: 119–20). By the logic of that concept, a sonless widow's relationship to her husband's property could only be custodial: as her husband's representative after his death, she was to maintain it intact for his future heir, one that she herself was obligated to adopt. By the same token, as her husband's representative, she had the supreme power to select an heir for him. In Shiga's view, those were hard-and-fast rules in both law and custom throughout the period from the Song through the end of the imperial era.

---

1. It will be remembered that the term "patrilineal succession" refers to those principles and practices that governed inheritance in families where there were no birth sons.

My disagreements with Shiga's static picture are threefold. A close look at the available evidence suggests that, in the Song, a widow had the right to inherit her husband's property outright, not restricted by any legal imperative to preserve it for some future heir. It was only in the early Ming that she was relegated to a custodial role. What Shiga misses was the shift in her rights that came with mandatory nephew succession.

Beyond that, a widow's authority in the selection of an heir clearly did not remain the same throughout the period. Where Song law gave a widow great latitude in the matter, law from the early Ming on not only compelled her to adopt an heir, but also dictated whom she should adopt. Shiga's concept of the husband-wife unit leads him to exaggerate a widow's powers of appointment in the Ming and Qing, portraying them as no different from what they had been in the Song.[2] What he misses here was the contraction in her powers under the tightly structured regime of mandatory nephew succession.

Finally, Shiga focuses his attention on the legal principles of a widow's property rights, without regard to actual legal practice. A close examination of court cases shows another major force of change also not considered by Shiga. The adoption of mandatory nephew succession in the early Ming was accompanied by the growth of the cult of widow chastity. That cult, paradoxically, actually empowered widows, as judges came to enlarge their custodial powers in reward for their virtue.[3]

Thus, where Shiga sees continuity, I argue for fundamental changes in a widow's property rights over time. They contracted sharply with the adoption of mandatory nephew succession in the early Ming, but subsequently expanded with the rise of the chastity cult and the Qing legislation giving a widow the prerogative to reject an heir she did not like.

2. Although Fuma Susumu (1993) challenges Shiga's conception of the supreme power of the widow in succession matters, he does not provide an alternative construct for understanding the nature of a widow's powers or the changes over time.

3. Scholars like Holmgren (1985), Fuma (1993), Birge (1995), and Sommer (1996) emphasize the ways in which the cult of widow chastity restricted women's access to property. Although that was undeniably an important effect, far too little attention has been paid to the other side of the coin—the ways in which widow chastity also empowered women. For other important studies of widow chastity, see Elvin 1984; Mann 1987; T'ien 1988; and Carlitz 1997.

Widows and Litigation Over Patrilineal Succession

Although household division was the more common mode for the intergenerational transmission of property in imperial China, taking place in perhaps 80 percent of families, patrilineal succession in fact generated far more litigation—accounting for fully 79 percent of the cases (340 of 430) on which this study draws.[4] And, as Table 2 shows, by far the greatest number of those cases, 204, involved widows. This was, in fact, the single largest category of litigation over inheritance. To explain this phenomenon, two questions need to be addressed. Why was litigation more frequent over patrilineal succession than over household division? And why did widows find themselves the most frequent focus of litigation over patrilineal succession?

We need not linger long over the first question. As Philip Huang has demonstrated, household division was governed by well-established and clear-cut community norms and procedures that helped to minimize litigation. Once the decision to partition the household had been made, several respected middlemen, drawn from neighbors and kin, were called in to oversee the process and to ensure its fairness. After setting aside portions of the property for the old-age maintenance of any surviving parent and the dowries of any unmarried daughters, the remaining property would be divided into shares of equivalent value and distributed to the sons, often by drawing lots. A household division document (*fenjiadan*), listing in minute detail what property went to whom, would then be drawn up and signed by all the recipients as well as by the middlemen. The process, by virtue of its strict attention to detail and equality among brothers, left little room for future discord. Should a dispute nevertheless subsequently arise, the first recourse would be to the middlemen, who more often than not were able to settle the problem. Disputes over household division thus tended to be resolved in the community, rarely escalating into a lawsuit at the local yamen (P. Huang 1991, 1996: 25–28, 60–61).

The potential for conflict was much greater in patrilineal succession for a number of reasons. First, whereas the fundamental principle of household division was equality, the essence of patrilineal

4. The 80 percent is based on the rate of heirlessness in Ming and Qing China, roughly 20 percent, as discussed in the Introduction.

TABLE 2
Litigation over Patrilineal Succession and
Household Division, Song–Qing

Litigant	Patrilineal succession cases	Household division cases	Total cases
Husband	18	—	18
Widow	204	39	243
Family/lineage members	118	51	169
TOTAL	340	90	430

SOURCES: Baodixian dang'an; Baxian dang'an; Cheng He n.d.; Dai Zhaojia 1721; Dan-Xin dang'an; Dong Pei 1881, 1883, 1884; Fan Zengxiang 1897, 1910; Gao Tingyao 1862; Gui Danmeng 1863; Hu Xuechun 1851; Huang Wensu n.d.; Kuai Demo 1874; Li Jia 1904; Li Jun 1833; Li Yu 1667; Li Zhifang 1654; Liu Kezhuang n.d.; Liu Ruyu 1860; Lu Chongxing 1739; Lu Jianzeng 1725; Lu Weiqi 1893; Lu Ying 1746; Pan Shaocan 1688; Panqiao Yeren 1835; QMJ; Qufu shifan xueyuan lishixi 1980—; Shen Yanqing 1862; Sichuansheng dang'anguan 1991; Sun Dinglie 1904; Taihu Wu Guangyao 1903; Wu Hong 1721; Xu Shilin 1906; Zhang Kentang 1634; Zhang Wuwei 1812; Zhong Tizhi 1890.

succession was inequality. One branch of the lineage would benefit at the expense of the others. The benefit was twofold: not only would the heir himself receive all of his adoptive father's property, but his loss of any right to his birth family's property meant a greater share for his brothers. In this zero-sum situation, where one branch's gain was every other's loss, it was little wonder that the appointment of an heir set relatives against each other.

Second, whereas family division was the internal affair of just one household, patrilineal succession drew in the wider network of patrilineal kin. Each potential heir-giving family within the lineage had a vital stake in the succession, and the more people involved, the greater the likelihood of conflict. At their most contentious, fights over patrilineal succession rivaled intrigues at the imperial court, with the formation of factions (dang) around different candidates, the buying of needed support with the promise of payoffs, and the escalation of the dispute into violence against both property and people (Li Jun 1833, 1: 10a–11b; Qufu shifan xueyuan lishixi 1980—, 3.1: 428–37, 441).

Third, patrilineal succession was not just about the distribution of property; it was also about the creation of a parent-child relationship. The adopted heir was to become the full-fledged son of his adoptive parents, and, if they were still alive, was expected to share the same residence and to care for them in their old age. Because of the legal and ritual requirement that the adopted heir be just one generation removed from the adoptive father, the candidates were not always adorable little boys who invited and gave affection easily. For those adopting later in life, the candidates were more likely to be married men with wives and children of their own; some could even be quite elderly, such as Liu Yi, of Boping county (Shandong), who was well into his seventies when he became the son of the reluctant Mrs. Liu (née Zhang), herself over eighty (Hu Xuechun 1851, xia: 41a–43a). With adult men, genuine affection for the adoptive parents could not be taken for granted, and a couple in need of an heir understandably looked long and hard at the character of the candidates, desiring one who had their best interests at heart and was not just after their property. This need for an affectionate relationship between the parties made the selection of an heir a particularly contentious issue.

It also essentially ruled out a single guiding principle for patrilineal succession, like the one that governed household division (equal division among all sons). How did one balance the needs and desires of the adoptive parents and the claims of lineage members? The very nature of patrilineal succession made it an ambiguous process at best, one that by its very uncertainty invited conflict. Codified law itself was not immune to the ambiguity, coming, as we shall see, to embody contradictory principles of selection that the savvy litigant attempted to exploit to his or her own advantage. The eighteenth-century official Zhang Zhentao was not too far off the mark when he complained that "with the establishment of more laws [on succession], the abuses only multiply" (*fa li bi sheng*; Zhang Zhentao n.d., 59: 8a).

Finally, disputes over patrilineal succession easily outstripped a community's capacity for mediation. From the state's perspective, conflicts among lineage members were ideally to be handled within the lineage, but here the lineage itself was a principal in the dispute. Also, fights over patrilineal succession were not always confined to the arena of an individual village, town, or city, but drew in patrilineal kin residing in other places. In those circumstances, a single community's mechanisms for mediation would be hard pressed to contain the conflict, and the parties would be likely to take their case to the local magistrate as a higher authority who stood above them all.

Within the patrilineal succession process itself, the greatest source of conflict was a widow's designation of an heir. Of my 340 succession cases, 35 percent were disputes among patrilineal kin after the death of both the husband and the wife. Another 5 percent were disputes between a man and his relatives over his particular choice of an heir. But the majority, 60 percent in all, were between the widow and members of her husband's kin (Table 2).

Of particular interest here is the fact that the widow appeared as the principal in litigation twelve times more frequently than the husband. The death of a sonless husband precipitated an immediate and grave succession crisis. An heir had to be appointed as soon as possible to serve as chief mourner in the funeral rites and take over the sacrifices to the ancestors. Since succession as ritual heir also meant succession to property, prospective candidates and their families had a keen interest in the integrity of the deceased's estate, fearful that if the widow had charge of it for too long, she might spend more than was necessary for her daily living expenses or, more malevolently, that she might seize the opportunity to conceal contracts, sell land and housing for more easily hidden cash, or give everything away to personal favorites. There was thus tremendous pressure on the widow to adopt an heir right after her husband's death. When the process of selection did not go smoothly, it was not uncommon for the burial to be delayed for months on end. Accounts of succession disputes frequently contain phrases such as "disrupting the funeral, fighting over the succession" (naosang zhengji); "obstructing the encoffining, forcing the succession" (zulian qiangji); and "stopping the funeral, obstructing the burial" (tingsang zuzang; Zhang Wuwei 1812, shiyu: 20a–21b; Qufu shifan xueyuan lishixi 1980–, 3.1: 428–36).

The death of a wife before the husband was just not as ritually or economically significant. He, after all, could still hope to acquire a son of his own either through a concubine or through a successor wife (jishi). There was also no compelling need for him to adopt an heir to attend to his wife's ritual needs. A lineage nephew could be designated as the honorary chief mourner at her funeral, a position that did not confer automatic status as a patrilineal heir, and sacrifices to her spirit did not begin anyway until the husband died, and their tablets could be placed together on the ancestral altar. So far as the couple's property was concerned, the death of a wife in no way affected the husband's rights. All in all, a husband did not experience anywhere near the same pressure to appoint an heir after his wife's death as she experienced after his.

Finally, a widow was much more vulnerable than her husband to challenges from his agnatic kin. Brothers or cousins who would not think of dragging each other into court did not show the same restraint when it came to widows. Indeed, a full 15 percent of the 204 widow-related succession cases were disputes in which kinsmen took the woman to court to contest her husband's adoption of a particular heir before his death. Not daring to challenge him about his choice directly, they had bided their time, holding their fire until he had died and they could aim their sights on his widow, the more vulnerable target. In the other 85 percent of the cases, the widow was challenged by her husband's kin over her own choice of heir. Whatever a widow's authority in succession by law, it should not be confused, as Shiga tends to do, with her actual authority in practice. What the statistics show most conclusively is that a widow's choice was open to contestation in a way that a husband's was not.

Widows in the Song

Turning now to the question of historical change over time, we again take Song law as our starting point, looking first at the nature of a sonless widow's receipt of her deceased husband's property and then at her powers in the appointment of an heir.

Inheritance Rights

The Song code (following Tang law) spelled out the widow's right to her husband's property in its statute on household division. It read:

Whenever real estate and other property is to be divided, it shall be divided equally among brothers. . . . If a brother has died, his son(s) shall receive his share. . . . A widow without son(s) is to receive her husband's share. . . . That refers to a woman who maintains her chastity [*shouzhi*] in her husband's household. If a widow remarries [*gaishi*], she cannot take any bond-servants, slaves, land, or housing with her. [That property] is to be divided equally among the coparceners (*yingfenren*). (Niida, comp. 1933: 245–46; Song: 197)

Thus, if a deceased man had sons, they were to receive (*cheng*) his share of family property at the time of household division. If a man had no sons, his widow was to receive his share, but was permitted to keep it only if she did not remarry.

What was the precise nature of a sonless widow's receipt of her husband's property under Song law? Shiga, in keeping with his view that only a man's patrilineal heirs could succeed to his property, argues that a widow did not in fact inherit in the same way that a son did. Although she became the legal owner of the property, entitled to its product as well as responsible for its taxes, her ownership was not absolute. She merely served as the "conduit" through which property flowed down a patriline. Both law and custom restricted her rights of disposal so as to safeguard the property for her husband's future heir.

Evidence from the *Qingmingji* would seem to support Shiga's position. Two cases from the 1240's cite a specific regulation prohibiting widows from disposing of their husbands' property. The first reference mentioned both widows without sons or grandsons and widows with sons or grandsons who had not yet reached their majority:

In law [*zai fa*], if a widow has no sons or grandsons or if they are under 16 years of age, then she is definitely not permitted to mortgage or sell the land or housing (*tianzhai*).   (*QMJ*: 141)

The second reference mentioned only widows without sons and grandsons:

In law, should a widow without sons or grandsons arbitrarily [*shan*] mortgage or sell the property, she will be punished with 100 blows of the heavy bamboo, and the property will be returned to her as the owner. If the buyer and/or the guarantor was aware of the situation, he will be punished in the same manner.   (*QMJ*: 304–5)

In other *Qingmingji* cases, the judges, though they did not cite this regulation, nevertheless also prohibited widows without sons or grandsons or with only minor sons or grandsons from selling or mortgaging their deceased husbands' property (*QMJ*: 143–46, 164–65, 234–37, 592–93).[5]

On the basis of these references, it would be easy to assume, as Shiga does, that the same rationale informed both situations—that just as a widow with young sons had to preserve their patrimony

5. As for a widow with adult sons, Song law stipulated that the sons could not dispose of the property without their mother's express permission. The proper procedure for such transactions was for the contract to be drawn up in the mother's name, with the sons affixing their signatures or seals at the end of the document (cited in *QMJ*: 301). If a son disposed of property behind the widow's back, she was

until they came of age, a widow without sons had to preserve the patrimony of her husband's future heir. It is an assumption shared by other scholars (Birge 1992; Ebrey 1993).

But if we separate out the evidence pertaining to widows with young sons from the evidence pertaining to widows without sons, it becomes evident that the principles underlying the two proscriptions were not the same at all. Although the prohibition against disposal by a widow with minor sons derived from a concept of custodianship, the prohibition against disposal by a widow without sons had an entirely different origin altogether, one that had nothing to do with patrilineal succession.

The widow as custodian was clearly the rationale behind the prohibition concerning a widow with young sons. One official explained it in terms of the "thrice followings" (*sancong*): "It is based on the principle that after her husband's death, a woman is to follow her son [*fu si cong zi*]. A woman does not succeed to a share of the property, so how can she privately mortgage or sell it?" (*QMJ*: 141). Another, capturing perfectly the custodial nature of a widow's management, ruled in a case before him that the property in dispute was to go to the widow to manage until her son reached his majority. In the meantime, she was not permitted to mortgage or sell any of it (*QMJ*: 237). The regulation was intended to protect a youth's patrimony from dissipation by the widow.

It was also intended to protect both the widow and her children from avaricious relatives and unscrupulous land grabbers, who, unconcerned for their welfare, might well strip them of what little property they possessed. As one official put it:

Even before the deceased's body has grown cold, brothers, uxorilocal sons-in-law, and other relatives, without attending to the funeral arrangements, set out to cheat and bully the widow and her children. Sometimes they steal property, sometimes they take away contracts, sometimes they illegally sell the land, and sometimes they forcibly cut the harvest. . . . Forgetting righteousness [*yi*] in their quest for profit [*li*], they are utterly heartless. This practice is most despicable.   (*QMJ*: 236)

Also despicable were relatives who pressured a widow into mortgaging or selling property to them (*QMJ*: 234–35), as well as "local

---

entitled to go to court to have the transaction annulled (see, e.g., *QMJ*: 301–2, 596–99). But a widow could not dispose of the property without the consent of her adult son(s) either. On that score, the law stipulated that if a senior (*zunzhang*) illegally sold (*daomai*) the land of a junior (*beiyou*), the property was to be returned to the junior and the money returned to the purchaser (cited in *QMJ*: 599).

despots" (*haomin*) who accumulated land without regard to the consequences, enriching themselves at the expense of others (*QMJ*: 301, 317–18). The prohibition thus was also intended to ensure that a transaction entered into under duress could be canceled.

Shiga takes the custodial logic behind the prohibition concerning widows with minor sons and assumes that it also explains the prohibition concerning widows without sons. The problem with such an interpretation is, first, that it conflicts with the evidence set out in the last chapter that patrilineal succession was not at the forefront of the Song's concerns. The Song did not legislate mandatory succession: a widow was not legally obligated to establish an heir for her deceased husband, nor were his relatives legally obligated to do so after her death. Moreover, in the case of extinct households, the state kept more of the property for itself than it gave to a posthumous heir. If an heir did not have to be appointed, either during a widow's lifetime or after her death, and if the state itself claimed much of the property, it makes little sense to suppose that the prohibition was intended to ensure that the widow conserve it for some future heir.

Second, other evidence strongly suggests that preserving the property for an adopted heir was not the reason for the proscription. Two cases from the *Qingmingji*, for instance, involve the right of disposal of a widow without sons, and though the presiding official in each applied the prohibition, neither did so in the name of patrilineal succession. In the first case, from Jianyang county (Fujian) in the 1240's, the sonless widow Qiu A Liu brought suit against her husband's cousin, who had appropriated and then sold off land that had belonged to her husband. The judge voided the transaction and ordered the cousin to return the money to the buyer and the buyer to return the land to the widow. He also expressly forbade Qiu A Liu to mortgage or sell the property "without good reason" (*feili*). He did not make any mention of an adopted heir (*QMJ*: 144–46).

In the second case, from Jian'an county (also Fujian), after Weng Tai died sonless, a woman, Hu Wujie (Fifth Sister Hu), came forward claiming to be his wife and requesting that Weng's property be turned over to her. For reasons that are not clear, the judge was suspicious of her claim, demanding that she provide proof of the marriage. If she could not do so, then Weng Tai's property would be declared, as was required by law, extinct household property and confiscated by the government. If she could substantiate her claim, then the property would go to her management. But she would only be permitted to live off of the interest. She could not mortgage or sell the property. To ensure that she would not be tempted to do so, the land contracts were to be placed in the county treasury for safe-keeping (*QMJ*: 143–44). There is no surviving record of the outcome of this case, but nowhere in the account is there any suggestion that the property was being held for a future heir. Rather, the overwhelming sense of the case is that the county was most concerned that the property eventually end up in its coffers.

The Song government's priorities can also be seen in its policy on "calling in a husband" (*zhaojie jiaofu*), the practice whereby a widow, upon remarriage, had her new husband come live with her in her household rather than, as was the usual custom, going herself to live with her new husband in his family's household. In the early Northern Song, it was stipulated that if the widow of a sonless man who had already divided up the family property with his brothers and established a separate household called in a second husband, the land was to remain registered under her name as the head of the household. Upon her death, her household was to be declared extinct. The regulation specifically prohibited the property from being registered under her new husband's name, since the transfer would put it beyond the reach of the state and its extinct household policies. The purpose of the regulation was not to secure the property for some future heir to her first husband, but to secure it for the state (*Song huiyao jigao*: 5902).

That policy remained in effect during the Southern Song. By the 1220's at the latest, the Board of Revenue had issued a regulation that, in keeping with the ceilings it had come to place on bequeathed and extinct household property, placed a cap of 5,000 guan on the amount of property a "calling-in" widow could retain of her previous husband's estate. Property over that amount was to go to the state. It also stipulated that should the widow decide to join her husband's family or should she die, her household and its remaining property would be treated as extinct (*QMJ*: 273). In this later regulation as well, no mention was made of any need for the widow to hold the property intact for a future heir.

Finally, the law permitted a widow without sons the same right to bequeath property to others through a will that it granted a widower without sons. The relevant regulation specified that "in cases where property has no coparcener [*chengfen zhi ren*], should [the owner] wish to bequeath it to paternal or maternal relatives above the fifth degree of mourning, then let the owner report the matter to the authorities, who shall issue an official certificate to that effect" (*QMJ*: 141–42, 304–5). By the letter of that law, a widow could, if she so chose, leave the property to an heir for her husband, but she also could leave it to any number of other relatives, subject of course to the ceilings the Song imposed on wills.[6]

Clearly, the state put its own fiscal concerns above patrilineal succession. The prohibition against a sonless widow disposing of property was intended, at least in part, to protect the property for its own coffers, and not for some future heir.

It also served the state's interests in another way. As we have seen, the Song state designated households headed by widows with no male descendants, whether natural or adopted, as a separate category—the "female household"—in its household registration system, deserving, like "official households" (*guanhu*), "single male households" (*danding*), "temples and monasteries" (*siguan*), and "households of the aged and infirm" (*laojihu*), of exemptions from labor service and/or land tax because of their special circumstances. Except for a brief spell during Wang Anshi's New Policies reforms between 1068 and 1085, female households were wholly exempt from labor service and relieved of some portion of the land tax (*Song huiyao jigao*: 6218; Yanagida 1993.)

Female households were often the focus of state concern over tax and labor service fraud (Yanagida 1993). The purchaser of a widow's land might not, as was required by law, register the transaction at the local yamen, thereby retaining for his own benefit the exemptions on the property. Or he might bribe yamen underlings and, with their collusion, pay the land tax and render labor service at the widow's lowered rates. The thirteenth-century regulation could well have been intended to cut off the problem at its source by prohibiting widows from disposing of their property in the first place.

Finally, as vulnerable as a widow with minor sons might be, a widow without sons was even more so, for she had no one to rely on for her livelihood. Should she dispose of her husband's property, either willingly or under duress, she faced a bleak future and a very uncertain old age. The prohibition was thus intended also to preserve the property as the source of the widow's livelihood.

6. Note that there is no contradiction here between the Song state's self-interested confiscatory extinct household policies and its permitting a sonless widow to bequeath property to others in a will. As with a sonless man, the extinct household laws only went into effect when he had not formally arranged for the disposition of his property after his death.

It should also be mentioned that the 1240's references in the *Qingmingji* are the only evidence of such a prohibition. There is absolutely no evidence to suggest that widows without sons were similarly restricted earlier in the Song.

Contrary to Shiga's assumption, then, a widow without sons did not possess merely custodial rights over her husband's property in the Song. Throughout most of the period, she enjoyed the same freedom of disposal as any other property owner, unconstrained by state law. When a prohibition was imposed in the thirteenth century, it had more to do with the state's fiscal policies and its paternalistic concern for the weak and the helpless than with any presumed emphasis on patrilineal succession. Under Song law, a widow without sons possessed the right to inherit her husband's property. The custodial logic did not obtain. Nor could it, for it derived from mandatory (nephew) succession, not yet established in the Song.

The Appointment of Heirs

As with inheritance rights, widows possessed much greater powers in the appointment of an heir in the Song than they were to have in the Ming and Qing. Those powers were a direct result of the Song government's posture on patrilineal succession. As we saw in the last chapter, Song law (like Tang law) nowhere required the appointment of heirs for men who lacked birth sons. In that, it was influenced, however distantly, by the classical descent-line ideal, which did not prescribe mandatory succession for the five-generation, lesser-descent line model that served as the basis for mourning and ancestral rites.

Song laws spoke in terms of "letting" or "permitting" people to establish an heir for a man who lacked birth sons. The Song code stipulated: "Let [*ting*] those without sons adopt a male of the proper generation from the same lineage [*tongzong*]" (Song: 193). An edict issued in the mid-1160's elaborated:

Those without descendants are permitted to adopt as son or grandson a male of the proper generation from the same lineage [*tongzong*]. . . . He who wishes to succeed to an extinct household [*jijue*] and who has been so ordered [*mingji*] by the extinct family's close senior relatives [*jinqin zunzhang*] shall be allowed to do so. When the husband is dead but the wife is still alive, then follow his wife [*fu wang qi zai, cong qi qi*]. (Cited in QMJ: 220, 247)

Under Song law, then, establishing an heir was not a legal obligation, but a legal prerogative.

That prerogative extended to widows as well. "When the husband is dead but the wife is still alive, then follow his wife" was the established principle for the adjudicating of succession disputes involving widows. And as cases from the *Qingmingji* amply document, judges did indeed follow the wife. Although they frequently represented a widow's adoption of an heir as a moral obligation, they did not see it as a legal one. They left the decision entirely up to the widow herself. In fact, no judge in any of the 20 widow-related *Qingmingji* cases forced a reluctant widow to adopt an heir for her husband.

What is more, if a widow did choose to adopt an heir, the decision on which lineage nephew to adopt was also hers alone to make, free of interference from her husband's kin. The official Cai Hang (*jinshi* 1229) made this clear in a case he heard while serving as the judicial commissioner of the Jiangnan Eastern Circuit in the late 1240's and early 1250's. The widow, a Mrs. Li, had selected one heir, and the lineage seniors (*zhong zunzhang*) another. Commissioner Cai did not even bother to assess the qualifications of the two candidates. He ruled solely on the basis of the widow's authority as family head after her husband's death:

By law, the establishment of an heir must be based on the source of the decision. Since Mrs. Li is the family head [*jiazhang*], the establishment of an heir must lie with her. . . . It is clear that the establishment of [the lineage's choice] came from the private plotting of the lineage and not from Mrs. Li's own intentions.   (*QMJ*: 244)

The legitimacy of a succession, in other words, depended entirely on whether the heir had been chosen by the person with the authority to make the selection.

The widow's authority in this domain constrained not only the actions of lineage elders, but also those of officials. Hu Ying expressed that well in a case he heard while serving as the supervisor of relief granaries for Hunan in the early 1240's. Zheng Wenbao had adopted Yuanzhen, a little boy of a different surname, to be his heir. After his death, his elder brother, Zheng Fengji, brought suit, hoping to replace Yuanzhen with one of his own two sons. Hu Ying reminded the plaintiff that current law permitted the appointment of an heir of a different surname so long as the adoption had taken place when the boy was under the age of three sui, as had been done in this case. Perhaps the widow would agree to appoint one of Fengji's sons to serve jointly (*bingli*) as Wenbao's successor, he suggested, but that was strictly up to her:

If Fengji . . . dislikes having someone not of the same lineage as [his younger brother's] heir, fearing that the ancestral spirits would not accept sacrifices from such a one, he should reason with his younger brother's wife so that she would select an heir of the appropriate generation from the lineage to be established jointly with Yuanzhen. . . . If she does not listen to his advice, according to the law, when the husband has died but the wife is still alive, then follow his wife. *There is no principle permitting compulsion by lineage seniors or officials.* (*QMJ*: 245–46; italics added)

In another case, the presiding judge, dead set against the widow's choice of heir for her deceased son, wrote (with a palpable sense of regret) that "officials . . . can only let her do as she proposes" (*QMJ*: 271–72).

Finally, the widow's authority in this matter meant that no male agnate, no matter how closely related to the deceased, had any legal claim whatsoever on the succession. Hu Ying was far from alone in dismissing the suits of even brothers and their sons on the grounds of the widow's exclusive prerogative to select her husband's heir. In a 1215 case from Ningdu county (Jiangxi), for instance, the judge rejected Xie Wenxue's suit against his widowed sister-in-law, ruling that she was entirely within her rights in selecting a distant lineage nephew over Xie's son (Huang Wensu n.d.: 605–6). Similarly, in a succession dispute in Tongcheng county (Hubei) in the 1250's, the presiding official ruled that the widow could keep as her husband's heir a different-surnamed son she had adopted when he was a little boy, instead of selecting one of the 11 sons of her husband's three brothers (*QMJ*: 217–23).

In the Song, the only constraint on this wifely prerogative was the greater authority of parents to select an heir for their son. Song law did not define the respective rights of a widowed daughter-in-law and her parents-in-law, probably because it was just taken for granted that in this matter, as in all matters, a daughter-in-law would defer to the wishes of her parents-in-law.[7] Officials in the

---

7. Song written law merely specified that when both a husband and wife died heirless, the legal right to select an heir for the husband passed to his close senior relatives (*jinqin zunzhang*) (*QMJ*: 220, 247). In Shiga's conception of the husband-wife unit, the right to select an heir belonged first and foremost to the wife as her husband's representative. Consequently, a man's parents and grandparents had to fall into the category of "close senior relatives," and a widow's prerogative had to take precedence over theirs (1967: 330–35, 367). However, both the wording of that law and the logic behind it indicate otherwise. "Close senior relatives" had the right only to "order the appointment of an heir" (*mingji*) for an extinct household. Since no household was considered extinct as long as it contained a deceased man's widow or his parents or grandparents to constitute a taxable unit, parents or grandparents,

Qingmingji shared that expectation, automatically vesting the authority to appoint an heir in the parents rather than the widowed daughter-in-law.

Take, for instance, the case of the widow Liu and her three sons, who lived together in an undivided household. When the eldest son died, leaving a wife, but no sons, a grandnephew of Mrs. Liu's husband came forward to claim the succession for himself, thereby provoking a lawsuit. The official presiding over the case dismissed the grandnephew's claim, ruling that it was up to Mrs. Liu to decide whom she wanted to adopt as a grandson, if she chose to adopt anyone at all. Although the official was well aware of the widowed daughter-in-law's existence, he did not feel it necessary to take her wishes into account (*QMJ*: 211–12). In other cases where a man was survived by both his wife and his parents, the judges likewise just assumed that the senior generation would be making all the decisions (*QMJ*: 214–15, 247, 269–70, 271–72).

The authority of parents-in-law over a daughter-in-law, however, should not distract us from the otherwise broad powers a wife did have in the appointment of an heir under Song law. In its noncompulsory succession regime, a widowed wife was not even legally obligated to adopt an heir for her husband, much less to adopt his closest nephew. It was the Song's stance on patrilineal succession that gave a widow such wide latitude in the appointment of an heir.

Widows in the Ming and Qing

The adoption in the early Ming of mandatory nephew succession transformed a widow's codified rights in patrilineal succession. The crucial law, issued in 1369, read:

A woman without sons who preserves her chastity after her husband dies [*furen fu wang wuzi shouzhizhe*] is to receive her husband's share of property [*he cheng fufen*] and must [*xu*], through the agency of the lineage head [*ping zuzhang*], select a nephew of the appropriate generation as heir. (*Da Ming huidian* 1587, 19: 20b)

This new law explicitly linked a widow's receipt of her husband's property to her adoption of an heir. In so doing, it extended the principle of custodianship, limited in the Song to a widow with minor

---

by the state's own definition, cannot be included among the "close senior relatives." In his analysis, Shiga considers only one meaning of the term "juehu"—the extinction of a patriline—and overlooks the other—the extinction of a taxable unit.

sons, to a widow without sons. She could no longer inherit her husband's property but was merely to receive it to hold in trust for her husband's heir, one that she herself was now legally obligated to adopt.

This law also established a new standard for a legitimate succession. Where under the Song a widow did not even have to consult her husband's patrilineal kin over her choice (her parents-in-law excepted) for a succession to be considered legitimate in the eyes of the law, she was now required not only to consult the lineage head but to obtain his consent to the appointment.[8]

It was a change reflected in the legal discourse of the Ming and Qing. A distinction was drawn between "an agreed-upon appointment of an heir" (*yiji; yili*) and "a private appointment of an heir" (*siji; sili*). The term "agreed-upon" (*yi*) conveys the sense of a consensus reached through discussion, and meant in this context that the widow had consulted with the lineage head and had obtained at least his agreement, and ideally the agreement of her husband's closest agnatic kin as well. The word "private" (*si*) carried the connotation of "selfish" or "self-interested," and meant in this context that the widow had willfully ignored her husband's kin and had adopted an heir without seeking the advice or consent of the lineage head (Baodixian dang'an: 182, 1866.2, 183, 1894.1; Xu Shilin 1906, 3: 65a, 67a; Sichuansheng dang'anguan 1991: 185–87).

From the state's perspective, the lineage head was the ideal person to oversee the "agreed-upon appointment." As one who most likely had no material stake in the succession himself, he presumably could be counted on to put ritual propriety ahead of profit-seeking, and the larger interests of the entire lineage ahead of the petty claims of individual branches. And as the designated leader of the group, he presumably commanded the respect needed to settle the squabbles and to build the consensus for an appointment that would minimize the chance of future conflict and litigation. So important were lineage heads in the selection of an heir that officials

---

8. The phrase "ping zuzhang" in the regulation, which I translate as "through the agency of the lineage head," has often been misinterpreted in Western scholarship to mean that the widow was to rely on the lineage head to select an heir for her, thus endowing him with the sole authority to designate an heir (e.g., Jamieson 1921: 14; Holmgren 1995: 11; Farmer 1995: 93). But as the Daliyuan, China's highest court in the 1910's and 1920's, noted, "ping" here is shorthand for *pingzheng* or "to serve as a witness for" (*DPQ*: 266, 272). The fact that a widow needed the consent of the lineage head for her candidate did not mean that she had to surrender all authority in the matter to him.

of the Ming and Qing routinely turned to them for assistance in resolving succession disputes that had come to court.

A widow's power of appointment in the mandatory succession regime was constrained even more importantly by the principle that the nephew(s) most closely related to the deceased had a legal claim to the succession and through it, to the property of the deceased. The move toward a "required heir" came in another 1369 Ming law:

> He who is without sons is permitted to have a nephew of the same lineage [tongzong] and of the appropriate generation succeed as heir, giving priority first to the sons of his brothers and next to the sons of his first cousins, then the sons of his second cousins, and finally the sons of his third cousins. Only if none of those exist may an heir be chosen from a distant branch or from the same surname [tongxing].   (Da Ming huidian 1587, 19: 20a–b)

By the letter of this law, the widow had no choice but to adopt the required heir.

A major modification came in 1500, when a new principle of selection was set out in law, providing an alternative to succession based on lineage order:

> If the appointed successor [jizi] cannot get along with his adoptive parents, then they can report the matter to the authorities and appoint another in his place. Should they then select as heir one of virtue and talent and of whom they are particularly fond, provided the proper generational sequence is not disrupted, lineage members cannot bring suit to dispute their choice on the basis of order [cixu, i.e., the required succession sequence]. (Da Ming huidian 1587, 19: 21a)

The selection of the worthy and the beloved came to be known in legal discussions as "succession out of affection" (aiji), or preferred succession, and the person so selected "the person one appoints out of affection" (aiji zhi ren), or the preferred heir.

This so-called revocation law clearly gave precedence to the required heir over a preferred heir, since it assumed that the existing heir had been chosen on the basis of lineage order. Thus, an heir was first to be selected on the basis of closeness of relationship, and only if that did not work out, could one be chosen on the basis of affection. Required succession was to be the general rule, and preferred succession the exception only in the event of disharmony between the required heir and the adoptive parents. Anyone who reversed that order by appointing a preferred heir without first trying out the required heir would be guilty of "transgressing the succession" (*yueji; Xinke fabi tianyou* n.d., xia: 50a; Taga 1960: 751, 822; Qufu shifan xueyuan lishixi 1980—, 3.1: 431–32).

The revocation law of 1500 was the last major succession law to go on the books in the Ming dynasty. The Qing incorporated all of the above-mentioned laws into its code without adding any of its own until the end of the Qianlong reign, a subject to which we will return below.

Succession and the Cult of Chastity

With the introduction of mandatory succession in the early Ming, then, a widow was legally obligated to adopt an heir for her husband during her lifetime. What is more, she was legally obligated to adopt as heir "the person who ought to succeed" (*yingji zhi ren*). On the face of it, a widow seemed to be left with little, if any, say in the matter.

This severely constrained role for the widow, however, was countered by new, unintended tendencies resulting from the growing cult of widow chastity. Officials in fact went well beyond the law to reward widows for not remarrying. Indeed, I did not find a single instance in my 43 late Ming–early Qing widow cases in which the presiding official ruled against the widow's choice, even when she had jumped over the closest nephew in favor of a more distant one. In no instance, in other words, did a judge dismiss the widow's preferred heir (unless he was of the wrong generation) in favor of the required heir.

The most an official did to accommodate the claims of the "person who ought to succeed" was to appoint both him and the widow's choice as joint heirs (*bingji, bingli*). This was the solution of Prefect Li Qing to a succession dispute in Ningbo sometime during the last decades of the Ming. The widow, Mrs. Zhang (née Hu), wanted a second-order nephew (*tangzhi*) as heir for her deceased husband, Zhang Shilu. Challenging her on the basis of lineage order was a first-order nephew (the son of Shilu's brother), by law the required heir. In his decision, Prefect Li ordered that both nephews be appointed as heirs, and the property divided equally between them (Li Qing n.d., 2: 107; see also Li Yu 1667, 13: 17a–18a).

On occasion, an official might award a small part of the deceased's property to the required heir as token compensation, as in the following late Ming case from Jiashan county (Zhejiang). What prompted the lawsuit was the elderly widow Qian's decision to adopt as heir a distant nephew, Qian Feng, over her husband's brother's son, Qian Hao. In his decision, Magistrate Li Chenyu explained that since Qian Hao was the required heir and Qian Feng only the preferred heir, Qian Hao did indeed have the superior claim on the succession. Nevertheless, the magistrate thought special consideration should be given the widow, who not only had suffered tremendously in the nearly half-century since her husband's death, but also, at an age of over 70 sui, did not have many years left. He therefore let stand the widow Qian's appointment of Qian Feng, but ordered her to give the disappointed Qian Hao 30 taels of silver from her deceased husband's property (Li Chenyu 1636, yanyu 3: 103).

The officials in these cases were well aware that in privileging the preferred over the required heir, they were going against the strict letter of the law. And to justify that departure, they resorted to a creative interpretation of the revocation law. The following explanation from an early-eighteenth-century prefect was typical:

> Succession [*ji ren hou*] is not just to offer sacrifices to the dead. It is also to provide a residence and sustenance for the living. If a mother is forced to establish someone as heir against her will, how can the two ever be at peace with one another? The code says that if the appointed successor cannot get along with his adoptive parents, they can select another. This refers to an heir that has already been established. Shouldn't this apply even more to someone who has not yet even been appointed?   (Xu Shilin 1906: 3: 65b; see also Panqiao Yeren 1835, 6: 10a–11b; and Qufu shifan xueyuan lishixi 1980–, 3.1: 428–37)

In this way, judges elevated preferred succession to equal standing with succession based on lineage order. To their minds, the selection of a preferred heir should be just as valid as the selection of the required one from the very outset.

Part of the reason for the judges' actions no doubt was that they tended to be deeply suspicious of anyone who brought suit to contest a succession. The explicit linking of property inheritance to patrilineal succession blurred the boundaries between "profit" (*li*) and "duty" (*yi*), a blurring that made officials uneasy. However careful the challengers might be to cast their claims in terms of ritual propriety, the judge could not help suspecting that their real intention was to get their hands on the deceased's property. One magistrate wrote: "Today's so-called patrilineal succession [*chengzong*] is in most cases just a scheme to fight over property [*zhengchan*]" (Li Yu 1667, 20: 35). Another official complained that "disputes over succession [*chengji*] among ignorant rustics [*xiangyu*] are disputes over property. [To them,] property is important, but benevolence and obligation [*enyi*] insignificant." (Hu Xuechun 1851, xia: 41a). Yet another castigated a litigant with this biting remark: "You keep saying 'family property is insignificant, morality is important' [*jia-chan wei qing, lunli wei zhong*]. Who do you think is going to be fooled by such pretty words?" (Zhang Wuwei 1812, pici: 81a–b).

Those who sought to impose their will on widows were often depicted in unflattering terms. Most common were words that evoked images of unrestrained hunger. One official, for instance, described a widow's covetous brother-in-law as a tiger slavering (*chuixian*) over her property (Shen Yanqing 1862, 4: 10a–11a). Another accused a claimant of seeing the property of a sonless deceased man as "meat on the table" (*jishang rou*), making a play on the phrase "a pearl in the hand" (*zhangshang zhu*), often used to refer to a beloved adopted heir (Xu Shilin 1906, 3: 63b). This distrust of the motives of challengers, including the required heir and his immediate family, helped to shift official favor toward the widow and her candidate.

But the more important reason for the shift, as touched on earlier, was the ever-growing normative power of the chaste widow ideal in the late Ming and early Qing.[9] Widow chastity added a whole new dimension to officials' perception of the purpose of succession. To them, ensuring a widow's sexual fidelity to her deceased husband became as important as ensuring the continuity of the man's descent line. And a widow's ability to safeguard her chastity depended on selecting an heir with whom she shared a particular bond of affection, one whom she could trust not to make her life so miserable that remarriage seemed an attractive alternative.

The concern for a chaste widow's welfare can be seen in a dispute that Wang Huizu helped to resolve as legal secretary for the Chang-zhou county (Jiangsu) magistrate. In the 1730's, a young scion of the wealthy and prominent Zhou lineage died, leaving behind his 19-sui wife, who was pregnant with the couple's first and only son, Jilang. After her husband's death, Mrs. Zhou remained chaste, devoting her

9. The canonizing of chaste widows, though not unknown in earlier dynasties, began in earnest after 1304, when the Yuan Board of Rites stipulated that a woman who had lost her husband before the age of 30 sui and who had reached at least the age of 50 was eligible for an imperial testimonial, or *jingbiao* (*Shen ke Yuan dian-zhang* 1908, 33: 17a). She was to be rewarded, in other words, for resisting the great temptation to remarry or carry on an affair in her reproductive and presumably most sexually active years. The 30-50 formula persisted through the imperial period. The main innovation, in the early Qing, was the bestowal of honors on any young widow who died before the age of 50, provided she had been chaste at least 10 years before her death. In 1871, the minimum was reduced to six years (*Qinding libu zeli* 1845, 48: 11a–b; *Qing huidian shili* 1899, 403: 11a; 404: 24a; Liu Jihua 1934: 537–39.)

energies to raising her son. But the boy himself died at age 18 sui, one month before he was to have been married. The widow, worried that her son would have no heir and hence no one to sacrifice to him, wanted to adopt a son for him. Her husband's kin, however, wanted to establish an heir for her deceased husband instead on the very sound ritual grounds that an heir could not be appointed for a man who had died young and unmarried. The dispute came to court in 1753 but remained unresolved until Wang Huizu reviewed the case in 1760.

Wang's sympathies clearly lay with the widow. He suggested to the Changzhou magistrate that Mrs. Zhou be allowed to adopt the heir of her choice so that she could "fulfill her vow to be a virtuous widow" (*yi quan zhenfu zhi zhi*). When the magistrate demurred, fearful of offending such a rich and powerful lineage, Wang pointed out that an official, "as the father and mother of the people [*min fumu*], should not force a faithful widow [*jiefu*] to harbor regrets until the end of her days." The magistrate then finally agreed to allow Mrs. Zhou to adopt an heir for her son (Wang Huizu 1796, shang: 17b–19a).[10]

The impact of the chastity ideal on succession extended beyond this concern for a faithful widow's needs in life to a concern for her needs in death. The eighteenth-century scholar Liang Zhangju, for instance, attributed the nearly universal disregard of the great line–lesser line distinction of the classical descent-line ideal not to the patrilineal principle of a son for every man, but to the sacrificial needs of chaste widows. Heirs had always been established for younger sons, he wrote, out of concern that "faithful widows would be left with no one to offer sacrifices to them after their deaths" (Liang Zhangju 1875, 9: 10a).

From attention to the chaste widow's sacrificial needs, it was not so big a step to the notion that she was adopting an heir not just to succeed her husband but also to succeed herself, and that she therefore should be allowed to adopt any lineage nephew she pleased. And indeed, in the legal discourse of the time, we can find increasing references to the establishment of heirs for women. For instance, in the mid-eighteenth century, the official Zhang Zhentao

---

10. Wang was famous for his sympathetic treatment of chaste widows. As Susan Mann has suggested, this no doubt stemmed in part from his own experience: both of his mothers—his legal mother (his father's wife) and his birth mother (his father's concubine)—remained chaste after his father's death and were imperially canonized as faithful widows (1991: 217–19, 226).

(*jinshi* 1769) proposed "Three Unnecessary Disputes" (*san buzheng*) as a way to deal with the conflict between required succession and preferred succession by specifying under what conditions each should be applied. The third of his three disputes was "No need for disputes over the appointment of heirs to women" (*ji furenzhe bubi zheng*).[11] Zhang distinguished between two types of "women without sons" (*furen wuzi*). For a woman widowed young, the lack of sons bespoke her abiding fidelity to her departed husband. But for a woman widowed later in life, it reflected a profound moral deficiency. Not only had she failed to produce a son herself; her fiercely jealous nature had made it impossible for her husband to take a concubine and acquire a son that way. The young widow deserved to pick as heir anyone she liked from among the eligible candidates (*aiji*), whereas the older woman should be required to hold fast to the prescribed lineage order (*yingji*). Zhang made reference to the patrilineal principle behind succession only in connection with unworthy widows—"establishing an heir [*liji*] is for succession to the patriline [*jizong*]; it is not for succession to herself"—and so excluded them from his category of "the appointment of heirs to women." By implication, a worthy widow was included: her designation of an heir was as much for herself as it was for her husband's patriline (Zhang Zhentao n.d., 59: 8a).

That sort of thinking is evident in succession cases from the late Ming and the Qing as well. In fact, in some cases the only concern expressed was that the faithful widow herself had no heir. A complicated succession case in 1789 in Qufu (Shandong), for instance, involved in part a dispute over who was to be the heir to an imperially commemorated virtuous widow who had starved herself to death after the death of her husband (Qufu shifan xueyuan lishixi 1980—, 3.1: 442–48). Similarly, a case in Cheng'an county (Zhili) in the early nineteenth century involved the appointment of an heir for Mrs. Li (née Gao), who had returned to her natal home after the death of her husband. The magistrate upbraided her father and elder

---

11. The other two unnecessary disputes had to do with premortem and postmortem appointments of an heir for a man. Zhang argued that only living people had desires (*yu*) and hence strong likes and dislikes. Desires died when the person died. All that was left was "breath" [*qi*]. Since an ancestral spirit would accept sacrifices from anyone as long as he just shared the same breath (i.e., was patrilineally related), the chosen heir need not be someone the deceased had been fond of in life. In that case, it would be appropriate to adhere to the prescribed lineage order. By the same token, a man who was still alive should be permitted to choose someone he was particularly fond of. On the concept of "breath" and its relationship to patrilineal succession, see Shiga 1978; and Waltner 1990.

brother for being concerned only with her daily needs and not considering that "her chastity was without an heir [*qi shoujie zhi wu-hou*]" (Zhang Wuwei 1812, pici: 64a–65b). In neither of these cases was mention made of the deceased husband's need for an heir.

Other cases suggest that the chaste widow ideal was also having an effect on the relative authority of a widow and her parents-in-law in the selection of an heir. For instance, in 1882, Dong Pei, then magistrate of Dongxiang county (Jiangxi), ruled in favor of a widow against her father-in-law on the grounds of chastity. After the death of her husband, her father-in-law had forced her to leave his home and live separately. He then brought in a young male relative to live with him as the heir for his deceased son. In his ruling, Dong Pei emphasized the obligation of an adopted heir to live with and support his adoptive mother. He also chided the father-in-law for his selfish concern for his own well-being (noting that the man was well over 80, deaf in both ears, and not long for this world in any event) and his disregard for that of his chaste daughter-in-law. He ordered that the father-in-law's choice be returned to his own family and that the widow, along with an upright member of the lineage, select another heir of the proper generation (Dong Pei 1883, 1: 10a–b). Several other Qing cases document the weight officials came to give to chaste widows in succession disputes with their in-laws (e.g., Zhang Wuwei 1812, pici: 15a–15b; Dong Pei 1881, 1: 4b–6a, 1883, 2: 1b–2b).

The growing emphasis in legal practice on the appointment of heirs for chaste widows did not sit well with all officials. One early-nineteenth-century official reprimanded a man who was thinking of appointing a grandson as his chaste widowed daughter's heir, reminding him of his daughter's obligation to her husband to appoint an heir for him from among his own agnatic kin (Deng Yao n.d.). Another, of the late nineteenth century, felt compelled to point out to the litigants in a case before him that "since the purpose of the appointment of an heir is to continue the patriline [*zongtiao*], heirs are established only for sonless men, and most certainly not for wives or concubines" (Sun Dinglie 1904, 1: 6b). Obviously, the very fact that these men thought it necessary to reiterate the original purpose of succession shows just how widespread the notion of heirs for chaste widows had become.

None of this is to suggest that heirs for chaste widows supplanted heirs for men. After all, a widow's adoption of a son served both purposes at once, securing an heir for herself, as well as for her husband and his patriline. The point is simply that under a legal code that privileged the required heir, the normative power of widow chastity helped to tip the balance toward the preferred heir in legal practice.

Codified law finally caught up with legal practice in the 1770's, when the Qianlong emperor issued two edicts that placed succession out of affection on an equal footing with succession based on lineage order. The first was issued in response to a memorial submitted in 1773 by Hu Jitang, the Jiangxi judicial commissioner (*anchashi*). Commissioner Hu faulted current law on two points—that it created much of the litigation over succession and that it was extremely difficult for officials to enforce.

Lawsuits in Jiangxi are numerous, and particularly so are those brought to contest a succession. Whether prominent families and illustrious lineages or commoners who labor in the fields, whenever a sonless person has a little bit of wealth, relatives will immediately start to quarrel with one another, not satisfied until they manage to seize the property. Some claim required succession [*yingji*], and others preferred succession [*aiji*]. . . . If an heir has not yet been designated, and the sonless person normally does not get along with the person who ought to succeed [*yingji zhi ren*] or else if they had previously been involved in litigation, it is difficult [for an official] to compel the appointment of the one who ought to succeed, there being no affection between them. . . . If the official insists on upholding required succession, how could he guarantee that after the appointment is made the two would live together in peace?

The emperor promptly issued an edict embodying Hu's proposal that the sonless person be permitted to pass over the required heir if there had been a history of strong dislike between them (Hu Jitang 1773, 59: 5a–6a).[12]

Two years later, in 1775, the edict was incorporated as a substatute in the Qing code:

When those without sons adopt an heir, if they normally feel enmity [*xianxi*] toward the person who ought to succeed [*yingji zhi ren*], they are at liberty to select from agnates of the proper generation one who is worthy and of whom they are particularly fond [e.g., *aiji*]. If a lineage member, plotting to acquire the property, coerces them into accepting him as heir or otherwise attempts to influence their selection so that a lawsuit results, the local official is to punish him and to confirm as heir the one chosen for virtue or affection.   (Qing: 078-05)

12. It was also Hu Jitang's memorial that led to the legalization of combined succession (*jiantiao*). The Qianlong emperor's edict is reproduced in *Taiwan* 1961, 4: 642–44.

The other edict, issued in 1775 and later codified in the *Qing huidian* (Collected statutes of the Qing), specifically addressed the question of a widow's selection of an heir. Since appointing an heir was for the dual purpose of continuing the patriline and providing support for the living, the Qianlong emperor decreed, two considerations were paramount: that the generational order be maintained and that "the widow's heart be followed" (*shun shuangfu zhi xin*). Accordingly, a widow should henceforth be permitted to select whichever lineage nephew she liked, provided only that she did not mix the generations (*Qing huidian shili* 1899, 753: 308–9). A selection based on affection was to be as valid as one based on lineage order from the very outset. In this fashion, codified law was brought into line with legal practice.

Since officials had already been adjudicating in favor of widows, the change in the law did not produce a change in the nature of their decisions, but it did result in a change in the way in which they framed them. No presiding official in the 141 widow-related succession cases that postdate the 1775 revision felt obliged to justify passing over the required heir for the widow's preferred heir. All just routinely affirmed her candidate, and most went on to admonish her foes for attempting to usurp her prerogative to adopt the lineage nephew of her choice (e.g., Dong Pei 1884, 1: 16b–17a; Sun Dinglie 1904, 1: 3a; Fan Zengxiang 1910, 3: 1597, 1688).

The 1775 revision in codified law thus compromised one of the basic principles of mandatory nephew succession as set up in the early Ming. The required heir's loss was the widow's gain, for she now had the legal latitude to select whichever lineage nephew she pleased. Moreover, so long as her choice did not confuse the generations, the required heir or anyone else for that matter was not permitted to contest her selection in court. Although widows of the Qing still ended up with fewer rights in patrilineal succession than their Song counterparts had enjoyed, their powers within the mandatory succession regime were greatly expanded.

CHAPTER THREE

Widows and Patrilineal Succession in the Early Republican Period

The late Qing and early Republican years marked an exceptionally important period of change in China's judicial system. The Qing code was revised; civil and criminal matters were for the first time clearly separated; a civil code and a criminal code based on Western models were drawn up; a foreign-derived language of "rights" entered legal discourse; and strict procedural guidelines were introduced. But so far as inheritance and succession were concerned, all the laws in the Qing code remained in effect until the promulgation of the Republican Civil Code in 1929–30. This chapter goes in good part, consequently, to seeking an explanation for the following conundrum. On the one hand, the Daliyuan, China's highest court and principal interpreter of law, repeatedly affirmed the crucial link between patrilineal succession and property inheritance, as well as the continued validity of each and every one of the Qing code's stipulations on the subject. Yet on the other hand, it repeatedly handed down rulings on appeals cases that violated those very same laws, even to the extent of allowing illegal heirs (those of a different surname or of a wrong generation and so on) to inherit all of the property. How was this possible?

It was not that the Daliyuan said one thing but did another. Rather, the apparent inconsistency between word and deed was the inevitable result of the court's adoption of the underlying principles of modern Western civil law. Thus, although the specific laws on succession and inheritance remained the same, they came to be based on a juridical logic quite different from that of the Qing.

The contrast between the two logics is brought out clearly in case records from the early Republican period. The Daliyuan stood at the forefront of change, and its Western-derived juridical principles by no means represented the general legal practice of the time. Lower courts tended in the main to continue to operate on the Qing principles of old. The two logics and their very different consequences came into direct conflict in appeals cases that reached the Daliyuan's chambers.

The widow and her claims serve as the best prism through which to view these developments. As the focal point of litigation over patrilineal succession, she would experience any changes in the legal perception of patrilineal succession and property inheritance more acutely than any other. In the last chapter, we saw how the immense normative power of the chaste widow ideal in the Qing made it difficult for anyone to challenge a widow's appointment of an heir, so long as her choice met the legal requirements (of the same surname, of the proper generation, and so on). In this chapter, we shall see how the new Western-based juridical logic made it difficult for anyone to contest a widow's appointment of even an illegal heir. In the Daliyuan's regime, it became possible for someone to inherit all of a man's property without at the same time being legally recognized as his patrilineal heir. The court's repeated affirmation of the crucial link between patrilineal succession and property inheritance notwithstanding, the ultimate result of its rulings was, in fact, an incipient separation of the two.

Judicial Reform and the Role of the Daliyuan

An official movement toward judicial reform began in 1902 with an edict from the Empress Dowager calling for an investigation of foreign laws and legal systems and the revision of China's own. The project was entrusted first to the Bureau for the Compilation of Laws (*Falü bianzuan guan*), founded in 1904, and then to its successor, the Bureau for the Revision and Compilation of Laws (*Xiuding falü guan*), founded in 1907. The reformers associated with those offices, foremost among them Shen Jiaben, saw their task as twofold: to revise the Qing code as a transition measure and to create new codes based on foreign models that would replace the revised Qing code at the appropriate moment. In 1909, they produced what was called the "Criminal Code of the Great Qing Currently in Use" (*Da Qing xianxing xinglü*), which the imperial court put into effect in the following year, 1910. By then, they had also drafted two new codes that, unlike both the old Qing code and its revised version, clearly separated criminal and civil matters—the New Criminal Code (*Xin xinglü*), presented to the throne in 1907, and the Draft Civil Code (*Minlü cao'an*), presented in 1911 (Meijer 1950).

The New Criminal Code was provisionally put into effect in early 1912 by the fledgling Republican government as the New Criminal Code Temporarily in Force (*Zhanxing xin xinglü*). It remained on the books until 1928, when it was rewritten by the Guomindang. A successor—the Revised Criminal Code (*Xiuzheng xingfa*)—was issued in 1935. The Draft Civil Code, however, generated so much opposition for what was seen as its emphasis on the individual at the expense of the family and society that it was never implemented. Neither was the substantially revised version issued in 1925–26 (the so-called Second Draft) in an attempt to rectify the original's supposed excessive individualism (P. Huang forthcoming). It was only with the promulgation of the Republican Civil Code of 1929–30 that China acquired a civil code to match its criminal code.

Until then, the revised Qing code remained the functioning codified law on civil matters. Because of the fall of the Qing, the "Great Qing" (*Da Qing*) in its name was changed to "Former Qing" (*qian Qing*). Also, the word "Criminal" (*xing*) was dropped, because of the adoption of a separate criminal code and because of a belated recognition that the "Criminal" in its title had been a misnomer from the start, since it, like the old Qing code, covered numerous civil matters (Pan Weihe 1982: 28). The Criminal Code of the Great Qing Currently in Use thus became the Code of the Former Qing Currently in Use (*Qian Qing xianxing lü*) or more simply, the Code Currently in Use (*Xianxing lü*).

As Philip Huang demonstrates, in revising the civil sections of the Qing code, the legal reformers left most laws unchanged, deleting only those that were deemed anachronistic, principally the laws concerning compulsory labor service, the civil service examination system, and Manchu bannermen. On patrilineal succession and household division, the Code Currently in Use duplicated almost word for word the old Qing code. The same held true for the other major categories of civil disputes—marriage and divorce, land transactions, and debt (P. Huang forthcoming).

The life of the Qing code was thus extended, but with the important qualification that only the laws that were not in conflict with either the Republican form of government (*guomin guoti*) or "the spirit of the age" were to be applied; the others were to be abolished or revised (F. Cheng 1923: i; Pan Weihe 1982: 28). The task of deciding which laws were applicable fell to the Daliyuan.

Established in Beijing in 1906 as part of the late Qing judicial reform, the Daliyuan took its name from the Dalisi (the Court of Revision), one of the Three High Courts (*Sanfasi*) of the Qing. (The others were the Board of Punishments and the Censorate.) It was replaced by the Supreme Court (*Zuigao fayuan*) in late 1927 and then removed to Nanjing in early 1929. The Daliyuan functioned as the final court of appeals in the four-tiered modern court system (court of first instance or *chuji*, district court, superior court, and Daliyuan), as well as the final interpreter of law (Xu Xiaoqun 1997: 3). In both of those capacities, it was granted broad powers to amend the codified laws and to legislate new ones. Its rulings, in the form of judgments on important appeals cases (*panjueli*) and interpretations (*jieshi*) in response to queries from lower-level judges, were not added to the text of the Code Currently in Use but instead constituted a separate body of laws.[1] In any direct conflict between a Daliyuan ruling and a codified law, the court's opinion was to govern. It is therefore in the Daliyuan's rulings that changes in succession and inheritance must be sought.

The Daliyuan kept the fundamental principles of patrilineal succession and property inheritance intact. It held fast to the principle that patrilineal succession determined property inheritance. In adjudicating disputes over property inheritance (*yichan zhi chengshou*), the courts "must take patrilineal succession as the question to be settled first" (*DPQ*: 284; Daliyuan: 241-2373). The Daliyuan also adhered to the principle of mandatory nephew succession. Any sonless man who had married or, though unmarried, had a chaste fiancée or had reached his majority was to have a lineage nephew appointed as heir for him, assuming of course there was a candidate of the appropriate generation. This was to be done even if the man himself had left verbal or written instructions that no heir needed to be appointed:

---

1. Periodically throughout the 1910's and the 1920's, compilations of the Daliyuan's rulings were published so that judges and lawyers could keep up with their changing content. The most comprehensive are *Daliyuan jieshili quanwen* (1931), which contains the full text of the 2,012 interpretations the court issued from its first, in January 1913, to its last, in October 1927; and *Daliyuan panjueli quanshu* (1933), which contains short summaries of the key decisions made on appeals.

The succession laws currently in use attach the greatest importance to the continuity of a line. . . . The articles on the establishment of an heir for the sonless are all compulsory laws [*qiangxing fagui*]. Although a sonless man is at liberty to adopt or not adopt an heir during his lifetime, any instructions he leaves ordering that no heir be established for him after his death would clearly not be in accordance with the intent of the law and would be difficult to recognize as valid.   (*DPQ*: 260)

Also compulsory were the Qing's proscriptions against different-surname and wrong-generation succession and the requirements of combined succession (*jiantiao*). The succession laws were to prevail over all customs or lineage rules to the contrary (*DPQ*: 255).

Beneath this essential continuity, however, were numerous changes compelled in equal measure by the Daliyuan's "rights" approach, the clear separation of civil from criminal matters, and the introduction of Western procedures. The result was a radical rewriting of the circumstances in which the compulsory succession laws in the Code Currently in Use were deemed applicable. For widows, the changes proved particularly important, allowing them a virtual free choice in the selection of an heir, even in violation of the code's proscriptions.

In discussing the rights of widows in the Daliyuan's legal regime, we must take care not to confuse results with objectives. Although the court's rulings had the effect of broadening women's rights, that was not its explicit intent. The Daliyuan did not take gender equality under the law as one of its central tasks. Indeed, as we shall see in a later chapter, when it came to property, the court proved to be very conservative, resisting at every turn the Guomindang's early attempts in 1927–29 to dissociate property inheritance from patrilineal succession and to legislate equal inheritance rights for women. The court's posture on a widow's role in succession thus stemmed not from any particular commitment to women's rights as a whole, but from its commitment to establishing in China a modern court system based on Western principles.

As one would .expect, the Daliyuan's rulings on patrilineal succession and property inheritance came out in piecemeal fashion over time, as the court became increasingly aware of the diverse implications of its adoption of the basic tenets of modern Western civil law. It was not in fact until 1923 that all of the major elements of the new complex were in place. As one might also expect, in keeping with the Western tradition, the court explicitly used the language of "rights" (*quanli*) in its rulings. That language carried its own imperative to delineate precisely both who possessed what rights and the circumstances under which they could exercise them.

The Right to Choose an Heir

In its rulings on patrilineal succession, the Daliyuan laid out more clearly than Qing law had done the respective rights of a sonless man, his widow, his parents or grandparents, and his other agnatic relatives in the choice of an heir. The right to select an heir (*zeji-quan* or *zesiquan*) belonged first and foremost to the man himself and then, on his death, to his widow so long as she remained chaste. If both husband and wife were dead, the right went to his direct lineal ascendants (*zhixi zunzhang*, parents, grandparents, and so on). If they too were dead, a family council (*qinzu huiyi*), composed of all agnates or else representatives from each collateral line (*fang*), was to select an heir by majority vote. If the family council could not reach an agreement and the dispute resulted in a lawsuit, the court was empowered to designate an heir (*DPQ*: 265–68 passim, 276).

For widows, the Daliyuan's rulings transformed what had been conceived in the Ming and Qing codes as an obligation to her husband's family into a right on her own account. The relevant substatute, it will be recalled, read: "A woman without sons who preserves her chastity after her husband dies is to receive her husband's share of property and must, through the agency of the lineage head, select a nephew of the appropriate generation as heir." It was retained word for word in the Code Currently in Use (*Da Qing* 1909, 5: 19). The Daliyuan, however, chose to interpret this law not as a statement of a widow's obligation, but as a statement of her rights. The meaning of the law, it explained, was that "the right to select an heir rests exclusively with the widow" (*DPQ*: 261).

The Daliyuan typically characterized the widow's right to choose an heir for her deceased husband as an "exclusive right" (*zhuan-quan*), one that could not be infringed by others. Thus, it ruled that male agnates could not under any circumstance interfere with her selection, appoint an heir in her stead, or select another even if her choice violated the law (*DPQ*: 271, 279). Those prohibitions included even the lineage head, whom the widow no longer needed to consult over her choice or secure as the principal witness (*ping-zheng*) to the adoption (*DPQ*: 266, 272). If any of those relatives, the lineage head included, established an heir without her express consent, their selection was automatically invalid (*DPQ*: 264; *DJQ*: no. 599).

Moreover, a widow's exclusive right to choose overrode the prerogatives previously granted to her parents-in-law. But the Daliyuan could not completely ignore the opinions of her husband's direct lineal ascendants without violating another of its principles: that "family affairs are united under a senior" (*jiawu tongyi yu yizun*; *DPQ*: 269). It resolved the problem by emphasizing that a widow had the exclusive right to select an heir for her husband, and her parents-in-law (or grandparents-in-law) only the right of consent (*tongyiquan*). Yet even then, they had only a circumscribed say: they could only invoke the right of consent if the widow had broken the law in her selection, whether by picking someone of the wrong generation, or of a different surname, or in violation of the requirements for combined succession. In those circumstances, they were permitted to bring suit to have her choice revoked. If they withheld their consent merely because they disliked the widow's candidate, she could bring suit to have her choice confirmed (*DPQ*: 261, 269–70, 277–78; *DJQ*: no. 709).

Likewise, in instances where the parents-in-law violated the law by selecting an heir without securing her agreement, the widow could go to court to contest the choice, and if she could prove that she had not approved of the move in the first place, the succession would be declared legally void (*DPQ*: 271). In a case reviewed by the Daliyuan in 1914, for example, Mrs. Liu (née Liu), a 58-sui peasant woman of Huaide county (Fengtian), was challenging her mother-in-law's and lineage head's appointment of a particular nephew as successor to her husband, who had died in 1911. Both the Huaide county magistrate and the Fengtian Superior Court had denied her claim on the grounds that the mother-in-law had acted well within her rights. Though that decision would have been acceptable under the Qing, for the Daliyuan what mattered was whether Mrs. Liu had ever agreed to the appointment. The mother-in-law argued in her own defense that Mrs. Liu had expressed the wish for that particular nephew to be heir at the time of her husband's death and had been present when the succession document was signed. The Daliyuan determined, however, that she could not have been there since the two defendants and the designated heir had driven her out of the house some time before. It ruled accordingly that their choice had no legal validity, and that the widow could appoint an heir more to her liking (Daliyuan: 241-250).

Finally, a widow's exclusive right to appoint a successor also gave her the right not to appoint one. The Daliyuan's position on mandatory succession notwithstanding, it decreed that a widow could not be forced to select an heir by a certain deadline (*DPQ:* 273). Should she fail to choose someone during her lifetime, the court reasoned, the consequence would not be so great, for under the law that "the wife receives her husband's property" (*fu cheng fufen*), his property would at least have someplace to go. By the same logic, after her death, it had nowhere to go (*wu suogui*). Accordingly, the man's parents or grandparents or, if they were all dead, the family council were legally bound to appoint an heir immediately to prevent various abuses (e.g., illegal seizure of the property) and to ensure the continuity of the deceased's line (*DPQ:* 262).

The difference between the Qing's and the Daliyuan's approach to a widow's rights in succession can best be explained by looking at their respective positions on the "private appointment of an heir" (*sili* or *siji*). In the Qing, as noted in Chapter Two, a widow who had gone through the proper steps, gaining at least the lineage head's consent and ideally the consent of her husband's closest agnatic kin as well, had participated in the consensual process of the "agreed-upon appointment" (*yili* or *yiji*). One who adopted an heir without securing the agreement of at least the lineage head was guilty of "a private appointment of an heir."

In the Daliyuan's rulings, the phrase "private appointment of an heir," with all of its negative connotations, ceased to be used in reference to a widow. She, after all, now had the exclusive right to appoint an heir on her own. The phrase came instead to be used in the same negative sense for any appointment that had not received *her* agreement, whether made by the lineage head, her husband's agnatic kin (a family council), or even his parents or grandparents (*DPQ:* 264; Daliyuan: 241-250, 241-5012).

The Right to Bring Suit

The reverse side of the Daliyuan's delineation of the right to choose an heir was a delineation of the right to bring suit to contest (*gaozheng*) another's selection. The Ming and Qing codes had placed some restrictions on the right to bring suit over succession. The revocation substatute of 1500 stipulated that when adoptive parents dismissed an established required heir in favor of a preferred heir, "provided the proper generational sequence is not disrupted, lineage members cannot bring suit to dispute their choice on the basis of [lineage] order." The enmity substatute of 1775 similarly stipulated that when the adoptive parents passed over the required heir in favor of a preferred heir on the grounds of dislike, lineage members were not permitted to contest the selection. In that sense, the Daliyuan was but continuing an existing trend.

But the court pushed that trend to extremes unimaginable in the Qing. As will be examined in detail in the following pages, the cumulative effect of its various rulings on the right to bring suit was to make it virtually impossible for anyone, outside of direct lineal ascendants (parents or grandparents), to challenge another's selection of an heir in court *even when* that choice was in violation of the compulsory laws on wrong-generation and different-surname succession, or the requirements for combined succession.

By the Daliyuan's own account, its reason for limiting the right to bring suit was "to prevent litigation" (*fangzhi jiansong; DPQ:* 750). Its desire to do so was nothing new, for Qing officials had often complained about mounting caseloads and an ever-growing litigiousness among the people (P. Huang 1996: chaps. 6, 7; Macauley 1998: chap. 2). What was new was the comprehensive solution the Daliyuan came up with to deal with the problem. Where Qing courts had coped by footdragging or by turning cases back for community or kin mediation, the Daliyuan resolved to combat the problem at its source by restricting the very right to bring suit in the first place.

Although denying certain people access to the courts in certain circumstances was not unique to the early Republican period, the Daliyuan's solution owed less to the legacy from the Qing than to the new package of reforms, part and parcel of which was adopting court procedures based on foreign models. Both the Draft Civil Procedural Law of the Great Qing (*Da Qing minshi susonglü cao'an*) and the Draft Criminal Procedural Law of the Great Qing (*Da Qing xingshi susonglü cao'an*), though completed in 1910, were only enacted in revised form in 1922 as the Civil Procedure Regulations (*Minshi susong tiaoli*) and the Criminal Procedure Regulations (*Xingshi susong tiaoli*).[2] Until then, judicial procedure was regulated by the Provisional Regulations for the Courts of Different Levels (*Geji*

---

2. The Nationalist government promulgated the Civil Procedural Code (*Minshi susong fa*) and the Criminal Procedural Code (*Xingshi susong fa*) in 1928 and the Revised Civil Procedural Code (*Xiuzheng minshi susong fa*) and the Revised Criminal Procedural Code (*Xiuzheng xingshi susong fa*) in 1935.

shenpanting shiban zhangcheng), issued in 1907, as well as interpretations and important judgments rendered by the Daliyuan itself.

One essential ingredient of any civil procedural law is defining who can be parties (*dangshiren*) to a suit. In the Western models that China drew on, those parties were defined as people with rights granted to them in the civil codes. In China's case, in the effective absence of a foreign-inspired civil code until 1929–30, the Daliyuan had in its rulings translated the provisions in the Code Currently in Use into the language of rights. By the logic of civil procedural norms, only those people with rights as spelled out by the Daliyuan had the right to be parties to a suit.

The Restrictions on Male Agnates

In the Daliyuan's rulings, the "yingji zhi ren"—"the person who ought to succeed," or the required heir—of the Code Currently in Use was rendered into the person who had the "right to succeed" (*chengjiquan*). Predicating the right to bring suit on the right to succeed, the Daliyuan ruled on numerous occasions that (outside of direct lineal ascendants) only those who had the right to succeed or their parents or grandparents acting on their behalf could challenge another's choice of heir in a court of law. All other people, no matter how closely related, were forbidden from doing so, even if the chosen heir was of the wrong generation, of a different surname, or otherwise in violation of the law (*DPQ*: 267–74 passim, 279; *DJQ*: nos. 564, 897, 1003).

What this meant in practice, the Daliyuan explained, was that courts were to reject succession suits brought by people without the proper credentials. In such cases, judges need not even investigate whether the choice in dispute did or did not accord with the law (*DPQ*: 269). Moreover, since the suit itself was not legal, judges were expressly forbidden to use the occasion to declare an illegal selection invalid (*DPQ*: 273).

The consequences of these rulings can best be illustrated with some concrete cases. One good example is the suit against Mrs. Xu (née Dai), a 60-sui widow of Songming county (Yunnan). After she adopted her young grandnephew Xu Renhe (24 sui) as her deceased husband's heir, a great-grandnephew, Xu Shimeng, came forward to challenge her choice on the very sound legal grounds that Xu Renhe, being two generations junior to her husband instead of just one, was not of the proper generation. The Daliyuan, hearing the case on appeal in 1914, dismissed Shimeng's suit. Even though the widow's choice was indeed illegal, the court wrote, Shimeng had had no right to bring suit in the first place since he himself, being three generations removed, did not have any claim to the succession (Daliyuan: 241-1166).

The Daliyuan's exclusion of all but those with succession rights extended to even such close agnatic kin as a husband's brothers if they themselves had no eligible sons. In 1922 in Anci county (Zhili), Yang Yujing (26 sui), who, though married, did not yet have any sons, had brought suit against his widowed sister-in-law, Mrs. Yang (née Li, 49 sui), and her designated heir, Yang Tianyou, charging that Tianyou's succession to his deceased brother, Yang Yufa, was illegal. The plaintiff had the strict letter of the law on his side, for Yang Tianyou, as a third cousin, belonged to the same generation as the deceased. The Anci magistrate accordingly ruled that Yang Tianyou must be dismissed as heir. But much to the chagrin of Yang Yujing, who hoped to secure the succession for a future son of his own, the magistrate also ruled that should Yang Tianyou eventually have a son, that son, who would be of the proper generation, could become Yang Yufa's heir. If he did not have a son, Mrs. Yang was to select another heir of the proper generation from among her husband's male agnates. Who that would be was entirely up to her.

Yang Yujing appealed the Anci county decision to the Capital Superior Court (*Jingshi gaodeng shenpanting*) in Beijing.[3] That court found fault with the Anci magistrate's ruling on legal grounds, but nevertheless denied Yujing's appeal. The court noted that since Yujing did not have any sons, who otherwise would have had a claim, the legality or illegality of the widow's appointment of Tianyou had nothing to do with him. He had had no right to bring suit in the first place (Jingshi: 239-7995).[4]

---

3. The Capital Superior Court served as the court of first appeal for both the Capital District Court (*Jingshi difang shenpanting*) in Beijing and the magistrate courts in surrounding counties. In 1928, it became the First Branch Court of the Hebei Superior Court (*Hebei gaodeng fayuan diyi fenyuan*), headquartered in Tianjin (*Shenbao nianjian 1933*, 1: 14). The district court was renamed the following year, to become the Beiping [Beijing] District Court (*Beiping [Beijing] difang fayuan*).

4. The Superior Court faulted the Anci magistrate for misapplying the law on "leaving the position empty to wait for a successor" (*xuming daiji*). The Code Currently in Use (like the Qing code before it) permitted one exception to the general rule on proper generational order. If there were no appropriate candidates (e.g., lineage nephews) and if the deceased was an only son, a successor could be appointed for the man's father. Then, when that successor had a son, the boy could be made the man's heir. The exception was provided to ensure that the father's line would not die out (Qing: 078-05; *DPQ*: 255–56). The Anci magistrate had in effect ruled for such an arrangement by allowing the position of heir to the deceased Yang Yufa to remain

In 1918, to give another example, a peasant of 52 *sui*, Zhu Han-zhang of Shangqiu county (Henan), filed suit at the county yamen to contest the succession to his deceased elder brother, Zhu Huan-zhang. His widowed sister-in-law, Mrs. Zhu (née Qi), had selected Zhu Runde, the only son of the two brothers' first cousin Zhu Hanqi as heir. The plaintiff had valid reasons for his objections to Runde. As an only son, he could not be adopted out, nor was he qualified for a combined succession (*jiantiao*), since his own father, Hanqi, and the deceased Huanzhang were not brothers. More damningly, Runde was not even a Zhu, for his grandfather, Chunhe, had been adopted into the lineage from a different surname group.

As an alternative, the plaintiff Zhu Hanzhang proposed that his only son, Deming, be designated as the combined successor for both himself and his elder brother Huanzhang. But his claim on behalf of his son turned out to be illegitimate. Huanzhang had been adopted out to an uncle, so that by law the two were no longer brothers but first cousins. Thus only-son Deming, like only-son Runde, was not eligible for a combined succession.

Faced with two far from ideal claimants, the Shangqiu county magistrate decided to designate both as Huanzhang's successor, with Zhu Runde, the widow's choice, as the heir appointed out of affection and Zhu Deming as the heir appointed out of obligation. That compromise solution did not sit well with Hanzhang. He appealed the decision to the Henan Superior Court, which upheld the county magistrate.

Zhu Hanzhang then decided to appeal to the Daliyuan. He should have left well enough alone, for the Daliyuan in 1920 overturned both the county and the Superior Court's decisions, and affirmed Zhu Runde as Huanzhang's sole heir. Since Hanzhang's son, Deming, was not qualified for a combined succession, he had no right to succeed Huanzhang and hence he and, by extension, his father had no right to challenge the widow's choice. It did not matter that her choice was also unqualified for a combined succession and, worse yet, originally of a different surname. Zhu Hanzhang had not had any right to bring suit in the first place (Daliyuan: 241-6291).

The Daliyuan made no allowance even for concerned lineage heads. In 1916, the Jiangsu Superior Court inquired of the Daliyuan whether a lineage head could bring suit against a widow for adopt-

---

unfilled until Yang Tianyou had a son. But as the Capital Superior Court pointed out, the circumstances of the case did not fit the two necessary conditions. Yang Yufu had lineage nephews who could be appointed as his heir, and he was not an only son.

ing a young man of a different surname as her husband's heir. After all, the court reasoned, the lineage head only wanted to have an appropriate heir appointed; he was not out to seize the succession and the property for himself or his own descendants. Hewing to the course it had set, the Daliyuan replied that since the lineage head himself was not entitled to succeed and was not the direct lineal ascendant of anyone with such a right, he could not contest a widow's choice in court, however illegal (*DJQ*: no. 455).

The exclusion of lineage heads, more than anything else, tells of the radical changes the Daliyuan was attempting to effect. In the past, as we have seen, the inescapable tension between succession to property and succession to a patriline was perceived as a moral conflict between "profit" (*li*) and "duty" (*yi*). Male agnates who stood to gain property through patrilineal succession were seen as only too willing to sacrifice duty for profit. No matter how careful they might be to speak in terms of the deceased's need for an heir to continue his line and maintain the ancestral sacrifices, they could not escape the suspicion that their true motive was to get their hands on his property. A lineage head, by contrast, was considered the one lineage member who could be counted on to place righteous duty above profit-seeking, and magistrates routinely turned to them for assistance in resolving succession disputes. Under the Daliyuan's new legal regime, however, the involvement of a lineage head, or any other person without succession rights, was not to be countenanced. A direct material claim became the only acceptable criterion for bringing suit to contest a succession.

The Loss of the Right to Bring Suit

In addition to linking the right to bring suit to the right to succeed, the Daliyuan mapped out a range of circumstances in which a person could lose that right and, with it, the right to challenge a succession in court. The court defined those circumstances so broadly that it became nearly impossible even for a nephew with the right to succeed—the required heir—to assert that claim over a widow's objections. In the Daliyuan's legal order, her exclusive right to select an heir was to take absolute precedence over his right to be chosen.

In the last chapter, we saw how the introduction of the enmity law in 1775 elevated preferred succession to an equal standing with required succession. A widow could pass over the required heir and adopt the lineage nephew of her choice. So long as her selection did not confuse the generations, lineage members were not permitted to bring suit to contest the succession. By implication, of course, lineage members could challenge a selection if the chosen heir was not of the proper generation or of the same surname or not qualified for combined succession.

The Daliyuan went one step further. It decreed that a required heir passed over because of enmity did not even have the right to contest an illegal choice. The consequence of not being selected as heir in the first place was the loss of one's right to succeed and hence one's right to challenge any succession, even an illegal one (*DPQ*: 267–68).

Thus, in a Daliyuan case of 1915, the widowed mother, Mrs. Xue (neé Wang), and the widowed wife, Mrs. Xue (née Liu), of Xue Dekui of Wu county (Jiangsu) had chosen a lineage nephew, Xue Zhaorong, as heir. Disputing their choice was the dead man's third cousin, Xue Deqing (56 sui), who had the strict letter of the law on his side. Zhaorong was not only an only son but also the son of one of the deceased's cousins, thus rendering him ineligible for a combined succession (in which the heir had to be the son of a brother). Since the plaintiff himself was the only cousin who had two sons, the younger one ought to have been made heir. The Daliyuan, even though acknowledging that the widows' selection did in fact violate the law, ruled against Xue Deqing on the grounds of a deep enmity dating from an 1874 lawsuit between him and the two widows. The widows clearly did not want his son as heir. His son thus had no right to succeed, and Xue Deqing, as the direct lineal ascendant, had no right to bring suit on his behalf (Daliyuan: 241-1595).

Similarly, in a Daliyuan case of 1919, the peasant woman Mrs. Wu (née Yu, 56 sui) of Lin'an county (Zhejiang) challenged the choice of her 62-sui widowed sister-in-law on the grounds that it violated the law. She wanted her son Wu Zongtang, as the closest eligible relative, to be designated heir instead. But after the sister-in-law explained that she found Zongtang unacceptable because he had sold off part of her deceased husband's property without her permission, an unlawful act for which she had taken him to court, the Daliyuan found for her. In its written judgment, it explained that, by his actions, Wu Zongtang had incurred her enmity, thereby disqualifying himself as a possible heir. And since he no longer had the right to succeed, his mother did not have the right to contest her sister-in-law's choice. The Daliyuan so summarily dismissed Mrs. Wu's case that it did not even bother to mention whether that choice in fact did or did not violate the law (Daliyuan: 241-5043).

Moreover, the Daliyuan ruled that "enmity" did not have to be established by "objective facts" (*keguan shishi*), merely by the selector's "subjective intent" (*zhuguan zhi yisi*). She or he was not required to offer any explanation for the animosity or to provide documentation or witnesses as proof. It was simply enough that the person did not want the potential heir (*DPQ*: 269–70, 273, 274; *DJQ*: no. 846).

It was on those grounds that the elderly widow Shao (née Li, 75 sui) of Daxing county (Zhili) was able to defeat a kinswoman's attempt to secure the succession for one of her own four sons. The kinswoman (64 sui) claimed that her sons were the closest possible candidates for the position (although the precise degree of relationship is not stated in the records). But the widow refused to accept any of them because, in her words, "whenever they extend their hands, they hit; whenever they open their mouths, they curse" (*shenshou jiu da, kaikou jiu ma*). The Capital Superior Court, citing the Daliyuan's definition of enmity, held that there was no need to determine the truth of her accusations. Although they were indeed the closest candidates for the succession, her very unwillingness to accept any of them rendered them ineligible. That, in turn, meant that neither they nor their mother had the right to bring suit in the first place, even though the heir that the widow Shao had settled on was of a different surname (Jingshi: 239-7958).

Finally, a lineage nephew with a valid claim to a succession could lose that right if he did not exercise it at the time the appointment was made or shortly thereafter. In the Daliyuan's judgment, by in effect tacitly assenting to the selection, he forfeited his right to succeed and, with it, his right to contest the selected heir (*DPQ*: 270; *DJQ*: no. 814). It was for this reason that Wang Yucai (37 sui) of Beijing eventually lost his bid to become the heir of his recently deceased uncle, Wang Qiming (his father's older brother). In 1922, he brought suit at the Capital District Court against his uncle's widow, Mrs. Wang (née Jiang, 52 sui), claiming that she had willfully deprived him of the succession in favor of an heir of a different surname, Zhang Wending. The Capital District Court ruled in his favor, confirming him as heir and dismissing Zhang Wending.

That decision would have been perfectly in order in the Qing, but other considerations came to be taken into account in the early

Republican period, as Wang Yucai learned when Mrs. Wang appealed to the Capital Superior Court. It ruled that since Zhang Wending had entered the Wang household as heir long before, in 1906, and Wang Yucai had not seen fit to challenge the illegal appointment at that time, he had forfeited his right to succeed and hence his right to bring suit (Beijing: 65-5-256-259).

Taken all together, the Daliyuan's pronouncements rendered a widow's choice of heir virtually incontestable in a court of law. Aside from her husband's parents or grandparents, only agnatic kin qualified to succeed (or their direct lineal ascendants) had the right to challenge her choice, thus ruling out, among others, lineage heads and a husband's own brothers if they themselves did not have sons. At the same time, though, the Daliyuan defined the circumstances under which men with the proper credentials could lose the right to succeed and the attendant right to bring suit so broadly that even those candidates found themselves with no legal leg to stand on. If they did not exercise that right concurrent with or soon after a widow's adoption of an heir, they had by their very inaction given their tacit consent to her choice and thus lost the right to contest it later. More important, under the Daliyuan's interpretations of the relationship between required and preferred succession and of the nature of enmity, one lost the right to succeed and hence the right to dispute a succession, even an illegal one, simply by virtue of not having been selected in the first place.

Although the focus here is on widows, all of these rulings applied equally to a man if he selected an heir before his death, as well as to his parents or grandparents if both he and his wife were dead. In the Daliyuan's perception, the big divide lay between a man, his widow, and his direct lineal ascendants on the one hand and the rest of the husband's lineage as constituted in the family council on the other. Rights accorded the former were not necessarily accorded the latter. For instance, whereas any one of the immediate family was permitted to name a preferred heir, the family council had to follow the strict lineage order and select the required heir (unless the husband or his widow had expressed a clear preference for or against a possible candidate before their deaths; *DPQ*: 270–73 passim, 276–77). Moreover, a family council's selection was vulnerable to a wider range of legal challenges, for the Daliyuan permitted, in addition to men with rights of succession, people with a close personal interest in the outcome—such as the deceased's concubines, his daughters, or, if he himself had been an adopted-out son, his own birth parents—to bring suit to contest the council's choice (*DPQ*: 273).

A caveat is in order here. It would be wrong to infer from this discussion that the Daliyuan reflected general legal practice during the early Republican period. A great distance still separated its rulings from the decisions of lower courts, in which succession disputes tended to be adjudicated on the basis of the familiar Qing laws as now embodied in the Code Currently in Use. Never once, in a randomly chosen sample of 31 Daliyuan cases from the 1910's and 1920's in which a husband's agnatic relatives (excluding his parents or grandparents) disputed a widow's choice, did the Daliyuan rule against the widow, including instances when her choice blatantly violated the law. By contrast, the Capital Superior Court overturned the widow in six of 19 randomly chosen cases, mainly because of an imperfect application of the Daliyuan's new standards about the right to bring suit and a reluctance to turn a blind eye to illegal succession.

Courts of first instance, whether the district courts of the modern system or the magistrates' courts of old, were even more likely still to decide cases not on the basis of the Daliyuan's rulings but on codified law. They accepted suits from people without succession rights. They enforced the proper generational order and the conditions attached to combined succession. And they most especially kept a vigilant guard against the appointment of an heir of a different surname.[5] As the litigants and the lower courts were to discover when such cases were appealed, those decisions, though wholly consistent with both the legal code and past practice, were not acceptable under the Daliyuan's new legal regime.

The Legality of Illegal Succession

What, then, was the legal standing of these technically illegal successions? The Daliyuan issued three crucial rulings that together amounted to a de facto recognition of illegal succession. One has already been mentioned—the finding in 1917 that courts could not cancel an illegal succession if the suit challenging it was itself

5. For examples of court of first instance rulings based on the letter of the codified law, see Beijing: 65-5-256-259, 65-5-395-405; Jingshi: 239-5465, 239-6993, 239-7995, 239-8045, 239-9768; and Daliyuan: 241-1483, 241-2436, 241-3388, 241-4898, 241-6291.

illegal. This was the reason why the Daliyuan itself did not declare invalid the instances of "illegal succession" we have discussed, namely Mrs. Zhu's appointment of an heir of a different surname, Mrs. Xu's appointment of an heir from a wrong generation, and the two Mrs. Xues' appointment of an heir in violation of the requirements of combined succession. Judges who used the occasion of an illegal suit to annul an improper succession were, in the Daliyuan's estimation, "excessively interventionist" (guofen zhi ganshe; Beijing: 65-5-395-405). Those who refrained from doing so came in for particular praise (e.g., Daliyuan: 241-1595).

In the second ruling, in 1923, the Daliyuan attempted to modify this stance by drawing a line between throwing out an illegal suit and validating a patent illegality. "According to the law, people without succession rights of course cannot bring suit to contest the succession of another person, regardless of whether it is legal or not. But this just means that the bringing of a suit itself should not be permitted. It definitely does not mean that an illegal succession can therefore be recognized as legal" (DPQ: 282). Since the proscriptions against different-surname succession, wrong-generation succession, and so on in the Code Currently in Use were compulsory laws, a court could not give an illegal selection its stamp of approval. Equally important, it had to leave the door open for people with the right to bring suit, for once a succession received court validation, it could not subsequently be contested by other parties in a different suit (e.g., Jingshi: 239-4438).

For those reasons, a court was to take care to avoid even the appearance of conferring legitimacy on the illegitimate. In its own decisions on appeals, the Daliyuan framed its written judgments in two distinctly different ways, depending on whether the selection in dispute was legal or not. If the designation of an heir conformed to the law, the court included a positive statement of confirmation in its judgment. Thus, "the appellant [Mrs. Jian, née Dong] may select Jian Xianyi to be the heir for her deceased husband, Jian Chenglin (Daliyuan: 241-3388), or "The defendant [Mrs. Li, née Huang] . . . has the right to select the heir. Since her establishment of third-order nephew Zongmo does not confuse the generations, the appellant's suit itself does not accord with the law" (Daliyuan: 241-111). But if the designation of an heir contravened the law, the Daliyuan was careful to stay clear of any such statement of validation, concentrating instead on the illegality of the suit. It also avoided, especially in the case of different-surname succession, even passing references to the illegal appointee as an heir (*sizi*), electing instead to refer to him always as merely an adopted son (*yizi*).

In its third ruling on the matter, also in 1923, the Daliyuan specified that if a person or persons with the right to bring suit did not come forward to contest a succession, then it was to be considered legally valid. "In the appointment of an heir for those without sons, if the selection is made by a person who has the right to do so, then even if the selection violates the law, it is not necessarily invalid. If people with the right to bring suit do not do so to confirm the invalidity of a succession or to have it annulled, acquiring a judgment to that effect, . . . then it is not permissible to deny the validity of the selection" (*DPQ*: 282). Any succession was thus presumed valid unless successfully challenged in a court of law.

The Daliyuan's de facto recognition of illegal succession makes little sense from the perspective of the law as codified in the Code Currently in Use and indeed from the perspective of many of its own rulings as well. If the proscriptions against different-surname and wrong-generation succession and the requirements for combined succession were, as the Daliyuan itself kept emphasizing, compulsory laws, why did the court not allow judges to rectify the situation and declare an illegal heir invalid?

The answer is that, by this time, the succession laws were wholly and unequivocally civil laws, grounded in the Western notion of rights and governed by a body of strict procedural guidelines. In modern Western jurisprudence, three characteristics distinguish criminal matters from civil matters. Criminal laws provide for arrests and punishments, whereas civil laws call merely for restitution. Criminal laws are to be enforced at all times in all circumstances by agents of the state, whereas civil laws are not enforceable until someone brings suit. And finally, criminal laws function to protect society as a whole (hence the formulation of "The People versus . . ."), whereas civil laws aim to protect the rights of an individual party against infringement by another party. In general, the placing of certain acts in the criminal category and others in the civil defines what a state considers most important and in constant need of monitoring and what it considers less important and best left to the workings of society.

By that definition, even imperial Chinese law contained numerous statutes and substatutes that qualified as civil laws in the modern-day Western sense. As Philip Huang has demonstrated, Qing jurisprudence distinguished between "weighty matters" (*zhong'an*), such as murder, rape, and robbery, and "minor matters" (*xishi*), such as disputes over marriage, succession, property, and debt (1996: especially 5–10). Although the majority of the provisions on minor matters prescribed punishments for the offenders, magistrates seldom resorted to them in their handling of such disputes. Moreover, in theory at least, yamen runners, subcounty functionaries such as *dibao* and *baozheng*, and indeed the general populace through the *baojia* system were legally bound to report to the magistrate the commission of "weighty" crimes, but not infractions of minor matters. A magistrate had to attend to the minor matters only if one of the parties to a dispute had brought suit. Finally, as Huang has also shown, although the Qing code did not articulate a notion of "rights" in the Western sense of rights guaranteed by law and independent of the will of the ruler, in practice local courts consistently upheld legitimate property and contractual claims from encroachment by others (1996: chap. 4). Because of the great similarity between the Qing's minor matters and modern-day civil law, it was relatively easy for the legal reformers of the late Qing and early Republican periods to separate out the civil and the criminal in codified law and to establish a two-track system for civil and criminal affairs in the newly formed modern courts.

At the same time, however, the transition brought about a fundamental change in the state's relationship to its own laws and the role of the courts in enforcing them. In the imperial system, once a minor matter came before a magistrate, his task was not just to protect someone's interests, but also to correct behavior or actions in violation of the code. This point can best be illustrated with a concrete example. In the late 1860's, one Zhang Shunfa brought suit at the Changzhou county (Jiangsu) yamen, claiming that the young boy his widowed sister-in-law had adopted as heir was of a different surname and was therefore not entitled to inherit her deceased husband's share of the family property. Upon investigation, Magistrate Kuai Demo determined that the plaintiff himself was an adopted son of a different surname and thus had no claim on the Zhangs' property and no right to interfere in the Zhangs' affairs. That was not the end of the case, however, for the magistrate went on to order the widow to appoint an appropriate lineage nephew to be her husband's successor (Kuai Demo 1874: 6022-23). Magistrate Kuai thus in effect ruled against both the plaintiff and the defendant. In the Qing conception of minor matters, it was possible for both parties to be in the wrong, and it was incumbent on the judge, in theory at least, to remedy the situation in accordance with the code.

In the early Republican period, judges no longer had the blanket obligation to rectify situations in violation of the law in civil matters. In fact, as we have seen, they were explicitly prohibited from doing so if the plaintiff's claim was unfounded. In the modern Western concept of civil matters, a court cannot find against both parties. The issue was not whether the defendant had broken the law, but whether the defendant had broken the law in such as a way as to infringe the rights of the plaintiff.[6] If it turned out that the plaintiff's rights had not been violated or if he or she had no rights in the matter to begin with, that was the end of the case. A judge could not simultaneously deny the plaintiff's claim and rule that the defendant had committed some legal offense in need of correction.

It was this aspect of the Daliyuan's rulings that lower-court judges in the early Republican period found the most difficult to grasp, or at least proved the most reluctant to follow. They comprehended readily enough the concept that only those with the right to succeed had the right to bring suit to contest another's selection. And in their judgments they pronounced suits brought by people without the proper credentials to be contrary to the law. But they balked at carrying that finding to the conclusion the Daliyuan demanded—the illegality of the suit meant that they as judges were not permitted to correct any instance of illegal succession. The result was a raft of judgments that rejected the plaintiff's suit and at the same time ordered the defendant to dismiss the chosen heir and pick another—a completely unacceptable combination under the Daliyuan's rulings (e.g., Jingshi: 239-714, 239-816, 239-7958).

Illegal Succession and Property Inheritance

The Daliyuan's de facto recognition of illegal succession had important implications for property inheritance. Since the court still

---

6. In this regard, the distinction between criminal and civil matters in the 1907 "Provisional Regulations for the Courts of Different Levels" still bore traces of the Qing concept of minor matters. It read: "Criminal litigation seeks to establish whether a crime has been committed," whereas "civil litigation seeks to determine right and wrong" ("Geji shenpanting shiban zhangcheng," 1907: art. 1; translation from P. Huang 1996: 5). In modern Western jurisprudence, civil litigation does not seek to determine who is right and who is wrong according to the law, but only whether a party's rights have been violated.

firmly upheld patrilineal succession as the determinant for property inheritance, the presumption of legal validity meant that those heirs, however technically illegal, automatically acquired the right to inherit the property of their adoptive fathers. The deceased's relatives were expressly forbidden to withhold any of that property from an illegal heir (*DPQ*: 274). Conversely, they could not go to court to claim any of the property the heir might already have in his possession (*DJQ*: no. 591).

Thus it was that Chen Jinchong (60 sui; born Luo Jinxiong), the adopted son of Chen Mingxian of Guiyang county (Guizhou), eventually emerged the victor in litigation over his adoptive father's estate. Four of Chen Mingxian's kinsmen had brought suit against Jinchong, arguing that as a man of a different surname and thus an illegal heir, he was not entitled to succeed to Mingxian's property and should be ordered to turn it all over to them. Since there was no suitable candidate of the proper generation within the lineage to serve as Mingxian's heir, the four proposed that the property be converted into ritual property (*jichan*) for the upkeep of the lineage's gravesites and the performance of ancestral rites. The Guiyang court found for the plaintiffs: Chen Jinchong was to be given a share of the property and return to his own Luo lineage, and the rest of the property was to revert to the lineage as ritual property. Chen Jinchong subsequently appealed the decision, but the Guizhou Superior Court also ruled for the kinsmen. Those decisions were entirely in keeping with the stipulations in the Code Currently in Use.

Chen Jinchong then appealed to the Daliyuan, which, in late 1917, threw out the two lower courts' rulings. None of the four kinsmen had the right to succeed Chen Mingxian, nor did they represent any direct lineal descendant who did. They therefore did not have any right to bring suit against Chen Jinchong to contest the succession or, by extension, his possession of the property. The Daliyuan accordingly denied their request that Chen Jinchong be ordered to relinquish the property (Daliyuan: 241-2436).

An illegal heir's acquisition of property was the focus of a particularly hard-fought legal battle in Beijing from 1917 to 1922. The litigation pitted widowed Mrs. Chen (née Du) and her adopted son, Chen Yongzhi (30 sui), against her four brothers-in-law, Chen Wenkui, Chen Wenquan, Chen Wenhai, and Chen Wenguang. According to the widow, her husband, Chen Wenxiang, had held a post in one of the treasuries of the Qing Imperial Household Department, a lucrative position that had enabled him to purchase two stores and eight residential units, including a 52-room compound. Out of concern that his four younger brothers did not own any property themselves, Chen Wenxiang had permitted them to rent living space in that large compound. Since Chen Wenxiang and his wife were childless, they had adopted a young boy from a Wang lineage, renaming him Chen Yongzhi. After Wenxiang's death in 1903, Yongzhi took over his job in the treasury and continued to enjoy a perfectly harmonious relationship with his adoptive mother. In late 1916, when the widow decided to sell part of the 52-room compound to pay off some debts, her brothers-in-law refused to vacate the premises. The next year, 1917, she and her adopted son filed suit at the Capital District Court, requesting that the four brothers be ordered to relinquish the property.

The brothers promptly filed a countersuit, arguing that the property in dispute was undivided common property (*gongchan*) owned jointly by all the brothers, and not, as the plaintiffs contended, Chen Wenxiang's private property (*sichan*). In support of that claim, they sought to demonstrate that the treasury position he had held was an inheritable one that had passed from eldest son to eldest son within the Chen family. Their father had held the position, which meant that it constituted family property. Consequently, the income from the post belonged to all five brothers and not just the one who held it, and since the income from that post had been used to purchase the disputed property—10 residential and commercial parcels—it too was theirs. They therefore requested that the family now undergo household division, with all the property divided into five equal shares.

But that was not enough for them. They argued also that as a man of a different surname, Chen Yongzhi was not qualified to be Wenxiang's heir and thus did not have any claim on his adoptive father's one-fifth share. They therefore requested that Yongzhi be returned to his own lineage (*guizong*), and a proper heir be appointed in his stead. The brothers had two candidates in mind: Yonghui, the only son of Chen Wenkui, and Yongen, the only son of Chen Wenhai. (The other two brothers were sonless.) Although by law an only son could not be adopted out, thereby cutting off his own father's line, he could become the dual successor (*jiantiaozi*) to both his father's branch and Wenxiang's branch. Either one of those sons, the brothers maintained, could serve as Chen Wenxiang's heir.

The surviving record does not contain the Capital District Court's ruling, but whatever it was, it did not fully satisfy either side. Both parties appealed to the Capital Superior Court, which rendered its decision in May 1918. Although Mrs. Chen had died in 1917 during the course of the hearing at the Capital District Court, her wishes ultimately proved decisive.

The Capital Superior Court ruled against the brothers on the property issue. A direct request to the Imperial Household Department had elicited the information that the post in question was not inheritable, having in fact been held by a man surnamed Zhang several generations back. Consequently, the court held, it could not be considered family property that had passed into the brothers' joint possession when their father died. It was Chen Wenxiang's own private property. That said, the court then went on to give the brothers their way on the succession issue: Chen Yongzhi, as an adopted son originally of a different surname, was not eligible to succeed Wenxiang. As the court explained in its judgment, "Those who raise an adopted son [*yizi*] of a different surname may not establish him as heir [*si*] should they have no sons of their own. The Code Currently in Use, which remains valid at present, clearly prohibits it." Now that Mrs. Chen was dead and could not make the decision herself, the brothers were to select one of the two eligible nephews to be heir.

This was only a partial victory, though, for the court continued on to evoke the law that expressly forbade an heir or his birth parents to expel a different-surname adopted son who had been particularly beloved by his adoptive parents, and also permitted a different-surname adopted son to receive a share of the property, provided that the value did not exceed that of the heir's share. It accordingly prohibited the brothers from driving Chen Yongzhi out of the family and out of its primary residence. It also ruled that Chen Yongzhi was entitled to the 52-room compound and the two shops as his share of the property. The appointed heir was to receive the remaining seven pieces of property, or the bulk of Chen Wenxiang's estate.

The Capital Superior Court's ruling represented a strict application of the codified law on succession and different-surname adoption. Under the Qing, it would have been considered a completely legitimate decision. Indeed, Qing magistrates routinely arrived at the same solution when faced with the competing claims of adopted sons of different surnames and patrilineal heirs (see, e.g., Li Yu 1667, 20: 34a–35; Dong Pei 1883, 2: 1a–b; and Cheng He n.d.: 97). But such a solution, though fully in tune with the Code Currently in Use, violated Daliyuan rulings.

When the case reached its chambers in 1918, the Daliyuan overturned the lower court's decision and ruled decisively against the brothers. At that level, they learned that they had not had the right to dispute the succession in the first place. The Daliyuan explained that none of the four brothers had the right to succeed Chen Wenxiang themselves, and two of the four had no sons on whose behalf they could contest the succession. As for the two brothers with sons, they too did not have any rights in the matter. The only way for an only son to become heir for another was through combined succession, but one of the specific requirements of combined succession was that both sides be amenable to the arrangement. During questioning at the Capital District Court, Mrs. Chen had explicitly said that she did not want either nephew as heir. Since she was not willing, the requirements for a combined succession had not been met. Therefore, those two sons, as only sons, had no right to succeed and, by extension, their fathers had no right to represent their cause in court. Although Chen Yongzhi's succession violated the law, the Daliyuan concluded, it had to overturn the Superior Court's decision and deny the brothers' request to appoint one of their sons as heir.

This was far from the end of the dispute. The Daliyuan, not satisfied with the Superior Court's handling of the property ownership issue, had ordered it to retry that aspect of the case. It did so the following February (1919), again ruling, on the basis of more documentation, that Chen Wenxiang was the sole owner of the property in dispute. The brothers again appealed to the Daliyuan, which this time, in August 1919, affirmed the Superior Court's ruling. All of the property, including the 52-room house where the brothers were renting living space, had belonged to Chen Wenxiang and thus was to be turned over to Chen Yongzhi.

Their appeal options exhausted, the brothers tried something different. In February 1920, a man of 41 sui calling himself Chen Yongfu filed suit against Chen Yongzhi at the Capital District Court. He claimed that he was Chen Wenxiang's second-order nephew (a son of one of Wenxiang's first cousins), and that a family council convened by the Chen brothers had designated him to be Wenxiang's heir. As proof of his kinship with the family, Chen Yongfu offered into evidence the obituary the family had issued after Mrs. Chen's death in 1917, in which his name appeared as a mourner.

And as proof of his selection as heir, he presented a succession document (*jidan*) signed by, among others, the four Chen brothers. The much-beleaguered defendant, Chen Yongzhi, charged that Chen Yongfu was lying about his identity. Although he was in fact surnamed Chen, he did not belong to the same Chen lineage. He was just an agricultural tenant of one of the brothers, whose claim was a mere pretext for seizing Chen Wenxiang's property. The Capital District Court, accepting Chen Yongfu's story, confirmed him as Chen Wenxiang's heir and ordered that he be given two-thirds of the property, with the remaining one-third going to Chen Yongzhi as the different-surname adopted son.

Chen Yongzhi appealed to the Capital Superior Court, which was much more skeptical of Chen Yongfu's claim, especially after he failed to properly identify the members and generations of his supposed lineage. The court also dismissed the obituary as evidence, since that could all too easily have been forged. Agreeing with Chen Yongzhi that Yongfu's appointment as heir was just a ruse, the Superior Court overturned the lower court's ruling. Chen Yongzhi was to retain possession of all of his adoptive father's property. Chen Yongfu then appealed to the Daliyuan, which upheld the Superior Court.

The case still did not end. The next year, 1921, Chen Yonghui (43 sui), the only son of Wenkui, brought suit against Chen Yongzhi at the Capital District Court, claiming that the family council had now appointed him to be the dual successor to both his own father and Chen Wenxiang, and demanding that he be given all of his uncle's property. Since the Daliyuan in 1918 had already pronounced Chen Yonghui (as well as his cousin Chen Yongen) ineligible even as a combined successor, his suit did not have any chance of success.

Even as the Chen brothers pursued their fight for the succession through the impostor Chen Yongfu and then Chen Yonghui, they were engaged in a parallel battle to win the right to remain in the 52-room compound. It will be remembered that the first round of litigation between the brothers and Chen Yongzhi ended in August 1919, with the Daliyuan's decision that Chen Yongzhi had full ownership rights to all of Wenxiang's estate, including the 52-room residence. In September 1919, Yongzhi filed a request at the Capital District Court for the forcible execution (*qiangzhi zhixing*) of the Daliyuan's decision. The district court ordered the brothers and their families to vacate the premises immediately and let Yongzhi take possession. When they refused to do so, the court then ordered the property sealed and forbade them entry. Some of the family members tore off the seal and resumed occupation, at which point they were forcibly removed from the compound and detained in jail for a period of time for their defiance of the court order.

At the same time, they fought eviction through a series of appeals to the Capital Superior Court and the Daliyuan, protesting the original execution order and reiterating their claim on the succession. Repeatedly, they argued that Chen Yongzhi, as someone from a different surname group, could not be Chen Wenxiang's heir and thus had no right to his property. That argument fell on deaf ears at the Capital Superior Court and the Daliyuan, which upheld the lower court's eviction order on the grounds that none of the brothers or their sons had the right to be heir and thus any right to bring suit. The documents on the case end in 1922, with Chen Yongzhi, a different-surname adopted son, in full possession of Chen Wenxiang's entire estate, including the 52-room compound (Beijing: 65-5-395-405; Jingshi: 239-6546).

This case is significant not only for what was said and done, but also for what was not. In none of their decisions did the courts (including the Daliyuan) confirm Chen Yongzhi as Chen Wenxiang's patrilineal successor. Nor did they ever refer to him as an heir (*sizi*), insisting always on calling him an "adopted son" (*yizi*). Yet Chen Yongzhi ended up with legal possession of all of Wenxiang's property. In other words, Chen Yongzhi did not succeed to Chen Wenxiang's line, but he did succeed to his property.

The Chen brothers would have been on firmer legal grounds had they chosen to challenge Chen Yongzhi's right to function in the other capacities associated with patrilineal succession. In other of its rulings, the Daliyuan explicitly barred different-surname adopted sons and their descendants from presiding at ancestral sacrifices, from serving as lineage head, and, if the lineage was opposed, from being included in its genealogy. The court also specified that any concerned lineage member, and not just those with the right to succeed, could challenge any infractions of those proscriptions in a court of law (*DPQ*: 244, 279, 284).

Although the Daliyuan repeatedly affirmed that patrilineal succession determined property inheritance, it in practice interpreted the law liberally, with the effect of an incipient separation of the two. In its legal regime, one could, like Chen Yongzhi, inherit all of a man's property without at the same time being recognized as his legal patrilineal successor. In that sense, the Daliyuan's rulings anticipated the complete severance of patrilineal succession and property inheritance that was to come with the promulgation of the Guomindang Civil Code.

CHAPTER FOUR

Property Inheritance Under the Republican Civil Code

The Guomindang's codification efforts began in 1927, with the establishment of the Legal System Bureau (*Fazhiju*). In the following year, 1928, the bureau finished drafts of the "Book on Family" (*qinshubian*) and the "Book on Inheritance" (*jichengbian*; for both, see Zhang Xubai 1930: 71–133). Before it could turn its attention to the other three books ("General Principles," *zongze*; "Obligations," *zhai*; and "Rights Over Things," *wuquan*), it was disbanded, its function assumed by the newly established Legislative Yuan. In early 1929, the Legislative Yuan set up a Civil Law Codification Committee (*Minfa qicao weiyuanhui*), which completed the drafting process. Final approval rested with the GMD's main ruling body, the Central Political Council (*Zhongyang zhengzhi huiyi*; Pan Weihe 1982: 34–35). The books on general principles, obligations, and rights over things were promulgated in 1929 and were all in effect by May 5, 1930. The books on family and on inheritance were promulgated in December 1930 and went into effect on May 5, 1931 (*Liufa quanshu* 1932).

The inheritance book of the Republican Civil Code transformed the structure of legal claims to property.[1] At the root of the changes lay the GMD legal reformers' express desire to achieve gender equality in inheritance rights. Drawing heavily on foreign models, particularly the German Code of 1896 and the Swiss Code of 1907, they redefined the connection between patrilineal succession and property inheritance, the conception of "family," and, indeed, the very nature of property itself.

---

1. All references are to *The Civil Code of the Republic of China*, 1976 reprint.

This chapter examines that new Western-inspired inheritance regime to see how it differed from the patrilineal succession and household division laws of old. Our concern will be less with a point-by-point comparison of Republican and imperial law than with the very different logics that informed the two. More specifically, the chapter addresses three questions. How did the code conceive the relationship between patrilineal succession and property inheritance? How did its notion of property rights differ from imperial law's? And how did its concept of inheritance differ from imperial law's concept of household division? The implications that the two different logics had for women's property rights will be explored in subsequent chapters.

The Separation of Patrilineal Succession and Property Inheritance

In their redefinition of property rights, the GMD lawmakers struck deeply at the link between property inheritance and patrilineal succession. In so doing, they broke completely with the earlier draft civil codes, which had affirmed the essential connection between the two.[2] As the Legal System Bureau stated in explaining the 1928 draft of the Book on Inheritance, one purpose of the new laws was to abolish "feudal" patrilineal succession. In this, the lawmakers were heirs to the May Fourth critique of the patrilineal family and its emphasis on succession as the root of so many of society's ills, especially the devaluation of women and the prevalence of concubinage. The draft, the bureau proclaimed, not only did not openly recognize patrilineal succession, but in fact went out of its way to avoid words that might suggest any tacit acknowledgment of it. As used there, the bureau cautioned, the word "jicheng" referred only to property inheritance; it had nothing to do with patrilineal succession (cited in Zhang Xubai 1930: 70–71).

In the summer of 1930, the GMD's Central Political Council affirmed this approach to patrilineal succession and property inheritance in the name of gender equality:

[In patrilineal succession] only a man can have an heir; a woman does not have that right. Only a man can be someone's heir; a woman does not have

2. The 1911 draft declared that "the system of patrilineal succession and the system of property inheritance are identical." The 1925–26 draft held that "what this code refers to as inheritance [*jicheng*] takes patrilineal succession as its prerequisite" ("Da Qing minlü cao'an," 4: 45; and "Minlü cao'an jichengbian," 1, in *Falü cao'an huibian* 1973).

that right. From this we can see that patrilineal succession privileges men and devalues women [*zhong nan qing nü*]. That is clearly not in keeping with the times.

Accordingly, the Central Political Council concluded, property inheritance must be based not on patrilineal succession but on strict gender equality (*Jichengfa xianjue gedian* 1930: 19–21).

That the Central Political Council, and the Legal System Bureau before it, felt the need to distinguish so carefully between property inheritance and patrilineal succession reveals how truly "foreign" to China the new code's Western-based concept of inheritance was. Indeed, the very words used to denote property inheritance, "yichan jicheng," were not readily comprehensible within the prevailing systems of thought. Both "jicheng" and "yichan" had been used almost exclusively in reference to patrilineal succession. In that connection, "jicheng" (or its more common variant "chengji") had combined the three meanings of succession to a person, succession to ancestral sacrifices, and succession to property, and "yichan" (lit., "left property") had referred to the property of a deceased heirless man. Under the civil code, both words acquired quite different meanings. "Jicheng," shorn completely of its association with lineal/ritual succession, came simply to mean "inheritance," and "yichan" came simply to mean the property in a person's possession at the time of death. The two together—"jicheng yichan" or "yichan jicheng"— came to mean property inheritance.

The lawmakers had also to come up with an expression to convey the Western notion of "heir." Because of the strong association of property inheritance with patrilineal succession, the Chinese language at the time had no word or phrase that meant just "heir to property." The word "sizi" would obviously not do, since it referred only to sons and encompassed the meanings of heir to a man and heir to the ancestral sacrifices, in addition to heir to property. The lawmakers settled on the phrase "yichan jichengren" (lit., a person who inherits property) to express the Western concept. The code itself used the phrase for all heirs to property, whoever they might be. It also resolutely avoided using the word "sizi" for sons, lest that be taken as recognizing patrilineal succession.[3]

Yet to the bewilderment of many members of the legal commu-

3. The only exception to this general rule came in the "Law Governing the Application of the Book of Inheritance of the Civil Code" (*Minfa jichengbian shixing fa*), a set of 11 articles detailing which of the new inheritance laws were to be retroactive and which were not. Art. 7 explained the inheritance rights of patrilineal successors (*sizi*) established before the Book on Inheritance came into force in May 1931.

nity, who were accustomed to viewing property inheritance through patrilineal succession, the code did not prohibit the designation of a successor under "the old customs of the country" (*wuguo jiuli*; *Zuigao fayuan panli huibian*, 28: 108). It was just that any such patrilineal successor had absolutely no legal rights to the deceased's property on that account alone. The property was to go instead to the statutory heirs listed in the code. One puzzled judge in Yuhang county (Zhejiang) sought clarification from the Judicial Yuan in 1932:

China has always emphasized the patriline and the question of patrilineal succession. Therefore, whenever a man grows old without having sired sons or whenever a man dies without male issue, then a junior male of the lineage necessarily has to become his successor. Whenever there are disputes over the property [*yichan*] of a deceased man, they also necessarily have to take as their premise the question of patrilineal succession [*zongtiao jicheng*]. If the succession goes to A, then the property goes along with it to A. If the succession goes to B, then the property goes to B. The property is but an appendage [*fushupin*] to the patrilineal succession. Now the Book on Inheritance deals only with property inheritance and not at all with patrilineal succession. But litigation among the people still follows the old custom of using disputes over patrilineal succession to contest property inheritance.

Since the code was silent on the succession point, the judge wanted to know how the courts should handle such disputes. The Judicial Yuan responded that since the civil code did not recognize patrilineal succession, the courts should see such cases as disputes over property inheritance and adjudicate accordingly on the basis of the new laws (*SJQ*: no. 780).

What this meant in practice was, first, that courts were no longer to give succession disputes a legal hearing.[4] Thus, for instance, in 1933, in reviewing a case from Dongguang county (Hebei), in which two paternal first cousins (*tangxiong*) of a deceased heirless man were fighting over which of their sons was to become the man's successor, the Supreme Court ruled that the case should have been rejected outright. Since the civil code did not contain any provisions on patrilineal succession, courts were not to concern themselves with any matter relating to succession, including, as in the case before it, the competing claims of agnatic kin (*Zuigao fayuan panli huibian*, 25: 18–21).

4. The exceptions would be disputes in which the property-holder had died before the inheritance section went into force. The courts were to accept those suits and adjudicate them according to the laws in force before May 1931. See "Law Governing the Application of the Book of Inheritance of the Civil Code."

Second, that being the case, courts were obviously obliged to reject any claims to property based on patrilineal succession. This the Supreme Court made clear in another case it heard in 1933. Chen Kuigen, of Xinchang county (Zhejiang), died in July 1931, two months after the inheritance section of the Republican Civil Code came into force. He left two daughters, but no sons. His daughters convened a meeting of their father's relatives at which Chen Songyun, Kuigen's 57-sui nephew (a brother's son), was selected to be his successor and, as such, the heir to his property. A succession document (*jishu*) was drawn up to that effect. Soon after, three of Kuigen's grandnephews (another brother's grandsons) brought suit against Songyun on the grounds that his appointment was illegitimate under the new inheritance laws. Since Chen Songyun could not now be Chen Kuigen's lineal successor, they reasoned, he could not inherit his property.

When the case reached the Supreme Court's chambers, it set the grandnephews straight on the fine points of the law. True, it responded, the new code did not cover succession, but neither did it prohibit it. Chen Songyun was fully entitled to be Kuigen's successor. But, the court continued, since patrilineal succession no longer determined property inheritance, Songyun's status as Kuigen's patrilineal successor did not entitle him to any of the property. The estate must be distributed to the statutory heirs listed in the code—in this case the two daughters themselves (*Zuigao fayuan panli huibian*, 28: 105–9).

This is not to suggest, however, that a designated heir had absolutely no rights under the code. The appointment of an heir was, after all, a type of adoption. And the civil code did recognize adoption and accorded adopted children statutory inheritance rights. Thus, whether a designated heir had any rights at all to his adoptive father's property depended on when and how he had acquired that status.

Up to now, as we have seen, postmortem adoptions were both legal under the law and conventional in social practice. But the new civil code incorporated the principle from its foreign models that only living people could adopt children. Consequently, any heir a man's patrilineal kin might appoint for him after his death could not acquire the status of adopted son (*SJQ*: no. 907). It was for this reason that the Supreme Court ruled Chen Songyun was not entitled to a share of Kuigen's property. Under the civil code, he could not be the deceased Kuigen's adopted son.

The same held true for postmortem heirs adopted by widows. Where under Ming, Qing, and early Republican law, a widow had the legal obligation to adopt an heir if her husband had not had one, she now had neither the obligation nor indeed the right to do so. Only someone adopted jointly by a husband and a wife was legally considered to be the child of both (art. 1074). Any child a wife adopted after her husband's death would be her child and her heir (*jicheng ren*), not his, and hence entitled to inherit only her property (*SJQ*: nos. 851, 907).

By the letter of the code, only a male heir appointed by a man himself during his own lifetime could acquire the legal status of an adopted child. And it was solely on that basis that he had any statutory claims at all to his adoptive father's property. But his rights were no different from those of any adopted child, male or female. If, for example, his adoptive father also had daughters, his share of the property was to be only one-half of each daughter's share. If the adoptive father was survived by a wife, the adopted son had to split the estate equally with her. Only if the man had no daughters and no surviving wife could the adopted son receive all of the estate (art. 1142). The civil code therefore greatly restricted the amount of property that could go to even a premortem adopted heir.

Finally, the code limited the amount of property a man could leave to any successor he might appoint through a will. It was not uncommon for a man without sons, either birth or adopted, to designate an heir (*sizi*) in a will. That practice had been firmly upheld in imperial and early Republican law. But under the Republican Civil Code, a man who had direct lineal descendants (children, grandchildren, and so on) could not will his property to another person. So, for example, a will that bypassed daughters or even granddaughters was automatically invalid (art. 1143).

Moreover, even in the absence of lineal descendants, the man could not will the whole of his estate to a designated successor, for other statutory heirs—his wife, siblings, parents, and grandparents—had legal claims to at least part of it. Surviving siblings and/or grandparents were entitled to at least one-third of his property, and his surviving wife and/or parents to at least one-half. At best, then, a designated successor might get a two-thirds share (arts. 1143, 1223).

The Redefinition of Kinship

The severing of the link between patrilineal succession and property inheritance was grounded in a fundamental reconception of family relationships. In formulating the family and inheritance books, the chief lawmakers, the Central Political Council of the GMD and the Legislative Yuan's Civil Law Codification Committee, had first to decide what exactly constituted "family." They explicitly eschewed the traditional kinship system, which, they explained, had distinguished among three kinds of relatives: "internal relatives" (*neiqin*), or paternal relatives within the five grades of mourning; "external relatives" (*waiqin*), or maternal relatives within the five grades of mourning; and "wife's relatives" (*qiqin*), or relatives of a wife within the five grades of mourning (*Qinshufa xianjue gedian* 1930).[5]

In this system, strict patrilineal principles determined the closeness of kinship. Since a person was considered to be more closely related to paternal relatives than maternal ones, a son or an unmarried daughter, for example, was obliged to observe the one-year mourning with staff for a paternal grandparent, but only the five-month mourning for a maternal one. Likewise, since a wife was deemed to be more closely related to her husband's relatives than he was to hers, she was obliged to observe the highest degree of mourning, the three years' mourning, for his parents, whereas he had to observe only the lowest degree of mourning, the three months' mourning, for hers (Wu Tan ca. 1780: 69–92 passim).

The lawmakers eradicated this system and substituted in its place a different set of family relationships that emphasized equality over patrilineal hierarchy. They abolished the distinction between internal and external relatives, collapsing all consanguineous kinship into the single category of "relatives by blood" (*xieqin*). This meant that a person, male or female, was now related just as closely to maternal relatives as to paternal ones. Kinship by marriage (*hunqin*) was likewise equalized: a wife's relationship to her husband's relatives was now no different from his relationship to hers. Finally, the lawmakers set up as a distinct and separate kinship link the relationship between husband and wife (*peiou*). In short, the three main components of the patrilineal kinship system (paternal, maternal, and wife's relatives) were replaced by three new categories: relatives by blood, relatives by marriage, and spouses (arts. 967–971).

5. The five grades of mourning were three years (*zhancui*); one year (*zicui*); nine months (*dagong*); five months (*xiaogong*); and three months (*sima*). One-year mourning was divided into two categories: with staff (*zhangqi*) and without staff (*wuqi*). The former was the deeper type of mourning, for the staff was meant to show that the mourner was so doubled over with grief that he or she needed support. Note that the Chinese terms do not refer to time periods but identify the type of clothing mourners were to wear for the specified times.

TABLE 3
Degrees of Kinship Under the Republican Civil Code

Lineal relatives	Degree	Collateral relatives	Degree
Great-great-grandparents	4		
Great-grandparents	3		
Grandparents	2	Great-uncles/aunts	4
Parents	1	Uncles/aunts	3
Self		Siblings	2
		First cousins	4
Children	1	Nephews/nieces	3
Grandchildren	2	Grandnephews/nieces	4
Great-grandchildren	3		
Great-great-grandchildren	4		

SOURCE: *Civil Code* 1930: art. 968.

The lawmakers went on to divide consanguineous kinship into two subcategories: lineal relatives by blood (*zhixi xieqin*), or direct ascendants and descendants (e.g., parents, grandparents, children, and grandchildren); and collateral relatives by blood (*pangxi xieqin*), or kin related through a common ancestor (e.g., siblings, cousins, aunts, and uncles; art. 967). Here again, no distinction was made between paternal and maternal relatives.

Finally, the lawmakers adopted an entirely new standard for determining the closeness of kinship. They did away with the patrilineal mourning charts and their precise calculations of kinship, and adopted instead the Roman law method, in which, by the code's explanation, the degree of relationship between both lineal and collateral relatives was determined by the number of generations between oneself and a direct relative or common ancestor. Thus, as shown in Table 3, children and parents would be related to the first degree, grandchildren and grandparents to the second degree, siblings to the second degree, first cousins to the fourth degree, and so forth.

The redefinition of kinship relationships played a decisive role in the formulation of the new inheritance laws. First of all, it completely changed the generational order of inheritance. Previously, the direction of property inheritance had always followed the direction of patrilineal succession. Since that always proceeded downward generation by generation through a patriline, so too did property inheritance. But the civil code legislated not only downward inheritance (from parents to children) but also lateral inheritance (from one sibling to another), and even upward inheritance (from children to parents and grandparents). Children, a first-degree relationship, came first, followed by parents (also first degree), then brothers and sisters (second degree), and finally grandparents (also second degree). Such an ordering of rights, with its generational hopscotching, would have been utterly unthinkable in imperial times.

Equally unthinkable would have been the complete disregard for the distinction between paternal and maternal relatives and with it the assurance that property stayed within a man's patriline. In Chapter Six, we will see how such property became vulnerable to the new legal claims of daughters, both married and unmarried, but that was only part of the story. Under the new laws, property could flow outside a patriline through other avenues: from a widow to her children by another husband, to her siblings, or to her parents or grandparents; from a sister to her husband and children; or from a granddaughter to her husband and children. (It could also flow to the state in the absence of statutory heirs or a will; art. 1185. As the Legal System Bureau explained, the code's narrow range of statutory heirs was part of the GMD's policy of restricting private capital [*jiezhi ziben*] in order to reduce disparities of wealth. Such confiscated property was to be used to fund local development projects; cited in Zhang Xubai 1930: 76.)

The inheritance laws were significant not only for whom they included among the statutory heirs, but also for whom they excluded. Where agnatic nephews had once held first claim to the succession and hence to the property of a deceased heirless man, a nephew as such had no rights whatsoever to inherit from his paternal uncle. As defined by the code, only relatives to the first or second degree possessed statutory rights of inheritance.[6] This ruled out even the closest nephews (sons of one's brothers, a third-degree relationship), not to mention more distant ones. The exclusion of nephews, more

---

6. Art. 1140 stipulated, however, that "where an heir of the first order . . . has died or lost the right of inheritance, . . . his lineal descendants shall inherit his . . . portion in his place." In this way, third- or fourth-degree relatives (great-grandchildren, great-great-grandchildren) could inherit. A nephew could, of course, inherit from an uncle as an adopted son or testamentary heir, but even then, as we saw earlier in this chapter, his share of the property was limited by law.

than anything else, tells of the complete dissociation of patrilineal succession and property inheritance under the Republican code.

The Reconceptualization of Property

Underlying the separation of patrilineal succession and property inheritance was a fundamental reconceptualization of the nature of property ownership. The civil code did not think of property as above all familial in the manner of imperial law. What had been legally conceived of as family property became the individual property of the father. No mention is made of family property (*jiachan*) anywhere in the code; it had ceased to exist as a legal concept.

Superficially, the code's legal reconstitution of family property as the father's private property seems to suggest an essential continuity with the past. After all, imperial and early Republican law had also vested legal ownership in the father, since only he possessed the rights of management and disposal. But the question of legal ownership alone cannot convey the true significance of the code's formulation. A deeper transformation was at work, one that can be comprehended only by looking more closely at the nature of family property.

Useful in this regard is Shiga Shūzō's understanding of the classical expression *tongju gongcai*, which he translates as "common living, common budget." In his view, family property was at once individual and communal. It was the father's individual property from the perspective of legal ownership. But at the same time, it was also "everyone's" property from the perspective of the common living, common budget group. All household members belonged to that group, since family property was "a pooling of the fruit of the labor of all members of the household and the means of support of all" (1978: 149). In that sense, family property was the direct physical manifestation of the family economy. Participation in that economy conferred membership in the common living, common budget group, and with that membership came certain duties, such as the obligation to contribute one's labor and income to the group, as well as certain rights, including above all the right to be maintained by the family property.

It was this very connection to the household economy that made the property family property, and not merely the personal possession of the father. To understand the full import of this severing of the linkage between property and the household economy, then, we must look beyond the simple issue of legal ownership to what the elimination of "common living, common budget" produced: a restructuring of the conceptual foundations of both inheritance and maintenance.

Property Ownership

The code's designation of family property as the personal property of the father was by no means a foregone conclusion. Indeed, in reaching for a definition of property ownership, the lawmakers had to make a critical choice. As they themselves saw it, the question was whether to legislate a system of rights that retained a connection to the household economy or one that did not. Or, to put their choice in our terms of the dual-sided nature of family property, the question was whether to emphasize the communal or the individual.

Interestingly, the GMD lawmakers first elected to emphasize the communal. The 1928 draft of the inheritance book called for property to be shared by parents and their adult children. By way of explanation, the Legal System Bureau noted:

Actually in our country, the majority of parents and children engage in communal work [*gongtong gongzuo*] . . . and the property thus acquired through that labor in fact possesses the nature of communal property [*gongyou caichan*]. Although parents have the right to manage and the right to use [*shiyong*] that property, they can do so only to the extent needed to achieve the aim of a life in common [*gongtong shenghuo*]. Generally speaking, they do not have complete freedom of disposal. Taking this social condition into consideration, this draft . . . provides for communal property between parents and children.   (Cited in Zhang Xubai 1930: 112–13)

More specifically, the draft provided that adult children who continued to live with their parents and made contributions (*gongxian*, e.g., labor and capital) to the household's property were to be vested with co-ownership rights.

What was being proposed here was not the family property regime of old, but a revised system that did away with perceived inequalities. In the old system, only sons could claim shares of the property during household division. In the 1928 system, daughters were to be co-owners no less than sons and, as such, were entitled to the same rights during household division. In the old system, parents decided when the property was to undergo division. In the 1928 system, any co-owner was to be allowed to request his or her share at any time. In the old system, parents also had the ultimate right of disposal. In the 1928 system, if they disposed of it unwisely, children could go to court to request that the transaction be canceled. Finally, in the old system, sons were entitled to equal shares of the family property during division, regardless of their contributions to the family's economic life. In the 1928 system, the amount of each person's share was to be determined by what he or she had actually contributed as adults, thereby rewarding enterprise and discouraging sloth (Zhang Xubai 1930: 97, 112–13, 127–28). The Legal System Bureau thus sought to retain the principles of family property and household division but in a revised form that would eliminate the past inequalities in ownership and contributions.

The 1928 draft's linking of inheritance to contribution, which was intended to work against the excessive parcelization of family farms, was intended also to limit the scope of daughters' inheritance, despite the GMD's professed allegiance to gender equality. Luo Ding, the principal drafter of the 1928 provisions, admitted as much in a book he published in 1933 on the inheritance laws as ultimately enacted:

The overwhelming majority of the country's citizens are peasants. Among such peasants, fathers and sons, elder brothers and younger brothers, work together to maintain what little property they own. [Under the 1929–30 civil code] children of a deceased parent are each to receive exactly the same amount [of the estate], regardless of whether they had made any contribution to it and regardless of whether they are still living at home. . . . How can this be called fair? Moreover, this property is principally immovable property such as land and houses. Its division into excessively small parcels greatly lessens its utility. It was questionable enough before whether the principle of absolutely equal division among all sons was the best policy from the perspective of the national economy. Now that unmarried and married daughters are also to participate in the equal distribution of an estate, the degree of parcelization will be even greater. The more the property is divided, the tinier it becomes. How could its utility not also be accordingly reduced? As for a daughter who has married out, how could she, simply because she received a few mu of land and a few rafters of housing from her natal family, abruptly abandon her husband and children to return to her place of birth and make full use of her acquired property? (Luo Ding 1933: 3–4. For similar criticisms, see Wu Ruikai 1930: 25–26)

By retaining the link between property and the family economy in the 1928 draft, Luo Ding had hoped to prevent at least married daughters from inheriting. Because one's status and share as a co-owner depended solely on one's contribution to the property after reaching adulthood (20 sui), daughters, who had normally married out of their families by then, would have had little opportunity to contribute anything as adults and thus would have been entitled to little, if anything, at the time of household division.

As is obvious from Luo's remarks, the proposed communal property regime was not included in the final version of the code. It was dropped partly because it left little room for daughters to inherit and partly out of concern that the requirement of putting a monetary value to each co-owner's contribution would prove to be too contentious and result in too many lawsuits.

It was for much the same reasons that, in 1930, the Central Political Council, the GMD body with the final say on the content of the code, decided not to include a provision for compensation (*baochang*) in the Book on Inheritance. Such a law, drawn from the Swiss code, would have permitted children to request, over and above their statutory shares, reimbursement from the deceased's estate for any contribution he or she had made to it in the way of labor or capital. In its rejection of the proposed law, the council concluded that the system of "common living, common budget" (*tongju gongcai*) was so pervasive in China that to legislate compensation would only open up the door to endless litigation (*Jichengfa xianjue gedian* 1930). There was also concern that such a provision would put daughters at a disadvantage, thereby undermining the code's principle of gender equality (Luo Ding 1933: 3–4). In the end, then, the lawmakers opted for a system of property rights that was completely divorced from the family economy.

In the code as finally enacted, the reformulation of family property as the father's personal property came about not through any general statement of principle, but rather through a process of elimination. The code permitted minor children to own property, such as inheritance and gifts (art. 1087). It also allowed a wife to own property separate from her husband (such as dowry, inheritance, gifts, and remunerations she received for her own labor).[7] All property not owned by the children or the wife was perforce owned by

7. The code provided for four different matrimonial property regimes (*fuqi caichanzhi*), one statutory and three contractual (arts. 1004-1048). Unless a married couple specifically adopted one of the contractual regimes by a written agreement, the statutory one obtained by default. This so-called union property system (*lianhe caichanzhi*), modeled closely on Swiss law, constituted what the lawmakers considered "the most appropriate for the circumstances of our country," striking what seemed to them to be an ideal balance between the maintenance of a life in common (*gongtong shenghuo*) and the protection of the individual interests and rights of both parties (*Qinshufa xianjue gedian* 1930). It was embodied in art. 1016, which stated that "all property belonging to the spouses at the time of marriage as well as property acquired by them during the continuance of the marriage becomes their union

the husband and formed his estate on death. By extension, all property not owned separately by the other members of a multigenerational family living in the same household was, by definition, in the legal possession of the father in the most senior generation.

Inheritance

The new code rejected not only patrilineal succession, but also household division. The redefinition of the nature of property ownership necessarily led to a transformation in the method of its intergenerational transmission. The code conceived the passing of property from one generation to the next as purely a matter of postmortem inheritance (*jicheng yichan*). Until the father died, he retained exclusive ownership of "his" property. At the moment of his death, the property passed into the ownership of his heir(s) (*jichengren*; arts. 1147, 1148). Should there be more than one heir, they owned the property in common (*gongtong gongyou*) until its partition (*fenge yichan*; art. 1151). Any heir could demand such a partition at any time (art. 1164).

The code's provisions on inheritance created a great deal of confusion within the legal community. After the Book on Inheritance was promulgated in late 1930, the Judicial Yuan received a flurry of inquiries from local officials, judges, and lawyers' associations in the provinces, asking for clarification. Two questions put forward by the Qidong (Jiangsu) county magistrate in 1931 are representative of the lot. "When a father or mother divides property among their sons," he wanted to know, "is this the start of property inheritance [*caichan jicheng kaishi*]?" And in a similar vein, "if sons had received and managed [*chengguan*] the property when their parents died, but had not yet drawn up a document to divide the property, has inheritance already started or does it only begin later, when the sons divide the property among themselves?" (*SJQ*: no. 465).

Although slightly different in emphasis, these two questions represent attempts to fit the novel concept of postmortem inheritance into the familiar context of family division. Both ask whether inheritance as defined by the code was the same as household division

---

property [*lianhe caichan*]." But this was in fact a union of unequals, since most of the rights over the property were vested in the husband. The three contractual regimes were community of property (*gongtong caichanzhi*), unity of property (*tongyi caichanzhi*), and separation of property (*fenbie caichanzhi*). All four will be examined in my sequel volume on marriage and divorce in late imperial and Republican China.

as popularly practiced. To both, the Judicial Yuan responded that inheritance began with the death of the father and not with household division, regardless of when it occurred.

Thus, in the family property/household division regime, the crucial moment had been the division of property, which could occur before or after the father's death. Inheritance and the division of property were simultaneous, for it was through the very act of dividing the property that one inherited it. But in the individual property/inheritance regime, the crucial moment was the death of the property owner; inheritance, by definition, could only be postmortem, never premortem. Furthermore, inheritance and the division of property were seen as two separate matters, and the latter, if it took place at all, might occur years after inheritance. Postmortem inheritance and household division operated on two radically different logics.

Maintenance

The redefinition of family property had a more subtle, though no less significant effect. It changed the nature of family members' legal claims to maintenance. In imperial and early Republican law, each member of the common living, common budget group had the right to be supported by the family property regardless of which member of what generation happened to be in charge of it—whether a grandfather, grandmother, father, mother, brother, or so on. But the civil code did not recognize the existence of any claims on property based on membership in a common group. Family property, once conceived of as both the father's property and the property of all in the common budget group, had become the exclusive property of the father alone.

That change in turn necessitated a revision in the terms of maintenance. In the civil code's chapter on "Maintenance" (*fuyang*) in the Book on Family, four classes of people bore a reciprocal obligation to support one another financially: lineal relatives by blood; a spouse and his or her parents-in-law living in the same household; brothers and sisters; and the head of a household (*jiazhang*) and its members (*jiashu*; art. 1114).

The list can be simplified into two categories, one based on kinship and the other on co-residence. The first category consisted of one's closest consanguineous relatives: lineal ascendants (parents, grandparents, both paternal and maternal, and so on), lineal descendants still under their majority, and sisters and brothers. The concept of close kinship underlying this category, of course, was not the patrilineal one of old, but the new one as defined by the code, hence the inclusion of maternal grandparents as well as paternal, grandchildren through a daughter as well as a son, and sisters as well as brothers.

For all other relatives by blood and all relatives by marriage, a right to maintenance depended entirely on whether they lived in the same household as the provider, with, as the code put it, "the object of sharing a life in common permanently" (arts. 1122, 1123). If they lived outside the household, they were not legally entitled to maintenance.

At bottom, the code's formulations represented a radical change in the conceptual foundations of maintenance. Where once maintenance claims attached to property, they now attached to people instead, whether through close kinship or co-residence in a family head–family member relationship. Maintenance under the code and maintenance under past law were thus also based on two very different logics.

As envisioned by the GMD lawmakers, three large obstacles stood in the way of inheritance rights for women—patrilineal succession, the patrilineal family, and the concept of property as family property. They thus dissociated property inheritance from patrilineal succession, equalized kinship relations, and separated property from the household economy. They adopted wholesale the Western concepts of individual property and postmortem inheritance. In their rejection of the old and their embrace of the new, the lawmakers fully expected that their modern civil code would represent an unqualified advance for women.

CHAPTER FIVE

Widows' Inheritance Rights Under the Republican Code

Judging by the code alone, the GMD lawmakers accomplished what they had set out to do. The Book on Inheritance contains not a hint of gender differentiation, let alone of gender bias. Wives and husbands were spouses, daughters and sons direct lineal descendants, mothers and fathers parents, grandmothers and grandfathers grandparents, and sisters and brothers siblings. As one commentator pointed out, the principle of equality between the sexes was so deeply embedded in the very language of the laws that it was not even necessary to specify that they were to be applicable to all regardless of sex (*bufen nannü*; Liu Langquan 1931: 21). Absolute gender equality had been achieved in the written law.

Contemporary observers uniformly credited the code's provisions on inheritance with overturning several millennia of "feudal" oppression. One called it a "great unprecedented reform" (*Shishi xinbao*, May 24, 1929). Another applauded it as "great news for women" and as "a bolt of thunder from the blue sky that breaks through four thousand years of rotten air" (Liu Langquan 1931: 17). Even the code's detractors did not dispute that the Book on Inheritance was a big step forward for women: they merely questioned whether the cost to others, particularly sons, might be too high (*Shenbao*, Oct. 16, 1929; Luo Ding 1933: 3–4).

Those assessments of the code and its impact on women's legal rights to property proved to be too optimistic. The problem lay not in any failure of the courts to follow the new laws. Indeed, in not one single case in my study did the presiding judge willfully turn his back on the code and grant a woman less than what was now her rightful due. In that respect, inheritance cases differed from divorce cases, where the code allowed judges a certain amount of discretion. As I have examined elsewhere, judges tended to use that authority to deny women divorce, thus giving rise to a considerable gap between the lawmakers' declared intent of gender equality in marriage matters and actual legal practice (Bernhardt 1994). The inheritance laws permitted no such latitude, clearly spelling out in formulaic fashion the respective rights of the various statutory heirs. Inheritance cases thus evinced a congruency between codified intent and legal practice not found in divorce cases.

Rather, the problem lay with the code itself. The code did not simply extend *existing* property rights to women. An equally fundamental transformation was at work: the replacement of the patrilineal succession and household division complexes with a new property and inheritance regime patterned after Western models. Even as women were being granted equal inheritance rights, the very nature of those rights was being restructured.

Two principles thus informed the code, gender equality and the Western concept of individual property/postmortem inheritance. The lawmakers saw the two as inextricably connected. For them, it was an article of faith that gender equality could be achieved only through a wholesale adoption of Western notions of personal property. Little did they imagine that it would be precisely because they took this tack that women did not necessarily end up with full inheritance rights in the new legal order. Applied to the Chinese context, as we shall see, the two principles sometimes worked at cross-purposes.

An examination of female inheritance under the new civil code not only tells of the points of conflict between two of the document's basic principles, but also affords an opportunity to explore more fully the different property logics laid out in the last chapter. Although men did not remain untouched under the new laws, they still enjoyed full inheritance rights, as they had in the past. Thus a focus on their claims can only go so far in uncovering the very different conceptual underpinnings of the two systems. Because women's rights experienced the greatest change, it is there that we will find the sharpest contrast between the two logics.

Wives as Statutory Heirs

Under the new civil code, a wife had the right to inherit her husband's property, just as he had the right to inherit hers. In 1930, the

Central Political Council explained its reasons for breaking with past practice:

In the former laws of our country, a wife did not have the right to inherit property from her husband. The law that read "a woman without sons who preserves her chastity is to receive her husband's share" merely amounted to the temporary management of property. As for a husband inheriting from his wife, although there was no written law on the matter, customarily the wife's property was not separate from the husband's. When she died, her property immediately became his. . . . This patriarchal [*fuquan*] system is the first thing that is not in keeping with current thought. [Moreover,] in the former laws of our country, only those who succeeded to the patriline could inherit property. The two were inseparable. Therefore, a wife had no right to inherit property. From today's perspective, patrilineal succession concerns succession to the right to offer ancestral sacrifices, and property inheritance concerns the transfer of property. The meanings and purposes are different and need not be conflated. Patrilineal succession is the second thing that is not in keeping with current thought. (*Jichengfa xianjue gedian* 1930)

The principle of equality between the sexes, the council concluded, demanded that property inheritance be distinct from patrilineal succession, and that husband and wife have the same right to inherit each other's property.

The principle of equal inheritance rights between spouses having been established, the next order of business was to decide where to place a spouse in the list of statutory heirs. For the GMD lawmakers, the key question was whether to privilege children over spouses, as in the Japanese civil code, or to permit spouses to inherit along with their children, as in the German and Swiss codes (*Jichengfa xianjue gedian* 1930). They chose the second option, for reasons explained earlier by the Legal Bureau in the 1928 draft inheritance book:

It is quite difficult to determine which relationship is the closer—the husband-wife relationship or the parent-child relationship. Moreover, men receive help from their wives [lit., *neizhu*, "inner helpmate"] to acquire property and to establish themselves in business. . . . Once a husband dies, a wife must immediately rely on her sons and grandsons for her living expenses, so much so that sometimes to maintain peace and order in the family she has to take orders from them. This not only violates the principles of esteeming virtue and repaying merit [*chongde baogong*]; it is also something that human emotions seem unable to tolerate. (Cited in Zhang Xubai 1930: 77)

To achieve a balance between the needs of wives and the needs of children, it was imperative that wives be allowed to inherit concurrently with the other statutory heirs, children included.

In the code, a spouse's rights to the other's property was covered in articles 1138 and 1144. Article 1138 stipulated that "heirs to property other than the spouse come in the following order: 1. lineal descendants by blood [children, grandchildren, etc.]; 2. parents; 3. brothers and sisters; 4. grandparents." Article 1144 explained how the property was to be divided between a surviving spouse and these other statutory heirs. If a spouse inherited concurrently with heirs of the first order, or lineal descendants by blood, she or he was to receive a share equal to theirs. Thus, for example, a widow and three children would each receive one-fourth of the man's estate. If a spouse inherited concurrently with heirs of the second or third order, parents or brothers and sisters, then she or he was to receive one-half of the property and the others half. If a spouse inherited concurrently with heirs of the fourth order, or grandparents, then she or he was to receive two-thirds and the grandparents one-third. When there were no other heirs of any order, the surviving spouse would be entitled to the whole of the property.

A widow's ownership of her statutory share was absolute. It was hers to do with whatever she pleased during her lifetime. She could take it with her into a new marriage or sell it all off or give it all away to anyone she chose. When she died, the property was to pass on to *her* statutory heirs: her children, her parents, her siblings, or her grandparents.

On the face of it, the strict gender equality in the provisions for spouses might seem an unqualified advance for widows, just as the code's architects envisioned. But when the code is examined in conjunction with court records, a different picture emerges. These changes had at best very mixed implications for a widow's legal rights to property. The Western concepts of property and inheritance, when played out in the courtroom, produced results unforeseen, and unintended, by the lawmakers. In the end, their very modern civil code actually gave widows in certain situations less power than they had had in the much-maligned oppressive feudal past.

One of those unanticipated results was that not all widows ended up with the same set of rights. A distinction has to be drawn between widowed wives on the one hand and widowed daughters-in-law on the other. The sole difference between the two was the sequence of deaths in the family. A widowed wife was a woman whose husband died after his own father; a widowed daughter-in-law was a woman whose husband died before his own father. Up to this point in our discussion, there has been no particular need to distinguish between the two, since under earlier law, all widows had essentially the same set of rights regardless of the order of deaths. That such a distinction has to be made now is in itself indicative of the civil code's very different notions of property and inheritance.

Widowed Wives

In Chapter Two, we saw how the consolidation of mandatory nephew succession from the Song through the Qing had the paradoxical effect of increasing a widow's custodial powers over her husband's property, even while it deprived her of any inheritance rights. Here we shall see how the repudiation in law of patrilineal succession had the opposite effect of granting a widow inheritance rights to her husband's property, even while it deprived her of any custodial powers. Widowed wives lost even as they gained with the restructuring of rights under the civil code.

The implementation of the new inheritance laws on May 5, 1931, had a dramatic impact on the content of widow litigation over property. In the imperial period, as we have seen, succession disputes involving widows composed the single largest category of litigation over inheritance. Of the 430 cases studied, 79 percent concerned patrilineal succession. Widows were litigants in 60 percent of those disputes—or nearly half (47 percent) of all the cases.

In the GMD's new legal order, courts were no longer to accept such cases, since the code did not recognize patrilineal succession as a lawful mode for the intergenerational transmission of property. The evidence suggests that courts, at least those in large urban areas, hewed strictly to the new legal order, accepting only disputes over the estates of men who had died before the Book on Inheritance came into force. Five of 118 inheritance cases heard by the Beijing District Court in the 1930's and 1940's, for instance, concerned the designation of an heir for a man who had died before May 5, 1931, which the court dutifully adjudicated according to the Daliyuan's rulings. No case concerning the designation of a successor for a man who had died after that date shows up in the records. Patrilineal succession cases had virtually disappeared from the court's docket.

The removal of patrilineal succession from the formal legal realm created a huge gap between codified law and custom and, in so doing, deprived widows of a crucial source of support in their battles over the selection of an heir. The civil code notwithstanding, patrilineal succession continued as strong as ever in social practice (see, for instance, Niida, ed. 1952–58; and Taga 1960), as did the conflicting claims based on lineage order (*yingji*) and affection (*aiji*). To the extent that imperial and then early Republican law had come to favor the widow's right to select the heir of her choice, the courts had served widows well, consistently taking their side in disputes with their husbands' relatives. The withdrawal of that support under the civil code, we can surmise, made widows less able to resist the pressures from others.

What now filled the dockets of court judges were cases involving postmortem property inheritance. With this change came a change in the field of litigants. Previously, when patrilineal succession had determined property inheritance, a widowed wife faced as her principal adversaries in court those among her husband's agnatic relatives who had the greatest stake in the designation of an heir—her husband's nephews as potential heirs and their fathers (her husband's brothers and paternal cousins). Now, she most commonly was squared off against her children and grandchildren.

For instance, in 1942, the widow Yang Dong Yongzhen (60 sui) brought suit against her 29-sui son at the Beijing District Court, charging him with the dissipation of her deceased husband's property.[1] The only property remaining was the house (valued at 20,000 yuan), which she feared would also fall victim to her son's extravagance. She therefore requested that the house be sold, and the proceeds divided equally between them according to law. Her son agreed to the division, and the two signed a court mediation agreement to that effect (Beijing: 1942-6772).

Another widow who was ready to go to court to assert her newly acquired rights was Mrs. Chang (née Huang) of Beijing, who in the early 1940's successfully pressed her case for half of her husband's estate (consisting of a house, 5.2 mu of residential land, *jidi*, and 1,220 mu of farmland). Her husband, Chang Runfeng, had been a eunuch at the Qing court, and being childless, the couple had adopted the infant son of one of his brothers as heir. In 1935, Runfeng was kidnapped and killed by bandits. The following year, 1936, the adopted heir, Chang Zhentai, died, leaving a wife and two sons. Under past law, Chang Runfeng's entire estate would have gone into their possession, but under the new law, they had to divide it with his widow (Beijing: 65-22-1260).

1. In the Republican period, married women began to appear in the records under their full names—husband's last name, father's last name, and given name.

Though a widowed wife in this way gained the right to a portion of property, she at the same time lost the custodial powers she once had had over *all* of the family estate. In imperial law as well as in social custom, as we have seen, a widow, as her husband's representative after his death, possessed strong custodial powers over the family property. Sons, regardless of their age, were not permitted to dispose of family property without their widowed mother's express consent. Nor were they permitted to undergo household division without her approval. Since household division and property inheritance were simultaneous in the family property regime, her right to decide the timing of household division was tantamount to a right to decide when inheritance was to take place.

Under the civil code, widowhood ceased to be a special legal status with its own unique set of rights and responsibilities. Indeed, the code did not use the word "widow" or even "wife" in its inheritance laws, preferring instead the gender-neutral "spouse" (*peiou*). A widowed wife no longer enjoyed a special relationship to property. Legally, she was just one of her husband's heirs, with no more rights than any other heir.

And as just one of the heirs, a widowed wife could no longer dictate when the property was to be divided. In the logic of the code, inheritance and the division of property were two separate matters. Inheritance commenced with the property owner's death, after which time any heir could demand the partition of the property. A widow had no right to prevent this, which is to say, she was now legally defenseless against the demands of her sons, daughters, or any other heir for division.

The difference between the two regimes, and the place of widowed wives in each, lay at the heart of litigation in 1942 between the widow Mrs. Qi (née Han) and her married daughter. Mrs. Qi's husband, Qi Enqi, had died on November 25, 1941, leaving, besides the widow herself, four children, two sons and two married daughters. The following year, one of the daughters brought suit against her mother for refusing to turn over her rightful one-fifth share of the estate. Mrs. Qi based her defense on a widow's prerogative in household division. The property, she declared, was to be kept intact to provide for her livelihood and divided between the sons only after her death. In fact, she and her two sons had signed an agreement to that effect three days after her husband's death. No one had the right to demand the partition of the property, least of all a married daughter.

Such an agreement, as the written expression of a widow's custodial rights over family property, would have been perfectly legitimate under imperial law. But it was not under the civil code. In his decision, the District Court judge explained that under the new laws inheritance began with the death of the property owner. Thus, all of Qi Enqi's statutory heirs, his widow and his four children, had inherited his estate at the moment of his death. With inheritance came the right to demand one's statutory share at any time. She, as just one of the heirs, could not dictate when that was to occur. She especially could not, as the judge put it, mandate "that inheritance was not to begin until one of the heirs [she herself] had died." He thus ruled against the widow and for the daughter (Beijing: 1942-5210, 1942-5705).

Other widowed wives also discovered that they no longer had the right to decide when inheritance was to take place. In 1942, a 66-sui Beijing widow, Mrs. Liu (née Hu), lost a suit brought by her 23-sui grandson, Liu Wenzhi. She and her husband, Liu Xinting, had had three children, two daughters, now married, and one son, now deceased, the father of Wenzhi. Liu Xinting had died in 1939, leaving a 10-room house, 10 mu of land, a stationery store, and three rented-out storefronts. Against her grandson's claim, the widow argued, among other things, that after paying off all the debts her husband had incurred, what remained of the property would only be sufficient for her own livelihood. She therefore did not want it divided up.

In his ruling, the Beijing District Court judge informed her that inheritance had already occurred at the moment of her husband's death. Like she herself and her two married daughters, Liu Wenzhi, as the deceased son's only descendant, had come into an equal share. Moreover, he was entitled to withdraw that share from the common pot whenever he wanted. The judge accordingly ordered Mrs. Liu to hand over one-fourth of the property to the grandson (Beijing: 1942-1610, 1942-3931).

Although widowed wives most frequently faced their children or grandchildren in the courtroom, on occasion they confronted other statutory heirs intent on claiming their legal share of a husband's estate. As stipulated in the civil code, when the husband had no direct lineal descendants, then his widow had to share his estate with his parents, his siblings, or his grandparents. Thus, in 1942, a Beijing widow, Han Meng Youqing, was brought to court by her deceased husband's sister, Han Zengrong. Since the husband did not have any direct lineal descendants and his parents were dead, the sister, as a third-order heir, had the legal right to half his property, with the other half going to the wife. Bowing to the inevitable, the widow agreed to a mediated settlement dividing the deceased's property equally between them (Beijing: 1942-7629).

The widowed Mrs. Wu (née Cui), also of Beijing, faced a similar sort of challenge. Her husband died in 1941, survived only by the widow herself, two brothers, and a sister. In 1942, one of the brothers, Wu Zhongpei, brought suit against Mrs. Wu at the Beijing District Court, claiming a one-sixth share of the estate. He clearly had the law on his side. Since his brother had no surviving descendants or parents, the property should be divided in half, with one-half going to the widow and the other going to the three siblings, for a one-sixth share each. Not able to dispute a brother's legal claim in such a situation, the widow concentrated her defense on proving that Wu Zhongpei had been adopted out to another family when just a baby and had not, as he alleged, ever "returned to his birth family" (*guizong*). As it turned out, she won the suit, but only because she was able to demonstrate to the judge's satisfaction that Zhongpei was no longer a member of the Wu family and thus no longer a brother of her deceased husband (Beijing: 1942-4879).

This last case is instructive as much for what did not take place as for what did. In the past, a man intent on gaining control of the property of a brother who had died heirless had to plead his case on the basis of patrilineal succession. Since he himself, being of the wrong generation, did not have a right to succeed his brother and hence any right to inherit his brother's property, he had to bring suit on behalf of his own son, if he had one, or else one of his nephews. In this case, however, there was no mention of patrilineal succession or the rights of nephews, for the civil code recognized neither. Thus, Wu Zhongpei brought suit on his own behalf instead under the new law that granted siblings statutory inheritance rights (in the absence of heirs of the first and second orders—direct lineal descendants and parents).

Conversely, in the past, a widowed wife in Mrs. Wu's situation would have been legally obligated to adopt an heir for her deceased husband from among his nephews. But in this case, there was no talk of the adoption of a patrilineal successor. Indeed, under the civil code, she could not do so even if she wanted to, for any child she adopted would be her heir, not her husband's. Barred from adoption as a way to fend off her brother-in-law's claim, the widow Wu had to argue instead that he in fact was not her husband's brother. The dissociation of patrilineal succession and property inheritance under the code had changed completely the nature of disputes between a widow and her brothers-in-law.

Under the civil code, then, a widowed wife gained as an inheritor but lost as a custodian. The insistence on strict gender equality that informed the code ensured that a wife had the right to inherit a share of her husband's property, just as a husband had the right to inherit a share of hers. Yet at the same time, in overturning patrilineal principles, also in the name of gender equality, the code paradoxically removed the source of a widow's particular power: her role as the custodian of the family property after his death. A widow no longer enjoyed a special status as a widow; she had become just a wife.

Widowed Daughters-in-Law

If the Republican Civil Code proved to be at best a mixed blessing for widowed wives, it turned out to be a disaster for widowed daughters-in-law, those women who lived in undivided multigenerational households with their deceased husbands' parents. It not only deprived them of the custodial rights they had enjoyed under the old laws, but also failed to extend to them the inheritance rights accorded to widowed wives.

The complete dispossession of widowed daughters-in-law was a logical, albeit unintended, consequence of the radically different concepts of property and inheritance informing the code. In late imperial and early Republican law, property was conceived of as family property in which each son had a share (*fen*). If a son should die, his share was to go to his male heirs at the time of family division. If he had no male heirs, it was to go to the custodial control of his widow (so long as she did not remarry). A widow had this right to her husband's share in the family estate regardless of whether he died before or after his own father. Even if her husband preceded his father in death, she still retained the right to his share of the property when the household divided.

Under the civil code, however, if a married son died before his own father, his widow would not be entitled to any property upon the father's death. This exclusion of a widowed daughter-in-law from inheritance follows logically from the code's notion of individual property. Since family property was now seen as the exclusive property of the father of the household, a son did not have a share in it while his father was still alive. Thus, if he died before his father, he died without any property to bequeath to his widow. When the father then died, his property was to be divided among his statutory heirs only (his widow, his surviving children or grandchildren, and so on). A widowed daughter-in-law had absolutely no claim to it.[2]

This was the fate that befell a Beijing widowed daughter-in-law, Tu Jia Jingyuan (36 sui). In late 1941, she and her young son Tu Guifen (14 sui) brought suit at the Beijing District Court against her two sisters-in-law, Tu Baowen and Liu Tu Baofen, and her father-in-law's 57-sui concubine, Tu Liu Shi. At issue was the disposition of the property of her father-in-law, Tu Xun'an, a Qing dynasty official who had amassed much wealth in his long career and who had died two years earlier. The widowed daughter-in-law, Tu Jia Jingyuan, argued that her father-in-law's property should be divided into five shares, with one share for herself, one for her son, one for each of her two sisters-in-law (Tu Xun'an's daughters), and one for the concubine for her maintenance.

The Beijing District Court ruled against the widow Tu. Since her husband had died ten years before her father-in-law, she did not have a right to any of her father-in-law's property. She, just like her father-in-law's concubine, was entitled to no more than maintenance (a point to which we will return). The judge ordered the estate to be divided into three shares, with one share going to her son (as Tu Xun'an's grandson) and one share to each of her two sisters-in-law (Beijing: 1942-556).

To emphasize this loophole in the law, consider what would have happened if the widow Tu's husband had died after his father. When her father-in-law, Tu Xun'an, died, his property would have been divided into equal shares among his three children: his son (widow Tu's husband) and his two daughters. Then, when the son died, his share would have been divided equally between his widow and his young son Guifen. In this scenario, the widow Tu, as a widowed wife, would have received one-sixth of the family property (sharing equally with her son in her husband's one-third inheritance).

---

2. This was a change from a provision in the 1928 draft of the inheritance book allowing a spouse to inherit the other spouse's statutory portion in such a situation, just as children could inherit a parent's portion should that parent die before the grandparent (Zhang Xubai 1930: 80). This provision was subsequently revised to apply only to direct lineal descendants.

Instead, simply because her husband died before his father, she received nothing.

The difference between a widowed daughter-in-law's rights under the new laws and her rights under the old ones was made crystal clear in a case the Supreme Court heard on appeal in 1932. In that case, the widow Mrs. Ke (née Wei), who lived in Nanchang city (Jiangxi), brought suit against her two brothers-in-law and the widowed wife of a third brother-in-law for the division of her deceased father-in-law's property. She contended that, as a faithful and childless widow, she had the right to her husband's share of the family estate. Her in-laws argued that since her husband had died before his father, she had absolutely no legal claim to any of the property. For the Supreme Court judges who heard the case on appeal, the crux of the matter lay in the date of her father-in-law's death. If he had died before the effective date of the new inheritance laws, his widowed daughter-in-law, Mrs. Ke, would then have been entitled to her late husband's share of the family property, just as she claimed. If he had died afterward, then she would have no such right, just as her brothers-in-law and sister-in-law claimed. In the end, the judges, having verified that her father-in-law had died before the new laws went into force, granted her her husband's share under the old laws. Yet they also made clear that had her father-in-law died later, she would have received nothing (*Zuigao fayuan panli huibian*, 13: 21–24).

Widowed daughters-in-law with children fared much better than those without. As in the widow Tu's case, even though they could not inherit individual shares in their own right, their children, as the deceased father-in-law's grandchildren, could. So they were at least fortunate to the extent that they had someone they could depend on for their own livelihood.

Childless daughters-in-law did not have even this small fallback. Under the provisions of the civil code, they could not adopt children as a way to secure a share of their father-in-law's property. As mentioned earlier, any children a wife might adopt after her husband's death were not considered to be his children or his statutory heirs. By extension, they were not considered the grandchildren of her father-in-law and were thus not entitled to any of his property (*SJQ*: no. 851).

The most that a widowed daughter-in-law could claim under the code was continued maintenance from members of her husband's family, but even that was conditional. As explained in the last chapter, article 1114 stipulated that four categories of people had a mutual obligation to support one another: (1) lineal relatives by blood; (2) "spouse and the parents of the other spouse living in the same household"; (3) brothers and sisters; and (4) the head of a household and its members. The maintenance of a widowed daughter-in-law fell within the second and fourth categories. Those two categories shared the condition that the person to be maintained had to be living in the same household as the person required to provide the maintenance. Thus, a widowed daughter-in-law's right to support from either her parents-in-law (category 2) or, in the event of their death, from her brothers-in-law (category 4) depended entirely on whether she continued to live with them. Should she decide to live elsewhere, for whatever reason, their obligation to provide for her ended.

The Supreme Court made this clear in a decision of 1933. A young widow, Xiang Bencao (26 sui), of Yizheng county (Jiangsu), had brought suit against her father-in-law and brother-in-law (now living in Hanyang, Hubei), charging them with all manner of abuse and humiliation and requesting that they be ordered to provide her the wherewithal to live separately. The Supreme Court rejected her plea, noting that the obligation of a father-in-law toward his daughter-in-law, or of a brother-in-law toward his sister-in-law, existed only if they were living together. "If they do not live together, no matter the reasons, she cannot have the right to request maintenance" (*Zuigao fayuan panli huibian*, 27: 12–14).

In another 1933 decision, the Supreme Court went still further, to hold that a widowed daughter-in-law could not seek maintenance from her in-laws even if they had expelled her from the household. In those cases, the proper procedure would be for the widow to bring a cohabitation (*tongju*) suit to force her in-laws to accept her back into their household. Once that was accomplished, they would of course be legally bound to support her (*Zuigao fayuan panli huibian*, 21: 105–7).

With this strict cohabitation requirement, the civil code dealt still a further blow to widowed daughters-in-law. For previously, they could expect to receive maintenance from their in-laws if they set up on their own, provided the court found their reasons for doing so compelling. Thus, Fan Zengxiang, as magistrate of Xianning county (Shaanxi) in the 1890's, found in favor of a widowed daughter-in-law, Mrs. Weng (née Che), who was requesting that she and her two young daughters be allowed to live apart from her father-in-

law, Weng Shenxiu. Magistrate Fan reasoned that relations between
the widow and her in-laws had become so bad that forcing them to
continue to live together would only invite more trouble. He therefore ordered that Weng Shenxiu set aside three-tenths of the family
property to enable the widow and her daughters to live apart. He
also specified that she could only draw on the interest generated by
the property, and that she was not permitted to sell it, pawn it, or
pass it on to her daughters when they married or when she died (Fan
Zengxiang 1897: 43–44).

Early Republican law, like the Qing, left widowed daughters-in-
law some room to maneuver (*DPQ*: 254). In the mid-1920's, the
newly widowed Mrs. Ma (née Zhang) used substantially the same
argument to secure a settlement worth 13,500 yuan from her very
reluctant father-in-law, Ma Linyi. The Capital District Court, as well
as the Capital Superior Court and the Daliyuan on appeal, found
that Mrs. Ma could not possibly live with her marital family because of the hostility remaining after the exceptionally acrimonious
divorce suit that she and her husband, Ma Qian, had been involved
in several years earlier. Ma Qian, the initiator of the suit, had lost,
but he and Ma Linyi had still refused to accept her back into their
household. Ma Linyi, now professing his willingness to take her
back, argued that a father-in-law had no obligation to support a
daughter-in-law who lived elsewhere. In its decision, the Capital
Superior Court admonished him, explaining that an obligation to
support derived from one's status (*shenfen*). Mrs. Ma was still Ma
Qian's wife and Ma Linyi's daughter-in-law. So long as she retained
that dual status, she was entitled to support, no matter where she
lived (Jingshi: 239-7956; Beijing: 65-5-369-385, 65-5-458-463).

Once cohabitation became the sole criterion for determining
whether a widowed daughter-in-law was entitled to maintenance,
judges no longer even needed to inquire into the reasons for the estrangement or assess the prospects for at least a passably peaceful
coexistence. In a 1942 Beijing maintenance case, for instance, a widowed daughter-in-law, Deng Li Xiukui (30 sui), charged that her
father-in-law and his concubine had been so abusive and violent toward the young couple that her husband had sickened and died.
Fearing that she might suffer the same fate, she had returned to her
natal home in Tong county. Her in-laws retaliated by bringing a
countersuit, accusing her of having driven their son to his death
with her shrewish and high-handed ways and, with her bright clothing and frequent absences from home, of acting in a manner unbe-

fitting a widow. To the judge hearing the case, the truth of the accusations did not matter, nor did the palpable animosity between the widow and her in-laws. All that mattered was that she was no longer living with them. As required by law, he therefore denied her request for maintenance (Beijing: 1942-6931, 1942-7097).

This new requirement for widowed daughters-in-law resulted from the civil code's basic reconceptualization of legal entitlements to maintenance. In past law, a person's claim to maintenance was not based simply on kinship or simply on cohabitation: it was based on membership in the "common living, common budget" (*tongju gongcai*) group. As a member of that group, one had the right to be supported by the family property. In contrast to its usage in the civil code, "common living" (*tongju*) had not been used literally to mean actual physical coresidence in the same dwelling. As the Daliyuan had once explained in another connection, the opposite of common living was not just "separate living" (*yiju*) but "divided property, separate living" (*fencai yiju*; *DPQ*: 209; see also Niida 1942: 350–52; and Shiga 1978: 111–12). So long as the property remained undivided, a person would be considered to be in common living regardless of where he or she lived and, consequently, in full possession of the rights and obligations that membership in the common budget group conferred. It was on the basis of this logic that a widowed daughter-in-law in the past was entitled to maintenance even if she no longer lived with her husband's family. Short of rejoining the common budget group of her natal family or remarrying into a new one, she remained a member of her deceased husband's group and, as such, was entitled to claim support from its property.

But once family property became a father's personal possession, claims for maintenance became detached from property and affixed to people instead. The civil code's two criteria for maintenance—kinship and coresidence—shared that common characteristic. Thus, in maintenance based on kinship, a man unable to support himself was entitled to be supported by a brother: the claim was against the brother and not against any property under his control. From the perspective of the code, it did not matter whether the two belonged to the same common living, common budget group or whether they had already divided the family property and established their own separate common living, common budget groups.

Likewise, in maintenance based on coresidence, a family member (*jiashu*) was entitled to be supported by the family head (*jiazhang*): the claim was against the family head and not against any property under his or her control. Moreover, "tongju" as used in the new code meant literal physical cohabitation; it was never used as a shortened form of common living, common budget (*tongju gongcai*). That being the case, once cohabitation ended, so too did the family head's obligation to provide support. It was on the basis of this logic that a daughter-in-law under the civil code was entitled to maintenance only if she continued to live with her husband's family.

The claims of its architects notwithstanding, the civil code did not necessarily accord a widow more rights to property than she had had in the "feudal" past. To be sure, the new inheritance laws granted a widowed wife the right to a set share of her husband's property, but that came at the cost of a loss of custodial control over all of the property. The Western logic pervading the code had no place for the special authority a widow had exercised over family property in past law. That property was now conceived as the individual possession of her husband, over which she had no more claim than any of the other statutory heirs.

In a similar fashion, the Western-based logic of the code had no place for the property claims of a widowed daughter-in-law. Where once she stood to inherit her husband's share of family property even though he had died before his father, the reconceptualization of that property as the individual possession of her father-in-law meant she now had no legal claim to inherit any of it. She thus completely lost the custodial rights she had possessed under the old laws, yet at the same time did not gain the inheritance rights promised to wives in the new ones. By the same token, under the reconfigured maintenance claims, her right to be supported by her husband's family came to be restricted by the requirement of coresidency. A widowed daughter-in-law lost out doubly under the Republican Civil Code.

CHAPTER SIX

Daughters' Inheritance Rights Under the Republican Code

B y the letter of the Republican code, daughters acquired equal inheritance rights with sons for the first time in Chinese history. Yet in practice, just as with widows, the courts delivered to daughters less than what the code promised, and for much the same reason. The structure of rights that daughters were now to share equally with sons was not the one of old, but a new set based on the Western concept of individual property.

As we have seen, the GMD lawmakers simply assumed that gender equality could best be achieved by adopting the Western property logic. On an abstract level, there was nothing wrong with such an approach. But when imposed on a society long accustomed to the logic of family property, unexpected problems resulted.

This chapter will look first at the difficulties the GMD encountered in the late 1920's in its effort to establish the principle of equal inheritance rights for daughters. Determined resistance came from the Supreme Court, which, operating from the concept of family property, used its interpretive powers to thwart the GMD's efforts. In that story, we see one way in which the conflict between the differing logics of family property and individual property threatened the principle of gender equality.

The GMD emerged victorious in that battle, and the principle of equal rights for daughters became enshrined in its code of 1929–30. In our discussion of the resulting court cases, we will see that code and custom in fact came into conflict, with the result that daughters did not attain the full equality promised in the code. For all the good intent of the GMD lawmakers, this development was the inevitable outcome of the imposition of an individual property regime on a society that continued to operate by the logic of family property.

The Birth Pains of Equal Inheritance

The principle of equal inheritance rights for daughters predated the promulgation of the Book on Inheritance of the civil code by four years.[1] At the Second National Congress of the Guomindang, held in Canton in January 1926, the representatives passed a "Resolution on the Women's Movement" (*funü yundong jueyi an*). The document called for the greater participation of women in the revolution, but also recognized that the "vast majority of women [were] still locked in a prison of many sorts of oppression. They [were] too far removed from society." Thus, the women's movement, "in addition to leading the female masses to participate in the national revolution [*guomin geming*], must at the same time pay special attention to the liberation of their persons [*benshen de jiefang*]." To that end, the party and the government were to promote the principle of strict gender equality (*nannü pingdeng*) in the legal, economic, educational, and social realms. Among the slogans the resolution proposed for the women's movement were several relating directly to women's legal status: "Oppose polygamy" (*duoqizhi*); "Absolute freedom in divorce and marriage"; "Oppose the decisions of judicial organs that [uphold] the inequality of men and women"; and, finally, "Daughters [*nüzi*] must have property rights [*caichanquan*] and inheritance rights [*jichengquan*]" (cited in Zhang Xubai 1930: 6–12).

In October 1926, the Judicial Executive Committee of the Nationalist Government (*Guomin zhengfu sifa xingzheng weiyuanhui*) issued an order calling for the immediate implementation of inheritance rights for daughters in the provinces under GMD control (Guangdong, Guangxi, Hunan, and Hubei), and their enforcement in other provinces the day they submitted to the Nationalist government.

Neither that order nor the party resolution earlier that year defined the scope of daughters' inheritance rights. That task fell by default to the Daliyuan, renamed the Supreme Court (*Zuigao fayuan*) in late 1927. Not yet under GMD control at this point, the court

---

1. Far from granting daughters equal inheritance rights, both of the two pre-GMD draft civil codes had given them even more restricted rights than they had under late imperial law. Whereas under Ming and Qing law, the order of inheritance was (1) sons, whether natural or adopted; (2) wife; and (3) daughters, daughters were relegated to sixth place in the 1911 and 1925–26 drafts, after (1) sons; (2) wife; (3) direct lineal ascendants (parents and/or grandparents; (4) brothers; and (5) the family head ("Da Qing minlü cao'an," 5: 3–4; and "Minlü cao'an jichengbian": 6–7, in *Falü cao'an huibian* 1973).

used its powers of interpretation to systematically undermine the intention of the resolution. Working from the logic of family property, it first excluded married daughters from consideration and then limited the inheritance rights of unmarried daughters.

Interestingly, it was the resolution's use of the word "nüzi" that gave the Supreme Court the opening it needed to exclude married daughters. By the 1920's, "nüzi" had come to bear in Western-inspired reformist and revolutionary discourse two distinct meanings, depending on the context in which it was used. When paired with "nanzi" (men), it was understood to mean "women" in the broadest sense, that is, all persons of the female sex (*nüxing*) irrespective of age or marital status; when paired with "erzi" (son, sometimes also "nanzi"), it meant simply "daughter."

At the same time, "nüzi" had an older, more restricted meaning deriving from Confucian discourse. In that meaning "nüzi," or often just "nü," was juxtaposed not against a male referent, but against a female one—"fu." Here "nü" referred to an unmarried daughter, and "fu" to a married woman. In this usage, the compound word, "funü," meant precisely "married women and unmarried daughters."[2]

Given these competing notions of "nüzi" and the resolution's failure to explain exactly what it meant by the term, it is not surprising that one of the very first inquiries to the Supreme Court on the subject concerned definition. The query came in early 1928 from the head of the Jinhua District Court in Zhejiang, who asked whether the "nüzi" in the resolution referred to "funü" or whether it referred only to unmarried daughters (*guinü*). The Supreme Court, electing to employ the older set of meanings, responded that "nüzi" here meant "unmarried daughters," thereby barring *fu*, or married women (i.e., married daughters), from equal inheritance rights with their brothers (*Zuigao fayuan jieshili quanwen*: no. 47).

To justify its interpretation, the Supreme Court drew on the age-old analogy of a married-out daughter and an adopted-out son: "a daughter who has already married out [*chujia*] is no different from a son who has already adopted out [*chuji*]." Since an adopted-out son did not have any claim to his natal family's property, the court reasoned, neither should a married-out daughter (ibid.: nos. 34, 47). To make the analogy more compelling, the Supreme Court made curious use of the phrase "birth parents" (*suosheng fumu*) to refer to a married daughter's father and mother. The phrase heretofore had

2. For an illuminating discussion of the changing meanings of these terms, see Barlow 1991.

been used in both legal and popular discourse in conjunction with the phrase "adoptive parents" (*suoji fumu*). By calling a married daughter's parents her "birth parents," rather than using the conventional *fumu* ("parents"), the Supreme Court posited a greater degree of similarity between married daughters and adopted-out sons than had in fact actually existed in law, ritual, or popular custom. In so doing, it conveniently overlooked the claim (albeit a limited one) that married-out daughters had had in late imperial and early Republican law to extinct household property, claims not enjoyed by adopted-out sons.

The Supreme Court's exclusion of married daughters from equal inheritance rights with sons provided an excuse also to limit the rights of unmarried daughters. Although the court affirmed again and again that unmarried daughters possessed the same inheritance rights as sons, it interpreted that notion very literally to mean that they did so only as long as they remained unmarried. Once a daughter married, she automatically lost not only her legal claims to property, but also whatever she may have already inherited, the logic being that she would then be a married daughter and, as such, had no right to her natal family's property. Thus, the court held in a 1928 interpretation that any property a daughter inherited while unmarried became her individual private property (*geren sichan*), but that apart from what she needed for her dowry, she could not take any of it to her husband's family without the permission of her natal family: her parents, or if they were dead, her brothers, or if she had no brothers, the designated heir, or if the designated heir was still a minor, his guardian, or if there was no heir, her father's relatives (*qinzu; Zuigao fayuan jieshili quanwen*: no. 92). In other words, upon marriage, a daughter had no more claim on family property than she had had in the past: the right merely to a dowry (in an amount that was at the discretion of others).

In that same year, 1928, the Supreme Court found another reason to whittle away at the rights of unmarried daughters. Among the requests for clarification it fielded were several queries from the provinces concerning the status of patrilineal succession within the new regime of daughters' rights. Since patrilineal succession determined property inheritance and since daughters now had the right to inherit property (*jicheng caichan*), did they also have the right to succeed to the patriline (*jicheng zongtiao*)? If they did not, how then was property to be divided between an adopted male heir and unmarried daughters?

In its replies, the Supreme Court upheld the principle of male succession and spelled out the rights of an adopted male heir vis-à-vis unmarried daughters. If the parents had adopted a male heir before their deaths, then the property was to be divided equally among the unmarried daughters and the adopted son. If the parents died without having appointed an heir, then part of the family property was to be set aside as ritual land (*jichan*) to fund the sacrifices and another part set aside as the share for a posthumously designated heir. In this latter situation, the Supreme Court emphasized, unmarried daughters did not have the right to claim all of the family property (ibid.: nos. 87, 92, 163).

These pronouncements, particularly the court's exclusion of married daughters, provoked a great deal of opposition in the GMD party and government. In April 1929, the Nationalist government's newly constituted Judicial Yuan took matters into its own hands. Charging the Supreme Court with violating the spirit of the "Resolution on the Women's Movement," it recommended to the GMD Central Political Council that married daughters be accorded the same rights as their unmarried sisters. On July 31, 1929, the Central Political Council formally accepted the Judicial Yuan's suggestion and promulgated a new set of laws entitled "Detailed Rules for the Implementation of Retroactive Inheritance of Property by Married Daughters" (*Yijia nüzi zhuisu jicheng caichan shixing xize*; text in *Nüzi jichengquan xiangjie*: 14–21).

The "Rules" set out to undo what the Supreme Court had done. The court was in error in its interpretations. The Resolution on the Women's Movement of January 1926 and the Judicial Executive Committee's order of October of the same year were meant to apply to all daughters. Married daughters, like unmarried ones, should have acquired inheritance rights as of October 1926 in the provinces then under GMD control and in other provinces on the day they joined the Nationalist government. Accordingly, married daughters not only must be allowed to inherit in the future, but should even be permitted to exercise their rights retroactively within certain limits. If the family property had already been divided up, a married daughter could demand that it be redivided and that she be given her rightful share, but she had to do so within six months of the effective date of the "Rules."

The Book on Inheritance of the civil code superseded this and all other previous laws when it went into effect on May 5, 1931. Birth daughters, both married and unmarried, ranked along with sons as statutory heirs of the first order (art. 1138), meaning that they were entitled to the same shares as their brothers. The civil code also removed the restrictions that the Supreme Court had placed on daughters' inheritance rights. A daughter owned her inherited property absolutely, which meant that she could take all of it with her when she married or otherwise left her natal family.

Equally important, the code's uncoupling of patrilineal succession and property inheritance meant that a daughter's right could not be compromised as easily by the designation of a male heir. The Supreme Court's view that a daughter had to share the patrimony equally with a male heir adopted during the lifetime of the parents, as well as with any appointed after their death, was roundly rejected. Under the civil code, as discussed in Chapter Four, a daughter received twice the amount of property allotted to a son adopted by the father. Moreover, neither a son adopted by the mother after the father's death nor an heir appointed by relatives after both their deaths had any rights at all to the father's property.

Daughters and the Courts

The implementing of daughters' inheritance rights had its greatest impact among the wealthier classes of China's urban centers. Indeed, the Shanghai newspaper *Shenbao*'s roster of cases reads like a Who's Who of Republican China. Among the disputed estates were those of the fabulously wealthy late Qing industrialist and banker Sheng Xuanhuai (estate valued at nearly 13,000,000 taels in 1916); Li Hongzhang's son Li Jingfang (estate valued at 8,000,000 yuan in 1934); the Wuxi silk merchant Sun Xunchu (estate valued at 500,000 yuan in 1930); the Shanghai dye industry magnate Xue Baorun (estate valued at 3,000,000 yuan in 1931); Cai Fulin, a comprador with the British and American Tobacco Company; Dai Gengxin, the founder of the Huacheng Tobacco Company; and Ma Fuqi, the Shanghai "Nightsoil King" (*fen dawang*), holder of the monopoly for the collection of wastes in the foreign concessions (estate valued at 4,000,000 yuan in 1935).[3]

Lawsuits involving the rich and the famous naturally commanded the most attention in the press, but daughters of urban families of

3. The suits brought by Sheng's two unmarried daughters are cited in the text. Other litigation over Sheng's property, as well as the Li and Xue cases, are cited in subsequent notes. On the other cases, see *Shenbao*, March 17, 1930, June 4, 1930, April 21, 1935, and May 4, 1936.

more modest means, we know from both newspapers and case records, also went to the courts to press their claims. In 1930, three unmarried daughters in Shanghai sued their brother and the uxorilocal husbands of their two elder sisters for one-sixth shares of the family property of three houses and 3.4 mu of land (*Shenbao*, June 15, 1930). And in 1942, a married Beijing woman sued her natal family for a one-fifth share of her father's estate (total value 20,000 yuan), consisting of a six-room house, a four-room house, a rickshaw business with ten or so carts, ten or so pigs, clothes, and household furnishings (Beijing: 1942-5210, 1942-5705).

As one might expect, outside the big cities, the new laws had a minimal effect at best. Only very occasionally do daughters of small-town and village China appear in newspaper accounts or case records (e.g., Beijing: 1942-6908). In general, in all matters, the Republican Civil Code and its underlying gender ideology had only a small impact on the countryside, where knowledge of the new laws was limited, the new court system was not easily accessible, and women were more sheltered and hence less receptive to change. All that, plus the fact that litigation over property was the most costly type of lawsuit in Republican China, put the whole question of inheritance outside the experience of most small-town and rural women.[4]

The new laws were first put to the test in 1928, in litigation initiated by two unmarried sisters in Shanghai. The case commanded nationwide attention not only because it was the first of its kind, but because the litigants were the daughters of Sheng Xuanhuai. (The case became the subject of a drama, *Young Misses Fight Over Property* [Xiaojie zhengchan], performed at a Shanghai theater. *Shenbao*, Jan. 7, 1929.) Sheng had died in 1916, leaving an estate worth 12,956,000 taels, the equivalent at the time of roughly 10,000,000 U.S. dollars (Xu Dixin and Wu Chengming 1990: 851). His wife, née Zhuang, died in 1927, leaving anywhere from 600,000 to 3,000,000 yuan (the exact amount was in dispute). By the early 1930's, the Sheng-Zhuang fortune had been the target of no fewer than seven separate lawsuits, all of which were provoked by the changing laws on female inheritance. Two cases concerned unmarried daughters; one case, married daughters; two others, married granddaughters;

---

4. For the impact of the civil code in the countryside, see Bernhardt 1994; and P. Huang 1996: chaps. 2, 3. For information on court costs, see Bernhardt & Huang 1994a: 5; Bernhardt 1994: 195–98; and P. Huang 1996: 181–85. On lawyers' fees, see Conner 1994: 238–39.

and the remaining two, grandchildren through daughters.[5] The seemingly endless litigation among the Shengs earned them the title of "most litigious [family] of all Shanghai" (*quan Hu jiansong zhi kui*) in the newspaper *Shenbao* (May 28, 1933).

The property at stake in the unmarried daughters' litigation was the capital freed by the dismantling in 1927 of the family's Yuzhai charitable estate (*Yuzhai yizhuang*). Before his death in 1916, Sheng Xuanhuai had ordered that after appropriate set-asides for his widow's maintenance and his daughters' dowries, his property was to be divided into two parts, one to be distributed equally among his five sons, and the other to be used to establish the charitable estate. After his death, his widow and sons dutifully did as he ordered: the widow and the daughters got 1,350,000 taels' worth of property, the sons 5,803,000, and the charitable estate 5,803,000 (*Nüzi jichengquan xiangjie*: 57–61).

In 1927, the revolutionary Nationalist Jiangsu provincial government, as part of its campaign against "local bullies and evil gentry" (*tuhao lieshen*), ordered the Shengs to turn over 40 percent of the charitable estate's capital to the government for military use. The Sheng brothers complied, at the same time taking the opportunity to dismantle the estate altogether. In early 1928, they received permission from both Chiang Kai-shek and the Nationalist government's Finance Department (*Caizhengbu*) to keep the remaining 60 percent of the estate's capital, 3,500,000 taels, for distribution among themselves (*Shenbao*, June 22, 1928; see also Aug. 29, 1929, and May 28, 1933).

That summer, Sheng Aiyi, one of the two unmarried daughters, brought suit at the Shanghai International Settlement Provisional Court (*Shanghai gonggong zujie linshi fayuan*) against her three surviving brothers and two nephews, sons of her two deceased brothers, for a share of the freed charitable estate property.[6] Identified in *Shenbao* as a fervent GMD party member, a great admirer of Sun Yatsen, and an intimate friend of the Song sisters, Sheng Aiyi argued in her plaint that the action of her male relatives violated the GMD's 1926 Resolution on the Women's Movement and recent Supreme Court interpretations on the matter. Under current law, she, as well

5. See *Shenbao*, March 7 and June 5, 1930, Aug. 12 and 16, 1931, Dec. 3, 1931, Jan. 29, May 19, and June 11, 1932, May 28, 1933; and *Dawanbao* (Shanghai), May 20 and June 1, 1932.

6. The Provisional Court had replaced the Mixed Court of the International Settlement in 1927. It became the Shanghai First Special District Court (*Shanghai diyi tequ difang fayuan*) in 1930.

as her unmarried sister, Fangyi, were entitled to share equally with their five kinsmen (*Shenbao*, Aug. 29, Sept. 6, 1928).

The outcome of the case turned on the question of the legal ownership of the charitable estate property. The brothers and nephews claimed that it was their joint property. As Sheng Xuanhuai's legal heirs, they had inherited it, along with the other half of his legacy, at the moment of his death in 1916. Therefore, when they distributed the remaining 60 percent of the property in early 1928, they were simply dividing among themselves what was in fact already theirs. Since an unmarried daughter did not possess the right to inherit her father's property in 1916, Sheng Aiyi had no claim on the charitable estate property, just as she had no claim on the rest of her father's legacy (*Shenbao*, Sept. 6, 1928).

The Provisional Court saw the issue differently. The Sheng men were not the joint owners of the charitable estate. In his verbal instructions to his family before his death, Sheng Xuanhuai had explicitly placed half of his property outside the scope of inheritance for the purpose of establishing the charitable estate. Since the estate had been effectively set up as an incorporated foundation (*caituan faren*), the property belonged to the foundation, not to the defendants. It was only because of the special administrative decision allowing the dissolution of the foundation that the defendants could lay any claim to it now. But that decision had simply specified that the property should be handed back to the family, not how it was to be divided. That was up to the court to decide on the basis of current law. And under current law, Sheng Aiyi had as much right to the recovered property as her brothers and nephews did. Accordingly, the Provisional Court ruled in late September 1928, Sheng Aiyi was entitled to a one-seventh share, or 500,000 taels, of the property (*Nüzi jichengquan xiangjie*: 57–61; *Shenbao*, Sept. 21, 1928).

Within weeks of this ruling, Sheng Fangyi, following her sister's example, filed suit against her male kin at the Provisional Court. She too won her case, receiving one-seventh of the property (*Shenbao*, Oct. 18, Nov. 9, 1928). The Provisional Court's decisions were subsequently upheld by its appellate division in December 1928 and the Supreme Court in Nanjing in December 1929 (*Shenbao*, Dec. 7, 1928, Jan. 9, Feb. 18, 1929; *Nüzi jichengquan xiangjie*: 57–61; *China Law Review*, 4.5 [1930]: 176–80). For both of those courts, as for the Shanghai Provisional Court, the Sheng litigation represented the first case to come up on the issue of unmarried daughters' inheritance rights.

It is important to note here that the Sheng daughters were successful in their suits only because of the special arrangements that Sheng Xuanhuai had made for his property. They would not have had any claim at all otherwise, since he had died before daughters' rights were spelled out in the Judicial Executive Committee's 1926 order (which was only gradually extended, it will be recalled, as provinces came under Nationalist control). The implications of this cut-off date, putting numbers of daughters under the old inheritance laws, will be dealt with more fully below. Suffice it to say that the question of timing frequently frustrated daughters in their court battles. In the first suit to be pressed in Shandong, for instance, Qian Ruizhi of Jinan, a young (25 sui) unmarried woman and an active GMD party member, lost her case against her elder brother because their father had died in the spring of 1926, two years before Shandong came under the control of the Nationalist government (May 1928).[7] Other daughters also failed in their suits because of infelicitous timing (see, e.g., Beijing: 65-5-1660-1668; and *Shenbao*, Dec. 20, 1929, April 11, 1930).

More fortunate were the daughters of the wealthy Shanghai banking comprador Bu Jichen, who had died in late 1927, after Jiangsu province had submitted to GMD rule. He left an estate valued at over 100,000 yuan and a concubine, four sons, and three married daughters, Baoyu, Manyu, and Shengyu (dubbed the "Three Jades" [*sanyu*] in newspaper accounts). Soon after his death, the brothers had divided up the family property. In late 1929 or early 1930 (exactly when is not clear), the three sisters requested a redivision of the property as specified in the newly promulgated Detailed Rules for the Implementation of Retroactive Inheritance of Property by Married Daughters. And in July 1930, they won a judgment against their brothers at the French Mixed Court (*Fagongtang*): each was to receive, as was her due, one-seventh of the property (*Shenbao*, March 30, July 18, 1930).[8]

Also successful in their suits, to give several other quick exam-

---

7. In 1927, Qian Ruizhi left off her studies at Beijing Normal University to enroll in the GMD's Central Party School in Wuhan. In 1928, she accompanied the Nationalist army on its expedition to North China, serving for a time as the chair of the Hebei Provincial Committee on Political Tutelage. In 1933, reportedly still despondent over her legal defeat and aggrieved by the recent death of a close male friend, she drowned herself in the ocean at Yantai (*Shenbao*, Sept. 21, Oct. 18, 1929; *Shibao* [Shanghai], Sept. 25, 1933).

8. In 1931, that court reverted to Chinese control and was renamed the Shanghai Second Special District Court (*Shanghai dier tequ difang fayuan*).

ples, were Mrs. Yu (née Jiang) of Shanghai, who in late 1929 won a judgment against her brother for one-half (about 17,600 yuan) of the property of their mother (d. September 1927; *Shenbao*, Nov. 2, 1929); Li Wang Youlian of Beijing, who won a judgment in 1940 against her brothers for her one-fourth share of her father's (d. 1933) estate, consisting of five shops, seven houses, 105 mu of land, stocks worth 21,500 yuan, about 88,000 yuan in cash, and assorted jewelry and antiques (Beijing: 1947-227); and Gao Liang Yuxiu, who in the late 1930's and early 1940's won two separate suits against her step-mother and four half-brothers for a one-sixth share of her deceased father's (d. 1937) Beijing property (10 houses with a total of 152.5 rooms), as well as a one-sixth share of the property he owned in his native place in Tong county (an 11-room house, a store, and 47 mu of land; ibid.: 65-5-763-768; 1942-3279).

In other cases, the dispute was ended not by a court judgment but by a mediated settlement, either worked out in the courtroom with the judge as the mediator or outside the courtroom with lawyers and/or friends and relatives as the peacemakers. The incentive to settle, always present in civil suits, was particularly strong in property cases because of the great costs involved. By agreeing to a settlement, the disputants avoided not only the risk of escalating lawyers' fees, but also the risk of coming up the loser and having to pay all of the court costs.

Thus, in Shanghai in 1932, Fang Xu Meiying, a married daughter of the Daying Bank comprador Xu Qingyun, acquired 520,000 yuan of her deceased father's estimated 10,000,000-yuan estate in a mediated out-of-court settlement with her elder brother (*Shenbao*, Dec. 16, 1931, May 1, May 13, 1932). In Shanghai, in the mid-1930's, the three daughters of the tea merchant Zhu Baoyuan each secured from their two brothers 80,000 yuan of their father's property (*Shenbao*, March 26, 1936). In Beijing in 1942, the suit of a married woman, Zhao Chen Shuzhen, against her mother and four sisters and brothers resulted in a court-mediated agreement awarding her one-sixth of her father's property (Beijing: 1942-3271, 1942-3747). And in another 1942 Beijing court mediation, a married daughter, Zeng Zhou Shuzhen, received 1,500 yuan from her stepmother and her three half-siblings (ibid.: 1942-6509).

Daughters, whether married or single, were not the only ones to benefit from their acquisition of inheritance rights. Under the civil code, a daughter's direct lineal descendants—children, grandchildren, and so on—stood to inherit her share should she happen to die before her father—in the same manner that sons in the past had been entitled to a deceased father's share of family property. Daughters' inheritance rights thus had much broader implications than one might think, for it opened up opportunities for people to lay direct claim through their mothers to the property of their maternal grandparents.

In a 1931 Shanghai case, for instance, Hua Lihou brought suit on behalf of his children, a minor son and daughter, against their maternal grandmother and four maternal uncles. The property in dispute was the 3,000,000-yuan estate of the children's maternal grandfather, the dyestuff magnate Xue Baorun, who had died the year before. Although the children's mother, one of Xue's six children, had died in 1919, Hua claimed his children had the right to inherit her statutory one-sixth share.[9] Both the Shanghai First Special District Court, which first heard the case, and then the Jiangsu Superior Court on appeal found for the children. It was on these same grounds that Li Hongzhang's great-grandchildren won a judgment in early 1937 at the Shanghai First Special District Court for a one-eighth share of their maternal grandfather Li Jingfang's 8,000,000-yuan estate.[10]

In the case of adopted heirs, the code again made provision for appointments made before May 1931, but even heirs of long standing, like birth sons, were obliged to share the man's estate equally with any daughters. On just those grounds, two married daughters of a peasant family outside Beijing won a judgment in 1942 against their father's longtime adopted heir. The Beijing District Court ordered him to hand over a third of the father's property—consisting of an eight-and-a-half-room house and assorted furnishings, 15 mu of land, and three camels—to each of the women (Beijing: 1942-6908).

Otherwise, an adopted heir acquired only the legal status of an adopted child, with no more rights than any adopted child, male or female: entitled to half what any birth child, male or female, got (art. 1142). Two married daughters in Shanghai did not hesitate to take their adopted brothers to court under this provision: Xu Wenjuan and Wu Ye Ruizhen, who pressed their suits in 1932 and 1936, respectively (*Shenbao*, July 4, 1932, Oct. 13, Oct. 22, 1936).

9. The children of deceased daughters possessed the right to their mother's share even if she died before the implementation of female inheritance (*SJQ*: no. 1051).

10. For details of the Xue case, see *Shenbao*, April 17, Aug. 4, Sept. 10, Nov. 30, 1931, June 30, 1932; and *Dawanbao* (Shanghai), June 12, 1932. On the Li Jingfang case, see *Shibao* (Beijing), Feb. 20, 1937; and *Shenbao*, Feb. 14, 1936, Feb. 19, 1937.

A postmortem heir did not enjoy even the limited inheritance rights of an adopted child. As noted earlier, any person adopted by a widow was deemed to be her adopted child and heir. Neither he nor any person appointed by agnatic relatives after the death of both the husband and wife had any legal rights to his "father's" estate.

To cite just one example, Chen Qiaofen (23 sui) sued her 14 brothers and sisters at the Beijing District Court in 1942 for her rightful one-fifteenth share of the property of her father, Chen Jingzhai. Against her claim, her siblings, led by the eldest brother, Gongmeng, argued that her suit was procedurally incorrect since she had not listed, as was required by law, all of the statutory heirs as defendants. They had two other brothers, Gongzhi and Gongda, both of whom were now dead, but both of whom had adopted heirs who were entitled to shares of Chen Jingzhai's property. Gongzhi and his wife had both died soon after their marriage, whereupon the father, Chen Jingzhai, had designated Gongmeng's third son to be Gongzhi's heir. Gongda died in 1938, three years after his father, whereupon his mother had named Gongmeng's fourth son as Gongda's heir.

The judge dismissed the defendants' argument out of hand. Not only did they not have any proof of their assertions that their parents had in fact appointed heirs for the deceased sons, but even if they had, those "heirs" (*sizi*) had no right under current law to inherit their "fathers'" shares of Chen Jingzhai's property. That being the case, the judge ruled, Chen Qiaofen's filing was procedurally sound, and she was entitled to one-fifteenth of the estate (Beijing: 1942-4503).

Compulsory Portions in Wills

All the laws we have discussed up to now applied to the estates of people who died intestate. In constructing China's inheritance laws, the Republican lawmakers had also to confront the question of how wills were to be incorporated into the new legal regime. As explained by the Central Political Council in 1930, the choice facing China was whether to adopt the Anglo-American principle of complete individual freedom of disposal (*geren ziyou chufen*) or the continental principle of the preservation of familial relations (*weichi qinshu guanxi*). Both granted property owners absolute freedom of disposal during their lifetimes, but in the Anglo-American tradition a person could bequeath property to anyone he or she pleased, whereas in the other, a certain portion of a person's estate was to go automatically to the statutory heirs. In the end, the Central Political Council opted for the continental example, hoping in this way to strike a balance between the interests of the individual and the interests of family members (*Jichengfa xianjue gedian* 1930; see also Luo Ding 1933: 251–55).

The code's provisions on compulsory portions (*teliufen*) in wills protected statutory heirs, including of course daughters, from being completely disinherited. Article 1187 mandated that "a testator may freely dispose of his property by a will, so long as he does not contravene the provisions in regard to Compulsory Portions." As set out in article 1223, those portions were one-half the value of the statutory portions in the case of a lineal descendant by blood (children, grandchildren, and so on), a spouse, or a parent (i.e., half of what she or he was entitled to inherit had there been no will), and one-third in the case of a sibling or a grandparent. A will that failed to bequeath the proper amount could be challenged in court.

Compulsory portions figured prominently in a Beijing case brought in late December 1939, pitting three married sisters—Wang Shuxian, Wang Shufang, and Wang Shujing—and their widowed mother, Wang Cheng Yushu, against their father's concubine, Wang Zhou Shi, and the concubine's son. In their plaint, the sisters and the widow explained that the father, Wang Yatang, had taken Wang Zhou Shi as his concubine in 1926 and had then, after the birth of his son, moved out of their residence to set up a separate household with Wang Zhou Shi and the boy. On Wang Yatang's death the previous April, the concubine and her son had commandeered all of his property, refusing to give the daughters and the widow their rightful shares. They were therefore requesting that the court grant each of them one-fifth of the property as provided in law, with the remaining one-fifth going to the son.

Attention in the case fastened on a will Wang Yatang had drawn up two weeks before he died. In it, he referred to his wife and his three daughters as "extraordinarily villainous," and mentioned an eight- to nine-year court battle with his wife over living expenses and dowry provisions for their daughters that had finally ended in 1935 with an out-of-court settlement, in which he had agreed to give her 5,500 yuan on the condition that neither she nor their daughters ever asked for anything more. Turning finally to the matter at hand, he wrote: "Since I am now aged and my wife [his concubine] is young and my son a minor, and since I honestly fear that in the future they will be harassed by Wang Cheng [Yushu] and her daughters, the ownership of all of my property should go to my son, Wang Hualin, to inherit."

The sisters and their mother lost the first round of litigation, because the defendants were able to convince the Beijing District Court judge that Wang Yatang no longer owned the property in dispute, having sold it all to pay off debts. On appeal to the Hebei Superior Court, however, the women were more successful. It ruled that Wang Yatang in fact still owned most of the contested estate, and that any documentary appearances to the contrary were just subterfuges by the concubine to keep the property all to herself and her son. Moreover, Wang Yatang's attempt to disinherit his wife and daughters contravened the law. But since he had drawn up a will, they were not entitled, as they claimed, to full statutory portions, only to compulsory portions, or one-tenth apiece (one-half the statutory one-fifth share; Beijing: 65-5-692-693). Although the son still received the greater part of the father's estate (six-tenths), the code's provisions on compulsory portions in wills prevented the complete disinheritance of the sisters and their mother.[11]

Postmortem Inheritance Versus Household Division

Thus far this chapter has dealt only with daughter inheritance cases in which family circumstances and actions happened to coincide with the Western conception of individual property and inheritance informing the civil code—that is, the division of family property after the father's death. Under the code, that action would be interpreted as follows. The father, the individual property owner, dies, at which moment his statutory heirs as designated in the code inherit his property and own it collectively. At some point in the future, those heirs then decide to partition the estate among themselves. And provided the father died after the law on daughters' inheritance took effect, those legal heirs included daughters. Our cases thus document a large area of overlap between household division and inheritance as defined in the code. They also document that it was in that overlap that daughters acquired what the Resolution on the Women's Movement and then the civil code promised—equal inheritance rights with their brothers.

But there remained a large area of disjunction between popular

11. The will of any testator who died after May 1931, no matter when he or she wrote it, was subject to the requirement for compulsory portions ("Law Governing the Application of the Book of Inheritance of the Civil Code," art. 2).

practice and the new laws. In the family property/household division regime, the critical moment was the division of property, whether before or after the father's death. But in the individual property/ postmortem inheritance regime, the critical moment was the death of the property owner: inheritance could never be premortem, only postmortem. It was in this disjunction, as we shall see, that daughters discovered that their actual inheritance rights fell far short of the promised gender equality. The issue of daughter inheritance thus brings to the fore the very different logics of the two regimes.

For the purposes of analysis, the clash between the two can usefully be divided into two categories: postmortem household division/postmortem inheritance and premortem household division/ postmortem inheritance. Although there was, as noted above, a great deal of overlap between postmortem household division and postmortem inheritance, the fit was not absolute. Premortem household division and postmortem inheritance, on the other hand, were utterly incompatible.

Postmortem Household Division and Postmortem Inheritance

The conflict between postmortem household division and postmortem inheritance manifested itself concretely in lawsuits over the property of fathers who had died before the law on daughters' rights took effect. Superficially, as mentioned earlier in this chapter, the outcome of such litigation was due to infelicitous timing, but more fundamentally, it documents well the completely different logics behind postmortem household division and postmortem inheritance. The daughters framed their plaints on the logic of household division, whereas the courts responded from the logic of postmortem inheritance.

Three cases expose the problem. In the first, from Shanghai in 1932, two married sisters, Chen Fang Jinqing and Fang Fang Youqing, brought a complaint against their two brothers and two nephews (sons of their two deceased brothers), requesting that they each be given one-sixth of the 300,000-yuan estate of their deceased father, the sugar merchant Fang Rongzhou. They explained that their father had died in the early years of the Republic, and that the year before last, their brothers and nephews had divided up his property four ways. Since by that time, 1930, the GMD's "Rules" on married daughter inheritance had already been promulgated, they too had the right to equal shares of their father's estate (*Shenbao*, Nov. 28, 1932).

In the second case, in 1930 an unmarried woman of 24 sui, Lu Minwen, and her mother, Lu Wang Xinyi (56 sui), brought suit at the Beijing District Court against their stepbrother/stepson, Lu Yulong, for resisting their request for a division of the family property (*jiachan*). They explained that the father, Lu Shoucheng, had died in 1916, leaving the two children, his wife Lu Wang Xinyi, and a concubine, Lu Zhang Guilan. Even when Lu Shoucheng was alive, the mother had ably managed all of the family property. After his death, she continued to do so, so wearing herself out that she had fallen ill. Lu Yulong, on the other hand, was nothing but a lazy spendthrift. Last year, the mother, no longer able to manage the property, had sent him a letter suggesting that it be divided up. But he had just ignored her request. Now that daughters had the right to inherit, they were asking that the property be divided half and half between Lu Minwen and her stepbrother. They were also asking that two-fifths of each half-share (or four-tenths of the total property) be given to the mother and the concubine for their maintenance (Beijing: 65-5-222-226, 65-5-547-554).

Finally, we have the 1929 Beijing lawsuit of 18-sui Zhou Jiayu against her brother. Her father had died in 1911, but her mother had just died the year before, leaving a widowed daughter-in-law, a son, Jiayu herself, and one other daughter. In her request that she be granted one-fourth of the family property, Zhou Jiayu argued that, although her father had died before the implementation of the law on daughters' inheritance rights, the family property had remained intact under her mother's control. Consequently, the opening of inheritance occurred not with her father's death, but with her mother's. And since her mother died after daughters acquired inheritance rights, she, Jiayu, was entitled to a fourth of the family property (ibid.: 65-5-547-554).

Clearly, the women in these cases were operating from the logic of the family property/household division regime. For them, the critical moment in the intergenerational transmission of property was not the death of the father, but household division. Heirs "inherited" the family property not when the father died, but when the property was actually divided, whether that was before or after the father's death or before or after the mother's death. Inheritance and family division were simultaneous. Since division in these cases took place after daughters were proclaimed to have inheritance rights, that division would necessarily have to accommodate to the new law. In other words, the women in these cases assumed that equal inheritance rights for daughters meant that they had received the same rights as their brothers to family property at the time of household division. What they did not realize is that the conceptual foundations of property and inheritance had been legally restructured.

In the end, of course, the daughters here lost their cases. All of their fathers had died before the law took effect, and their brothers had inherited their fathers' property at the moment of their fathers' death. It did not matter whether the mother was alive or not, or whether she had died before or after the implementation of the law. Family property had become the individual property of the father, and widows no longer had a special relationship toward it. That the brothers had not yet partitioned their legacy among themselves also was not material. Inheritance and property division were now legally seen as two separate matters, and division could take place years after inheritance. Since the daughters in these cases had not inherited the property in the first place, they had no right to participate in its division.

The clash between postmortem household division and postmortem inheritance also manifested itself in the question of the voluntary forfeiture of inheritance rights. In the household division regime, a renunciation of claims to family property could take place at any time up to and including the moment of partition. But the civil code specified that any waiver of inheritance "must be effected by a written declaration to the Court, the family council, or the other heirs, within two months from the time" the heir became aware of the death of the property owner (art. 1174). So both any waiver signed before the death of the property owner and any signed after the two-month deadline were legally invalid.

The code's forfeiture law was based solely on the logic of postmortem inheritance. The waiver of rights could not occur before the death of the property owner because, strictly speaking, inheritance rights did not come into being until the moment of death (art. 1147). The short two-month deadline, patterned after the German code (which stipulated six weeks), reflects the assumption that the estate would be broken up and distributed to the individual ownership of the heirs within a relatively short period of time after the person's death (*German Civil Code* 1907: art. 1944). It did not make allowances for a situation in which the property would be held in common by the heirs for years, even decades, before being divided up.

The conflict between the two logics can be seen in the litigation over the estate of Ma Yusheng of Beijing. The father of two sons and five daughters, Ma had died in 1928, but the family property had remained undivided under the control of his widow. Over the next decade and a half, the two brothers and three of the five sisters died. Then, in 1945, Widow Ma herself died. Shortly thereafter, a family division document was executed granting the bulk of the property to the widows and sons of the two brothers and a smaller amount to one of the surviving sisters, Ma Quan. The document bore the chops of the other surviving sister, Ma Rulan, and the children of two of her deceased sisters. The following year, 1946, Ma Rulan and those children brought suit at the Beijing District Court against the other family members for denying them their rightful three-sevenths share of Ma Yusheng's property (with the children laying claim to their mothers' shares). They maintained that the division document was not valid, since they had been variously forced or tricked into affixing their seals to it by the defendants. For their part, the defendants maintained that the plaintiffs had willingly signed the document, thereby voluntarily waiving their inheritance rights. Despite their differences, both sides plainly believed that the critical moment was household division, not the death of the father, and that the outcome of the case hinged only on the question of coercion or consent.

For the court, that issue was beside the point. Even if the plaintiffs had signed the document willingly with the intention of forfeiting their inheritance rights, the document itself did not fulfill the legal requirements for a waiver of rights: it was not drawn up within two months of the knowledge of the death of the property owner, but years afterward, and it did not explicitly express an intent to waive their rights. On those grounds, the court found for the plaintiffs, awarding them each one-seventh of the property (Beijing: 65-22-1621).

The same dynamic was at work in a suit that a married woman, Gao Liang Yuxiu, brought against her stepmother and her four half-brothers in 1939. In her plaint to the Beijing District Court, she related that after her father's death in 1937, her stepmother and brothers had drawn up a division document in early 1939 without her knowledge or consent. In that document, the defendants split her father's property among themselves five ways, leaving her without her share of one-sixth of the estate. Against her claims, the defendants argued that she was so extravagant and wasteful and so often in debt that their father had ordered just before he died that she was to receive none of his property. They also argued that she had been present at the signing of the document and had agreed to it, thereby renouncing her right to inherit. In this case as well, both sides framed their arguments on the logic of household division. For both, the key issue was whether Gao Liang Yuxiu had been present at the signing and had given her verbal consent.

The Beijing District Court found for the plaintiff Gao Liang Yuxiu. It put no stock in the defendants' assertion about the father's deathbed wishes. It also noted that she had not signed the document, so that there was no proof that she had ever agreed to the division. But most important, the judge, in a strict application of the code's forfeiture law, ruled that even if she had signed it, the document could not stand as a valid waiver of her inheritance since it neither explicitly stated that she was forfeiting her rights nor conformed to the required two-month time limit. The defendants were ordered to give the daughter one-sixth of her father's property (Beijing: 65-5-763-768).

Premortem Household Division and Postmortem Inheritance

The gap between social practice and the new legal inheritance regime was most evident in the conflict between premortem household division and postmortem inheritance. Whereas the new legal order could to a large extent accommodate postmortem household division to postmortem inheritance, it could not do the same with premortem household division.

Legally, premortem household division came to be defined as gift-giving, and not as inheritance. In 1931, the Jiangsu Superior Court forwarded to the Judicial Yuan this question from the Qidong county magistrate: "When a father or mother divides property among sons, is this when the inheritance of that property begins?" The Judicial Yuan replied that such an action came under the category of gift-giving (*zengyu*), and that the inheritance of property began only at the moment of the property owner's death (*SJQ*: no. 465).

Since premortem household division was, by definition, not inheritance, it was not subject to the laws governing that procedure. The Judicial Yuan made this clear in 1932 in its response to a query from the chief judge of the Wuxian District Court in Jiangsu. The judge posed a hypothetical example. Several days before his death, a man draws up a gift document (*zengyu ziju*), giving most of his property to just two of his four sons. He then draws up a will (*yizhu*), arranging for the distribution of the rest of his property after his death. In both the gift document and the will, he specifies that the property he gave the two sons was to be their private property (*sichan*) and was not to be counted as part of their share of his estate upon death. Were the father's actions legal? the judge asked.

Supplying a possible answer to his own question, he pointed to the civil code's law on compulsory portions, which mandated that an heir of the first order, that is, direct lineal descendants by blood, get at least half of his or her statutory portion. The purpose of that law, the judge averred, was to protect the inheritance rights of all statutory heirs. Otherwise, he explained, a father "during his lifetime can go by his likes and dislikes and use the gift method to dispose of his property as he wishes, so that statutory heirs do not inherit equally. [He] can even give all his property to just one of the joint heirs, thereby causing the others to receive absolutely nothing. This not only violates the system of compulsory portions, but also violates the objective of the equal inheritance of property." The father, by drawing up the gift document and the will one after the other, clearly intended to evade the law on compulsory portions. For that reason, his gift of the bulk of his property to just two of his sons could not be deemed valid.

The Judicial Yuan disagreed. It explained that the law on compulsory portions applied only to wills, through which a person arranged for the disposition of his or her property after death. It did not apply to premortem gift-giving. When people gave away property during their lifetimes, they could give it to anyone they pleased. The father in the hypothetical example was thus perfectly within his rights.[12]

Moreover, the Judicial Yuan pointed out, a property owner's right of free disposal during life even overrode the code's provision on gifts. Article 1173 stipulated that any gifts a property owner had bestowed on an heir for the purpose of marriage, living separately, or starting a business, must be deducted from the recipient's statutory share of the inheritance (the assumption being that gifts for those purposes were normally made as a prepayment of inheritance). But attached to the law was an important proviso permitting the property owner to declare at the time the gift was made that it was not

12. The 1928 draft of the Book on Inheritance, foreseeing the possible use of this tactic to circumvent the inheritance laws, had provided that gifts made for whatever reason within one year before the property owner's death would be automatically counted as part of the recipient's share of the inheritance. It also provided that gifts made with "malicious intent" (*eyi*, e.g., to lessen the shares of other heirs) within three years before the property owner's death would be counted as part of the recipient's share (cited in Zhang Xubai 1930: 92; see also Luo Ding 1933: 262–64). The final version of the civil code contained no such restrictions on premortem gift-giving.

to be counted against the recipient's statutory portion, just as the father here had done. In that case, the recipient of the gift would be entitled to the same share of the estate as the other heirs (*SJQ*: no. 743).

Now what did the reconceptualization of premortem household division as gift-giving mean for daughters? It meant, first of all, that their right to inherit equally with their brothers was severely compromised. If a father decided to divide the property among his sons while he was still alive, a daughter had absolutely no legal right to a share of the estate. She could not contest the division before her father's death, nor could she contest it afterward, since the property had already passed to her brothers' individual ownership at the moment of division. To the extent that premortem household division tended to be the norm rather than the exception (P. Huang 1996: 24–28), daughters were to that same extent effectively excluded from exercising their newfound rights. Also, perhaps needless to say, the gift-giving rule provided an easy and perfectly legal way for fathers and brothers to cut daughters off completely.

It also provided, as the following case demonstrates, an easy and perfectly legal way to dodge the prohibition against the distribution of property to a posthumously appointed male heir. In mid-1936, a young married woman, Chen Zhu Shuying, initiated a lawsuit at the Shanghai District Court against her paternal grandfather, Zhu Haikang, accusing him of depriving her of her inheritance rights. She was the only child of the grandfather's eldest son, Zhu Dingchen. Both her father and her mother had died some years earlier. At the end of 1935, she related, her grandfather had made one of his grandsons her father's heir. He had then divided all of his property, valued at 40,000 yuan, among that successor and his other two sons. In doing so, she charged, her grandfather had defied the law on two counts. She, as her father's only direct lineal descendant, was his only statutory heir. At the very least, her grandfather should have given her the compulsory portion (*teliufen*) mandated in the code. Beyond that, by establishing a male successor for her father and bestowing on him the property that should have come to her, her grandfather had violated the legal prohibition against linking property inheritance to patrilineal succession.

Her arguments were entirely without merit in the eyes of the Republican code. Since this case concerned premortem household division and not postmortem inheritance, the code's provisions on statutory inheritance and compulsory portions did not apply. The property in question was the grandfather's to do with whatever he liked during his lifetime, including giving it to a posthumous heir for his son (*Shenbao*, June 12, 1936).

The conflict between premortem household division and post-mortem inheritance lay at the heart of a complex and protracted Beijing lawsuit in the late 1930's and early 1940's. The case bears relating in some detail, for it touches on several of the elements that qualified a daughter's right to property, namely, the legal conception of premortem household division as gift-giving, the differences between a division document and a will, the nature of compulsory portions, and finally, the use of premortem household division to keep daughters from inheriting.

The litigation began in 1938 with a complaint lodged at the Beijing District Court by three sisters against their two half-brothers over the property of their father, Gao Yunquan. What made this lawsuit particularly contentious was Gao Yunquan's marital arrangements and the resulting frictions among his offspring. After the death of his childless first wife, he had married a second wife, who bore him a son, the defendant Gao Chongqi. Then the second wife died, too, leaving the child in the care of Yunquan's concubine, Zheng Shi. When Zheng Shi herself had a son in 1904, the other defendant Gao Chongzhao, the delighted father announced at the one-month ceremony celebrating the boy's birth that out of gratitude, he had elevated Zheng Shi to the position of legal wife (*zhengshi*). Subsequently (exactly when is not clear), Gao Yunquan acquired another concubine, Wang Shi, who bore three daughters, the plaintiffs Gao Yufeng, Gao Yuzhen, and Gao Yulan. Wang Shi and the three girls did not live at the same residence as Zheng Shi and the two boys, but were maintained in a completely separate household.

Gao Yunquan died in the fourth month of 1935 (lunar calendar), leaving a large estate of 29 pieces of residential and commercial property. In their plaint, the three daughters accused their half-brothers of monopolizing this family property and refusing to give them their rightful shares under the law. They were requesting therefore that the estate be divided equally among the five children.[13]

---

13. Another initial point of contention in this case was the inheritance rights of Zheng Shi, the concubine whom Gao Yunquan had elevated to the position of wife. The sisters contended that Zheng Shi remained a concubine and, as such, was not entitled to any of their father's property, whereas the brothers contended that she had become a wife and, as such, was entitled to the same share as each child. The District Court did not rule specifically on this issue, but the appeals court did, holding that Zheng Shi was not in fact Gao Yunquan's wife, his recognition of her as such notwith-

Gao Chongqi and Gao Chongzhao contested their sisters' claim by arguing, among other things, that since their father had given all of his property to family members before his death, he had died absolutely penniless. As proof, the brothers presented to the court a division document (*fendan*) written by a scribe (*daibiren*), witnessed by the scribe and one other person, signed by their father and themselves, and dated 4.24.1924 (lunar calendar). The document read in part:

In recent years, because I have become old and enfeebled, I have found it very difficult to exert myself in the management of the family's affairs. I now want to rest and not tend to family matters any longer. I fear that among my children there is not one who has the ability to be as conscientious about family affairs as I have been. I fear even more that after I die, my wife, concubine, and children will fight among themselves and not follow my wish that they all live together and pass their days. I have thought it over very carefully [and have decided] that the best thing to do while I am still alive is to divide and give [*fengei*] all of the property I own to my wife, concubine, and children, so that in the future when I die, each will then have their own property and can contentedly pass their days.

The document then spelled out how the property was to be distributed: a certain amount of cash and immovable property was to be given to his "wife," Zheng Shi, and his concubine, Wang Shi, for their support; each daughter was to receive 1,000 yuan in dowry; and all of the remaining property was to be divided equally between the two sons. The document also specified that the two sons were to be responsible for their father's support until his death. Since all of their father's property had been disbursed as gifts before his death, the brothers concluded, there was no property left to be inherited.

The sisters marshaled four lines of defense against these arguments. First, they contended that the will was not authentic, that it had been drawn up by the two defendants in collusion with the scribe and the witness just before the start of litigation. They claimed that their father's signature at the bottom was a forgery. What is more, there was an important discrepancy between the document's

---

standing. To be valid under the civil code, a marriage had to be concluded in an open (*gongkai*) ceremony in the presence of two or more witnesses (art. 982). Gao Yunquan's announcement at the one-month celebration for his son simply did not fit the bill. Witnesses there may have been, but the ceremony was not an open one. (Here the court was applying the strict criteria laid down by the Judicial Yuan in 1933 that defined "open ceremony" as one that could be seen even by people not invited to attend; *SJQ*: no. 859.) As we shall see in the next chapter, a concubine had no inheritance rights to her husband's property.

date—4.24.1924—and the scribe's and witness's testimony that it had been written up at Gao Yunquan's request in the second month of 1935 and had been signed by him, the scribe, the witness, and the sons a few days before his death several months later. If that testimony was true and the document had been executed in 1935, why then did it bear the earlier date of 1924? The reason, they argued, was that their brothers, well aware that daughters had acquired inheritance rights in 1926 through the GMD's Judicial Executive Committee order, purposely affixed the 1924 date to guarantee that they would inherit nothing.

But even if the document was genuine, the plaintiffs argued, Gao Yunquan obviously meant it to be a will, and not, as the defendants claimed, a gift document. After all, if the testimony of the scribe and witness was to be believed, Gao Yunquan had it drawn up while he was gravely ill and signed it shortly before his death, just as might be expected of a will. Moreover, the text contained the stock phrase found in most wills expressing concern that one's family would fight over the property after one's death. Their father's intention clearly was to specify how his property was to be divided after his death so as to prevent future discord. This meant that he died with his estate intact under his own ownership. Contrary to the defendants' assertion, there was in fact property to be inherited.

The sisters did not stop their argument there, but continued on to dispute the validity of the document as a will, contending that it was illegal in both form and content. It did not meet the civil code's requirement that a dictated will (*daibi yizhu*), like any nonholographic legal instrument, had to be witnessed and signed by at least three people (art. 1194). There had been only two witnesses, the scribe and one other person. As for content, since the will bequeathed the bulk of the estate to the sons and only a pittance to the daughters, it violated the code's provision on compulsory portions, which guaranteed each of them at least one-half of their statutory portion, or each one-tenth of the property (art. 1223).

Finally, the sisters argued that daughters' right to inherit fell within the category of "imperative laws" (*qiangzhi guiding*), the infringement of which automatically rendered a juristic act invalid (art. 71). In this case, Gao Yunquan's act—again supposing that he had drawn up a will—should be declared null, since it was contrary to the imperative law on equal inheritance among all direct lineal descendants. The property, they concluded, should be divided equally among all five of his children.

The sisters' arguments failed to convince the Beijing District Court. It ruled that the document was both authentic and valid. It had indeed been drawn up at the behest of and signed by the father. So far as the court was concerned, the discrepancy between the witnesses' testimony and the date on the document did not support the claim of forgery and was an inconsequential matter that did not affect the document's legal force. As for the nature of the document, the court ruled that it was not a will, as the sisters claimed, but a sworn statement arranging for the premortem disposition of property, as the brothers claimed. And as such, it of course did not have to conform to any of the laws on wills about proper form and compulsory portions. Finally, the father was perfectly within his rights to do whatever he wanted with his property during his lifetime. Since he had given all of it away before his death, there was in fact no estate for the daughters to dispute.

Disappointed at this outcome, the daughters immediately appealed the District Court's decision. Once the case entered the appeals process, it became as much a battle of wills between the Hebei Superior Court and the Supreme Court as between the two sets of siblings, with the Superior Court supporting the sisters and the Supreme Court supporting the brothers. All together, the case went through six more hearings, three each at the two appellate courts.

In the numerous appeals hearings, the key issue remained the nature of the document and its framer's intent. The Hebei Superior Court held that the document was a will. As proof, it pointed to the stock phrases that commonly appeared in wills, such as Gao Yunquan's references to his fear that after his death his family members would fight among themselves and his wish that upon his death each family member would receive his or her own property (*ge cheng ge ye*). The court also argued that if the document was indeed a gift document, as the brothers claimed, one would expect it to list very precisely which brother was to receive which piece of the various holdings. But far from doing that, it merely stated that the brothers were to divide equally the property remaining after the special allocations for the "wife's" and concubine's maintenance and the daughters' dowries. Clearly, the father's intention was not to give his property to his sons before his death. This was a will and not a gift document.

Furthermore, the Superior Court held, Gao Yunquan obviously intended with that will to deprive his daughters of their rightful legacy. Unlike the Beijing District Court, the Superior Court found the discrepancy in dates to be of critical importance in assessing Gao Yun-quan's purpose. It noted that according to the scribe's own testimony, on the day the document was allegedly signed (Minguo 24.4.13), the father, reminding the scribe that daughters had acquired inheritance rights in 1926 (Minguo 15), ordered him to transpose the day and the year, thus making it Minguo 13.4.24 (or 4.24.1924). This, the Superior Court contended, clearly revealed Gao Yunquan's intention to circumvent the law.

Finally, the court concluded, the will was contrary to the imperative provision of the code that mandated equal rights of inheritance among all children. It therefore was legally void. Gao Yunquan's estate was to be divided equally among all five siblings.

As appeal followed appeal, the Supreme Court consistently overruled the lower court. The document in question, though admittedly ambiguous in some respects, nevertheless provided for the brothers' maintenance of the father for the remainder of his life—a feature one would hardly expect to find in a will. Moreover, one should judge Gao Yunquan's intentions not just by the document itself, but by his subsequent actions. The brothers had submitted during the appeals process certain evidence (account books, among other things) that purportedly proved their father had indeed transferred the property to their ownership before his death. The Superior Court had dismissed that evidence as forgeries, but the Supreme Court ruled it genuine. Taken together, the document itself and the father's subsequent actions confirmed that his objective was not to arrange for the division of his property after his death, but to dispose of it before his death. Since the document was a premortem gift document, it obviously did not have to conform to the laws on wills or equal child inheritance. And since Gao Yunquan had given away all of his property before he died, there was nothing left for any of his statutory heirs to inherit. Whether or not he intentionally sought to defraud his daughters was not an issue. The property was his to do with whatever he liked. In the end, the Supreme Court's view prevailed, and the sisters lost their suit (Beijing: 65-5-2600-2601, 65-5-2899-2901, 65-5-3295, 65-5-3306).

This case speaks well to the larger issue of the interaction of the two principles of gender equality and individual property rights. Though not inherently incompatible, those principles can work at cross-purposes when superimposed on a society that does not readily recognize either. In the case of Republican China, the new legal order of individual property rights and gender equality operated in a social climate where the principles and practices of household division and patrilineal succession remained predominant. When that new legal order and those customary practices met in the courtroom, the fate of daughters' inheritance rights depended on the degree of disjunction between the two. Where the gap between social practice and the code was the narrowest—between postmortem household division and postmortem inheritance—daughters were able to exercise their new rights. But where the gap was the widest—between premortem household division and postmortem inheritance—daughters found their rights all too easily undermined by the principle of individual property rights and the freedom of disposal that it entailed.

CHAPTER SEVEN

The Property Rights of Concubines
in the Imperial and Republican Periods

In contrast to wives and daughters, the effect on concubines of the property and inheritance laws under study here was only indirect, filtered through an ever-evolving marriage logic. Overall, two broad trends are discernible. From the Song through the Qing, we see an elevation in the legal status of concubines—from little more than a sexual servant to a kind of minor wife. By the Qing, a concubine was entitled to some of the same rights accorded any wife, including, after the death of her husband, custodial rights over his property, as well as the right to designate an heir if the man had died without sons. But then, in the Republican era, with the firm commitment to the "modern" ideal of monogamy, concubines came to be denied any legal existence at all. When set against the background of the Western-inspired property logic of the civil code, that lack of a legal identity had important implications for a concubine's rights to property.

Concubines in Imperial Times

As is well known, imperial Chinese law forbade polygamy, but not polygyny. A man could have only one wife (*qi*) at a time, but any number of concubines (*qie*).[1] The code-makers took the distinction seriously, spelling out in myriad ways the inferiority of a concubine

---

1. The successive codes from the Tang on did attempt to limit the number of concubines among members of the imperial family and officials, but those laws were not vigorously enforced (*Zongfan tiaoli* 1565: 567–69; Chen Peng 1990: 681–705 passim). As for commoners, under both Yuan and Ming law, they were not allowed to take a concubine at all, except for sonless men over 40 sui. This prohibition, however, lacked any real teeth, for though a violation brought 40 lashes of the light bamboo

and the superiority of the wife. Because of her status as the wife's
junior, a concubine was subject to a heavier punishment for any
crimes she committed against the wife than the wife got for the
same crimes against her. The different positions also came with different legal rights and responsibilities.

To a very large extent, popular practice as well maintained a clear
distinction between a wife and a concubine. In the first place, their
very entry into a household differed markedly. A wife went through
the formal betrothal and marriage rites, including the exchange of
wedding gifts and culminating in her presentation to her new family's ancestors. A concubine was most often purchased outright and
came into the household with little, if any, pomp and circumstance,
the only ceremony being her service of tea to the wife on bended
knee, symbolic of their relative positions. Within the household,
the patterns of daily life, ritual duties, even forms of address, all reinforced a concubine's subordination to the wife. The distinction
between the two continued after their deaths, with different funer-
ary and mourning rites, different placement of their tablets on family altars and in ancestral shrines, and different representations in
lineage genealogies (for general discussions, see Ebrey 1986, 1993;
Jaschok 1988; and Watson 1991).

Shiga Shûzô sees the "husband-wife unit" as lying at the heart of
these conventions. It was not only the source of a wife's authority;
it was equally the source of a concubine's lack of authority. Since a
man could have only one legal wife (*diqi*) at a time, a concubine
never could be and never was anything approximating a wife. By the
same logic, not ever having been a man's wife during his lifetime,
she was disqualified from serving as his representative after his
death and thus could not and did not exercise any of the prerogatives of widowhood. Those were the sole preserve of a wife (1967:
551–68 passim).

But a concubine's position in imperial China was in fact much
more ambiguous than the "husband-wife unit" would suggest. Legally, she existed somewhere between a maidservant of the household on the one hand and a full-fledged legal wife on the other.
Where exactly she was located along that continuum was open to
varying constructions, depending on the circumstances. To be sure,

---

(*chi*), the man was not required to expel the concubine (Chen Peng 1990: 698–99;
Ming, 6: 9a–10). The early editions of the Qing code incorporated the prohibition, but
it was deleted in 1740 (Wu Tan ca. 1780: 445).

neither codified law nor judicial officials looked kindly on a concubine who attempted to usurp the wife's authority while she was still alive. But they were much more ambivalent when it came to a concubine's rights and duties after the wife was dead. After all, contrary to Shiga's assertion, a concubine often did assume the role of family matriarch after the wife's death and the role of de facto head of the household after her husband's death, whether because of age or sheer force of personality, or simply because there was no one else around to take on the job. However much officials may have wanted to affirm the distinction between a wife and a concubine in such situations, practical realities sometimes demanded that they make accommodations in order to preserve the family and its property. The "husband-wife unit" does not fully capture the range of roles a concubine assumed in the household.

Moreover, the "husband-wife unit" was not, as Shiga suggests, a timeless concept untouched by historical change. As a description of a concubine's lack of authority, it is more appropriate for the Song than for later times. By the Qing, what counted most was not whether a woman was a wife or a concubine, but whether she was a chaste widow. For concubines, widow chastity became a source of authority that overrode the exclusivity of the husband-wife unit.

The Tang and the Song: Exalted Servants

Tang and Song law left little room for ambiguity over the respective rights of concubines and wives in property and succession matters. The Tang regulation on household division makes no mention of concubines, stating only that "widowed wives [*guaqi*] without sons are to receive their husband's share" (cited in Niida, comp. 1933: 245–46). Elsewhere the code explicitly ruled out concubines as coparceners of family property. As the law on the murder of a master or mistress [*zhu*] by a servant explained, concubines could not be considered "mistresses," since that category included only household members who had legal claims to shares of family property, and concubines enjoyed no such right. The Song code, following Tang law, also excluded concubines from sharing in the division of family property (Tang: 328; Song: 197, 274–75).[2]

2. Curiously, in its provisions on household division, the extant version of the Song code, though otherwise following Tang law to the letter, contains the phrase "widowed wives and concubines" (*guaqiqie*) and not just "widowed wives" (*guaqi*). The character for "concubine" here was probably not part of the original version of the Song code, but inadvertently added in a later one (Niida 1942: 476; Nakada 1943: 1342–1343; Shiga 1967: 262). Two facts, in particular, support this view: the Song

Concubines were similarly excluded from succession matters. No Tang laws apparently existed on the respective rights of family members to appoint an heir for a deceased sonless man, but pertinent Song law was unambiguous: "when the husband is dead but the wife is still alive, then follow his wife [*fu wang qi zai, cong qi qi*]." If the wife was also dead, then the power of appointment went directly to the husband's close senior relatives (*jinqin zunzhang*). After a wife's death, a widowed concubine did not succeed to her exclusive right to appoint an heir.

Cases from the *Qingmingji* demonstrate that legal practice followed written law in the matter. The death of one Wang Ping, for instance, provoked a succession dispute between his elder brother and his first cousin. Even though Wang Ping was survived by a concubine, the official presiding over the case did not consider her wishes in the matter at all (*QMJ*: 512–17). In another case, a widowed concubine purposely represented herself as a wife to officials to gain the right to appoint an heir of her own choosing. The judge saw through her ruse and dismissed her candidate (*QMJ*: 268). In neither of these cases was the widowed concubine treated as a surrogate wife.

Concubines in the Song not only were denied the property and succession rights accorded wives, but were also much more vulnerable to arbitrary expulsion from the household. They did not come under the protection of the "seven outs" (*qichu*) and the "three not-goes" (*san buqu*), which laid out the grounds upon which a man was permitted to divorce his wife.[3] Their position was the more precarious because they were apparently not covered by the legal prohibition against the forced remarriage of an unwilling widow by her marital family. As documented by Patricia Ebrey, concubines who had not borne children were particularly vulnerable to expulsion by the husband, and after his death, by his family (1993: 227–33).

This is not to say, however, that concubines were entirely bereft

---

code's verbatim adoption of the Tang law on the killing of a master or mistress by a servant, which, as noted, specifically ruled out concubines as coparceners of family property; and the Song officials' routine citing of widowed wives only in connection with household division (e.g., *QMJ*: 220).

3. The "seven-outs" were the failure to bear a son, adultery, unfilial conduct toward the parents-in-law, loquacity, theft, jealousy, and incurable illness. The "three not-goes" specified that a husband could not dismiss his wife for any of the "seven-outs" (except for adultery and incurable illness in the Tang and Song and adultery in the Ming and Qing) if she had performed the three-year mourning for her parents-in-law, if her husband had been poor when they first married and had since become rich, and if she had no natal relatives to take her back (Tang: 268; Song: 223; Ming, 6: 37b–38b; Qing: 116-01).

of safeguards under Song law. Those who were fortunate enough to have borne children for their masters acquired a social and legal legitimacy that childless concubines lacked. Although the man's principal wife (*diqi*) exercised full legal parental rights over a concubine's children, she herself enjoyed the status of "birth mother" (*shengmu*) toward her own children and the status of "concubine mother" (*shumu*) toward all of her husband's other offspring, whether by the legal wife or by other concubines. (A concubine who bore no children could not be the "concubine mother" of any of her husband's other children.) It was through her status as a mother that a concubine acquired some rights under the law.

Most intriguingly, the available evidence suggests that, in certain circumstances, a concubine had the right to succeed to the property of her child. A biography of the twelfth-century official Cheng Jiong in the *History of the Song* includes a brief account of a property dispute he adjudicated while serving as the Yangzhou prefect in the 1160's. Ten years earlier, a Taixing county man of some means and prominence had died without any other survivors but his concubine and their daughter. At this late date, someone (who exactly is not specified) had brought suit against the concubine to contest her control of her deceased husband's 1,000 mu of land. The upshot was that Taixing officials had confiscated the entire estate, and what is more, were demanding that she compensate the county for the rent she had collected during the past 10 years on the grounds that she had not had any right to the property in the first place. When the case reached Prefect Cheng, he ruled that the property was to be returned to the daughter and, should she die, it was then to go to the concubine as her birth mother (*shengmu*; *Songshi*, 437: 12949).

Moreover, two mid-thirteenth-century cases in the *Qingmingji* from two different officials cite a specific regulation concerning concubines: "if the man last in his line [lit., "extinct household person," *hujueren*] lived with his birth mother or birth grandmother, the property will be allowed to go to her as its owner" (*caichan bing ting wei zhu*; *QMJ*: 251, 268). For various reasons, the two cases themselves do not tell us much about the specific intent and scope of the law. But we can surmise that its purpose was to exempt such property from state confiscation. As we saw in Chapter One, the more widely cited Song laws on extinct household property specified that it should go to the man's daughters and his posthumously appointed male heir, and that in the absence of either, all of the property would then go to the state. These laws had made no allowance for the continued maintenance of a mother or grandmother who happened to be a concubine. The regulation cited above was intended to correct that oversight.

The way the regulation was applied in one of the two *Qingmingji* cases suggests that a concubine birth mother acquired, along with her son's property, the right to select an heir for him. The case was adjudicated by Fang Dacong (*jinshi*), most likely during his service as a prefect (*QMJ*: 268).[4] Three parties were fighting over the designation of an heir for one Ding Sunsan, each proposing a different candidate: a woman who claimed to be Ding's wife (not identified by name); Deng Shi (also called An'an), his father's concubine; and a group of his kinsmen (*zuren*).

In his ruling, Prefect Fang laid out the respective rights of the contenders in descending order. He considered first the woman claiming to be Ding Sunsan's wife. If she was actually his wife, he wrote, then she of course would have the exclusive right to appoint an heir for him (*fu wang cong qi*). But given that she had entered Ding's household only on the day he died, he did not believe that the two had ever married.

Next the prefect turned to Deng Shi, the father's concubine. Citing the law that "if the man last in his line lived with his birth mother or birth grandmother, the property will be allowed to go to her as its owner," he explained that her right to choose the heir depended on whether she was in fact Ding Sunsan's birth mother. He decided that she was not. Although she referred to Sunsan as her deceased son (*wangnan*) and to herself as "concubine mother" (*shumu*), that in itself was not proof of maternity, since the sons of a wife and other concubines would also call her "concubine mother." Furthermore, by the testimony of another relative, Deng Shi had had only one child, a now-married daughter.

Only after considering the claims of first the pretender wife and then Deng Shi did Prefect Fang turn to the group of kinsmen. He disqualified their candidate for several reasons, but primarily because of a history of animosity between him and Ding Sunsan and the adamant opposition of Deng Shi and some other relatives.

Since none of the parties had a perfect claim on the succession, Prefect Fang came up with what he hoped would be a workable compromise. He ruled that two heirs were to be established for

4. He served in both Guangzhou prefecture (modern-day Guangdong) and Longxing prefecture (modern-day Jiangxi; *QMJ*: 684). The account of the case does not tell us where it took place.

Ding Sunsan: the concubine Deng Shi's candidate and another to be selected from among the Ding kinsmen. Although Prefect Fang dismissed Deng Shi's claim to be Ding Sunsan's birth mother, the way he framed his account of the case leaves no doubt that had she been, the choice of an heir would have been entirely up to her.

Other cases from the *Qingmingji* suggest that widowed concubines with children acquired certain other rights under the law. As concubine mother to all of her husband's children, she was entitled to receive maintenance from all of the heirs to his property, not just from her own sons (*QMJ*: 303–4). And as birth mother to her own children, she could manage any property they may have inherited while still minors (*QMJ*: 232–33, 251–57), but only if their "legal mother" (*dimu*) was dead. The widowed wife otherwise had the legal right to handle the affairs of all of her husband's children, whether borne by her or borne by concubines.

The powers a concubine acquired through maternity notwithstanding, a vast divide still separated concubines and wives in Tang and Song law, with concubines possessing few of the legal privileges and safeguards enjoyed by wives. That divide in turn reflected the strict status boundary between the two. As is well known, imperial law provided for three broad status groups, applying to each different moral standards and different criminal penalties: officials (*guan*), commoners (*liangmin*, lit., "good people"), and people of debased or "mean" hereditary groups (*jianmin*). These three general categories obtained throughout the imperial period, the major change over time being the reduction of the number of groups assigned to the "mean" category and, as we shall see, the increasing permeability of the status boundaries set by marriage and concubinage.

In the Tang and Song periods, the debased groups included, most notably, slaves (*nubi*), serf-tenants (*kehu*), and prostitutes (*yuehu*, lit., "music households"). The line separating those groups from commoners and officials was rigidly fixed, particularly by the prohibitions against intermarriage. For instance, an official or a male commoner who took a slave as his wife was subject to two years of penal servitude, and a male slave who took a commoner as his wife to one and a half years. The law similarly prohibited an official or a male commoner from taking a serf-tenant or a prostitute as a wife (Tang: 256–57, 269–71; Song: 214–15, 225–27).

The law was more lax when it came to the acquisition of concubines. As a general principle, an official or a commoner could take only a woman of *liang* or commoner status as his concubine, but the Tang and Song codes in fact allowed for exceptions. Either could, for example, take a slave as concubine if she had borne him a son or if he first went through the proper manumission procedures to raise her to commoner status. He was also free to acquire a serf-tenant or a prostitute as a concubine with no threat of legal punishment (Tang: 257; Song: 215–16).

Within a household, the status boundaries between a wife and a man's other consorts were absolutely impermeable. A wife could not be degraded to the position of concubine, and a concubine, serf-tenant, or slave could not at any time be elevated to the position of wife, even after the man was widowed. Any man who did so was to be punished with one and a half to two years of penal servitude, and the woman was to revert to her original status (Tang: 256–57; Song: 214–15). The commentary accompanying this law in the Tang and Song codes explained the reasons for the prohibitions:

A concubine is acquired through purchase, and her position is far apart [from a wife's]. A female slave is of the debased ranks and is of course not fit to be a wife. [To degrade the wife and elevate a concubine or slave] damages the proper way [zhengdao] of husband and wife, corrupts the eternal principles of human relations, inverts high and low, and causes disorder in the rites and regulations.   (Tang: 256; Song: 215)

This constellation of laws indicates that, in these two dynasties, the major divide lay between wives, on the one hand, and concubines, female slaves and serf-tenants, and prostitutes on the other. Although the position of concubine did not carry the stigma of "mean" legal status, she nevertheless could not easily escape the taint of being a purchased good, as the commentary above suggests. A concubine was considered too corrupting an influence ever to be elevated to the position of wife. The status boundary dividing concubines and wives was a rigid one.

The Ming and the Qing: Minor Wives

After the Song, concubines gradually came to be legally constructed less as exalted servants and more as minor wives. Part of the reason for that transformation lay in the general loosening of the strict status boundaries with increasing commercialization and social mobility in the Ming and Qing. Several scholars have studied the effects of that process on various debased hereditary status groups (Niida 1942; Ch'ü T'ung-tsu 1961; P. Huang 1985; Jing Junjian 1993; Sommer 1994; Mann 1997). Its effects on concubines were at least as great, if not greater.

In Ming times, the range of Tang-Song prohibitions against intermarriage among status groups was reduced to two. For commoners,
the only law remaining in force was the proscription against a female commoner marrying a slave (Ming, 6: 23b–36a). The law now
allowed marriage or concubinage between a male commoner and a
slave, serf-tenant, or prostitute. For officials, the only illegality was
to take a prostitute as either a wife or a concubine (Ming, 6: 30b–
32a). The Ming laws on marriage and concubinage between different
status groups were adopted wholesale by the Qing (Qing: 113, 115).

Also in the Ming, the law on the elevation of a concubine to wife
was revised. It was still illegal to downgrade a wife to concubine and
upgrade a concubine to wife while the wife was still alive, but a
man was now allowed to raise his concubine to the position of wife
(*fuzheng*) after his first wife's death. Moreover, unlike Tang and
Song law, Ming law did not prescribe any punishments for the elevation of a slave or serf-tenant to wife, thus suggesting that they,
like a concubine, could be so elevated after the death of the wife
(Ming, 6: 9a–10a). The Qing incorporated this statute into its code
as well (Qing: 103).

This relaxation of status boundaries was reflected in the respective dynasties' ritual mourning charts. In the Song, a concubine's
circle of mourning obligations was small. She was to wear mourning only for her husband, his wife, her own children, and her husband's other children by his wife or other concubine(s) (*Qingyuan
tiaofa shilei* 1203, 77: 3a–13b). By the end of the eighteenth century,
she owed, in addition, mourning to her husband's parents, his paternal grandparents, his daughters-in-law, his grandsons and their
wives, and his granddaughters, as well as her own grandsons and
their wives and her own granddaughters. With the exception of the
husband's parents, a requirement that was instituted in the early
Ming, all these additions came in the eighteenth century (*Da Ming
huidian* 1587, 102: 1a–13b; Wu Tan ca. 1780: 68–190 passim).

The range of mourning owed a concubine also expanded. As a
rule of thumb, throughout Chinese imperial history, a concubine
was not to be ritually mourned if she had not borne the family head
a child. Otherwise, in the Song, she was to be mourned only by her
own children as their "birth mother," by the family head's other
children through different consorts as "concubine mother," and by
her own grandchildren (*Qingyuan tiaofa shilei* 1203, 77: 3a–13b).
With the revisions in the eighteenth century, she was to be mourned,
in addition, by a birth son adopted out to another family, by the wives

of her own sons and the wives of her husband's sons by other consorts, by her husband's grandsons and their wives, and perhaps most
important of all, by her husband and his wife (Wu Tan ca. 1780:
68–190 passim). Although a concubine's position in the mourning
network, whether as a giver or as a receiver of mourning, came nowhere near to matching the depth and range of a wife's, the Qing
revisions clearly marked a greater incorporation into her husband's
family and a slight lessening of the ritual distance separating her
from his wife.

An equally important part of the concubine's rise in status was
her inclusion in the imperially sponsored cult of the chaste widow.
In the Song, widowed concubines were under no obligation to remain faithful to their deceased husbands, any more than was a maid
of the household who might have borne a child by the family head.
The *Qingmingji* cases, for instance, contain large doses of extravagant praise for faithful widowed wives and equally large doses of
harsh criticism for remarried ones but are utterly silent about the
fidelity of widowed concubines (e.g., *QMJ*: 211–12, 344, 365–66).
Nevertheless, from the very outset of the imperially sponsored cult
in the Yuan dynasty, concubines, no less than wives, were eligible
for the imperial testimonials of merit (*jingbiao*) awarded to "chaste
widows"—a fact that has generally been overlooked in the secondary literature on widow chastity. Moreover, over time, they came to
occupy a greater proportion of the total number of commemorated
widows. The extensive collection of chaste widow biographies in the
Imperial Compendium of Books of All Ages (Gujin tushu jicheng),
completed in 1725 and published in 1728, gives a good sense of that
development. Concubines accounted for only 0.6 percent of the 359
honored chaste widows of the Yuan, but for 1.0 percent of the 27,141
honored in the Ming and 2.2 percent of the 9,812 honored in the
early Qing (1644–1725).[5] Figures for Shanxi province show a similar
trend: concubines, unrepresented among the 61 honored widows of
the Yuan, constituted 0.7 percent of the 1,668 honored in the Ming,
and 1.6 percent of the 44,754 honored in the Qing (1644–early 1890's;
Shanxi tongzhi 1892: juan 162–178).

Aggregate figures, of course, mask a great deal of regional varia-
tion. In general, the more commercially prosperous the region and
the stronger the gentry presence, the higher the proportion of con-

5. *Gujin tushu jicheng* 1728: juan 121–325. My figures are higher than those provided by Dong Jiazun (1937), who used this same source, because his tabulations do
not include the supplementary biographies that are appended to the main ones.

cubines among canonized widows: the commercial wealth provided the means to purchase and support a concubine, and the strong gentry presence encouraged the flourishing of the cult. The lower Yangzi region, for instance, boasted a relatively high proportion of concubines among its chaste widows: 5.4 percent of the 2,601 in Haiyan county (Zhejiang) during the Qing, and 6.9 percent of the 1,692 in neighboring Pinghu county (*Jiaxingfu zhi* 1879: juan 73–76).

Concubines were by no means underrepresented in those counties. Indeed, if anything, they may have been overrepresented. On average, they accounted for 3.7 percent of the consorts in Liu Ts'ui-jung's study of 23 lineages in South and Central China during the Qing, or a ratio of 1:27 (1983: 288). The ratio of concubines to canonized widows in Haiyan and Pinghu—1:18 and 1:14, respectively—was higher. This discrepancy was no doubt due in part to a higher number of concubines among consorts in the two counties, but the effect of that would have been reinforced by the greater age difference between concubines and wives. Since concubines were much more likely than wives to be years, even decades, younger than their husbands, they were much more likely to be widowed before the age of 30 sui, the required lower age for chaste widow canonization.

In most respects, the biographical sketches of faithful widowed concubines in local gazetteers mirrored those of widowed wives. They, like chaste wives, were commended for their fervent acts of resistance to remarriage (cutting off all of their hair, maiming their faces, and threatening suicide); for their attentive care of aging parents-in-law; for their raising and educating of children, including any adopted male heir; and for their protection of the sons' or adopted heir's patrimony from rapacious kin. Those biographies, formulaic though they may be, make clear that in the absence of a widowed wife, a widowed concubine was called upon to perform the same function—to ensure the continuation of the patriline and safeguard its property.

Sometimes, the biographies specifically mentioned that, to those women, chaste widowhood was no less a virtue for a concubine than for a wife. For instance, the concubine Zhang Shi of Haining (Zhejiang), who was widowed at age 23 sui and canonized sometime in the mid-eighteenth century, was said to have declared: "Wives and concubines are different [in status], but their duty is the same" (*di shu you bie, yi ze yi*). She remained faithful to her husband up to her death 41 years later (*Minguo Hangzhoufu zhi* 1916, 158: 27b). Similarly, Shen Shi, a chaste widowed concubine of Jiaxing county

(Zhejiang), reportedly said in response to those who urged her to re-marry: "Although I cannot read, I have heard that a woman follows only one husband throughout her life [*congyi er zhong*]. I am not willing to transgress the rites [*li*]" (*Jiaxingfu zhi* 1879, 67: 39a).

A concubine, like a wife, was also eligible for imperial recognition as a "virtuous widow" (*liefu*), one who committed suicide out of grief over her husband's death or to resist a forced remarriage and hence the compromise of her virtue. For example, the young (34-sui) concubine Wang Zhu Shi of Qiantang county (Zhejiang) poisoned herself after her husband's death, a meritorious act for which she received imperial honors in 1903 (*Minguo Hangzhoufu zhi* 1916, 154: 23b). Two other concubines so commemorated were He Shi of Haining, who killed herself in the face of pressure from her husband's relatives to remarry, and Xu Shi of Wujiang county (Jiangsu), who killed herself rather than submit to the wife's plan to marry her off (ibid., 163: 18a; *Wujiangxian zhi* 1747, 35: 33a).

The dictates of widow chastity made a concubine's position much more legally secure. Somewhat ironically, in fact, she was more secure after her husband's death than before. Still legally unprotected from arbitrary expulsion by the "seven outs" and the "three not-goes," she was entirely at the mercy of her husband, who, as one commentary to the Qing code put it, "could keep her if he loved her and expel her if he detested her" (cited in Shiga 1967: 570). But after his death, she was legally protected by the law prohibiting the forced remarriage of widows, which by the late Ming had been amended to cover concubines as well as wives (Ming, 6: 15a; Zhang Kentang 1634, 3: 9a; Qing: 105; *Xing'an huilan* 1886, 9: 16a–b). A widowed concubine, like a widowed wife, could not be married or sold off against her will by either her natal or her marital family.

As a result of this growing emphasis on widowed concubine chastity, as well as the increasing fluidity of status boundaries, the source of a concubine's security was transformed. In the Song, whatever security she possessed came from being a mother—the birth mother of her own children and the concubine mother of all of her husband's children. By the Qing, it came from being a faithful widow to her husband. That in turn had important implications for a concubine's role in succession.

Concubines and Patrilineal Succession in the Qing

In the Qing, as in the Song, a widowed concubine had no legal say in succession so long as the wife was still alive. This point is brought out well in a complicated case that the official Li Jun heard while serving as the prefect of Henan prefecture (Henan). The way Prefect Li opened his account of the dispute indicates the nature of the problem:

> [Wang] Tianjian [of Luoyang county] first had Shen Shi as his principal wife [*diqi*] and Ma Shi as his "second" wife [*ciqi*]. In the fourteenth year of the Jiaqing reign [1809], he married again with Shang Shi as his wife [*qi*], and in the eighteenth year [1813] he married yet again with Yao Shi as his wife [*qi*]. By that time [his principal wife] Shen Shi had already died.[6]

Wang Tianjian's death in 1827 provoked a battle among the three surviving wives over the appointment of a successor, with the fourth wife, Yao Shi, supporting one candidate and the second and third wives, Ma Shi and Shang Shi, supporting another. When Yao Shi unilaterally brought her choice as heir into the household, Ma Shi and Shang Shi filed a plaint against her at the Luoyang county yamen on the charges of "worming herself into the succession" (*zuanji*) and being a "conniving concubine [who had wiped out] the principal wife and arbitrarily [assumed] control of family affairs" (*diaoqie miedi, shanzhu jiazheng*). Yao Shi retaliated by accusing the others of "seizing [the status of] principal wife and driving out the heir" (*duodi zhuji*).

The case reached Prefect Li's docket on appeal in 1829. After some harsh words for the dead Wang Tianjian for creating such a mess by failing to distinguish between wife and concubine, Prefect Li decided on the basis of what he himself saw as less than perfect evidence that Shang Shi most likely was the principal wife, and Ma Shi and Yao Shi only concubines. To his mind, he explained, Ma Shi had to be a concubine since she had lived in the household when Wang's first wife, Shen Shi, was still alive. As for Shang Shi and Yao Shi, their status depended on when Shen Shi died. If she had died before Shang Shi's entry into the household in 1809, then Shang Shi had to be the new wife, and Yao Shi only a concubine; if she had died after 1809 but before Yao Shi's entry into the household in 1813, then Yao Shi had to be the new wife, and Shang Shi only a

---

6. In popular practice, a *ciqi* was just that—a second wife a man married while the first was still alive. (The "ci" in the expression has the same meaning as the "ci" in *cizi*, second son, and *cinü*, second daughter.) She was also commonly referred to as an *erfang*, likewise translatable as "second wife." A man was most likely to marry a second wife if the first was incapacitated by illness and unable to fulfill her household and child-rearing duties. On the meaning of "ciqi" and "erfang," see Niida 1942: 715–20; Niida, ed. 1952–58, 1: 227, 239; and Shiga 1967: 559). This is one typical example of true multiple wives in popular practice.

concubine. In the end, Prefect Li, unable to verify the exact year of Shen Shi's death, settled on Shang Shi as the new wife on the grounds that she had entered the household before Yao Shi and had come into the marriage straight from her father's home, whereas Yao Shi had previously been married.

On this reasoning, the prefect felt that Shang Shi probably did have the right to select the heir. But perhaps distrustful of his own conclusion about which woman held what status and clearly eager to put an end to the litigation, he opted for a compromise solution: the candidates of both parties were to serve jointly as Wang Tian-jian's heirs; and the property was to be divided into five equal shares among the three woman and the two heirs (Li Jun 1833, 1: 10a–11b). Prefect Li's solution notwithstanding, the case leaves little doubt that when both a wife and a concubine survived a husband, the con-cubine was to have no legal say in the selection of an heir.

Less certain was the concubine's right when she alone survived the husband. Where Song law had clearly stated that a wife had the right to establish an heir after her husband's death, later law was ambiguous. The relevant Ming regulation and the Qing substatute on a widow's role in succession did not use the word "qi" (wife) but chose the more comprehensive "furen" (woman): "a woman with-out sons who preserves her chastity after her husband dies [*furen fu wang wuzi shouzhizhe*] is to receive her husband's share of prop-erty [*he cheng fufen*] and must, through the agency of the lineage head, select a nephew of the appropriate generation as heir" (*Da Ming huidian* 1587, 19: 20b; Qing: 78-02). The existing evidence suggests that officials in the Qing were by no means averse to interpreting the "woman" here to mean a faithful widowed concubine and grant-ing her the same authority as a widowed wife in the designation of an heir.

One such official was Xu Shilin (*jinshi* 1713), who was excep-tionally well versed in legal affairs, having served as a secretary (*zhushi*) for the Board of Punishments, a prefect of Anqing prefec-ture (Anhui), Jiangsu judicial commissioner, and Jiangsu governor. In his published collection of court cases, he recounted with ap-proval a suit he reviewed while serving in Anqing in the late 1720's and early 1730's. Wu A Wang, the widowed concubine of Wu Zhang-bin of Qianshan county, had brought suit against her husband's seventh-order nephew Wu Chao over the issue of succession. Wu Chao, backed by the lineage, insisted that his son, Wu Dayi, be appointed as heir to Xike, the deceased son of Wu A Wang and Wu Zhangbin, since he was the most closely related man of the proper generation. Wu A Wang insisted that no heir needed to be established for Xike, for she and her husband had a grandson, Kan'er, by the son they had adopted, to continue the line. The adopted son turned out to be of a different surname, thus rendering Kan'er ineligible for the succession, but the magistrate hearing the case did not for that reason rule for the concubine's adversaries. Instead, he disqualified Wu Chao's son Daiyi from the succession because of the hostility between Wu Chao and the widow engendered by the lawsuit and because Wu Chao's line was so distantly related to her husband's (the closest relative in common being Wu Chao's great-great-great-great-great-grandfather). Noting that since her son had died unmarried and no successor needed to be established for him, the magistrate ruled that an heir should be appointed for her husband instead from the 33 nephews within the five grades of mourning. The choice was to be hers alone. The magistrate directly ordered Wu A Wang to select any one of them she liked and present her choice to the court for confirmation. She did so, and the case was closed (Xu Shilin 1906, 2: 36a–39a). Wu A Wang's status as a concubine was not at all an issue in the litigation.

Xu Shilin showed the same sympathy toward concubines' wishes in a succession case that he himself adjudicated as Anqing prefect. The suit concerned the appointment of an heir for Wang Zongzhuo, identified as a well-to-do lower gentryman (*linsheng*, i.e., a *shengyuan* on stipend). Wang's first cousin Wang Zonghong claimed that his own son, Wenju, had the right to the succession (*yingji*) as the nearest possible candidate of the proper generation. But Wang Zongzhuo's widowed concubine, Song Shi, refused to accept him because of the abiding animosity she and her late husband felt toward the boy's father over a previous lawsuit. Prefect Xu, while conceding that, in terms of lineage order, Wenju did have the superior claim, nevertheless disqualified the boy on the grounds of enmity. He put no stock in Wang Zonghong's argument that enmity was not of concern because Wang Zongzhuo was already dead, and Song Shi could just live separately from the heir. And to his argument that "succession to a line [*chengtiao*] is a serious affair . . . and concubines must not insist on taking charge of the matter," Xu Shilin responded that "her husband's enemy is her own enemy," suggesting that she was perfectly within her rights to refuse an heir her husband himself would have refused. In the end, he ordered that the male relative proposed by Song Shi and the lineage elders be appointed heir (ibid.: 54a–55b).

Finally, we have the following case heard by Zhang Wuwei during his stint as the prefect of Guangping prefecture (Zhili) sometime between 1808 and 1811. Zhang Xiaoxian of Cheng'an county had taken a family servant (*shinü*) as his concubine. When he died, the concubine, Jia Shi, designated Zhang Erxiao, the adopted son and heir of Xiaoxian's deceased brother, to serve as her husband's heir. One of Xiaoxian's kinsmen, Zhang Jiyuan, brought suit to challenge the succession. He claimed that no concubine, much less one who had been a servant, could succeed to the headship of a family (*chengjia*) and select an heir. He also argued that her choice of Zhang Erxiao was illegal, since the boy was an only son.

In his ruling, Prefect Zhang chastised Zhang Jiyuan for his boorish disrespect of Jia Shi and commended her for her faithful performance of her duties toward her husband. Directly addressing the question of whether a concubine could succeed to the headship of the family, he explained that Jia Shi was to assist the "household head" (*jiazhu*, i.e., her husband) in death just as she had assisted him in life. That she was formerly a servant and now a concubine was of no importance: "Among the people there are those who have married the servants of gentry households [*dahu*] as wives and those who have purchased the daughters of poor commoner families as concubines." Thus, "the difference between wife and concubine is just one of roles [*mingfen*]: it is not a question of 'good' [*liang*] and 'debased' [*jian*]." That said, he went on to affirm Jia Shi's choice of Zhang Erxiao as an entirely appropriate instance of combined succession (Zhang Wuwei 1812, pici: 70a–71b). In his handling of the case, Prefect Zhang treated the widowed concubine just as if she were a widowed wife.

No less a legal mind than Shen Jiaben also believed that the relevant substatute in the Qing code could be applied to concubines. His thoughts on the matter took the form of a response to a letter from a friend who had asked whether the word "furen" (woman) in the phrase "furen fu wang shouzhizhe" (a woman who preserves her chastity after her husband dies) referred exclusively to a wife or whether a concubine could receive the husband's property (*he cheng fufen*) if the wife had already died.

Shen Jiaben's response was that the substatute did not distinguish between wives and concubines, but only between women who preserved their chastity and those who did not. "Of those able to maintain their chastity, a wife of course can receive [the property], but even a concubine can also do so. Of those unable to maintain their chastity, not only can a concubine not receive [the property], but even a wife cannot do so." The framers of the substatute had deliberately used "furen" to mean concubines as well as wives, for if only wives had been intended, they would have just used the word "diqi" (legal wife), as in the statute under which it fell. (Here Shen Jiaben was referring to that part of Statute 78 that reads, "if a man's legal wife [*diqi*] has not borne a son by the age of 50, he is permitted to establish his eldest son by a concubine as heir.")

For those people who might emphasize the differences between wives and concubines, Shen Jiaben went on, one might point to the similarities in their obligations toward a deceased husband. Each had to observe the same three years of mourning for him. And each bore the same moral obligation to remain constant after his death, as evidenced by the Board of Rites' listing of faithful widowed concubines as eligible for imperial testimonials.

Those obligations included also the duty to adopt a successor for an heirless husband. The substatute's main purpose, Shen Jiaben reminded his friend, was to establish a woman's legal obligation to appoint an heir for her deceased husband. Her acquisition of his property was subordinate to that larger concern. By that logic, denying a concubine the right to receive her husband's property would be tantamount to denying her the right to establish an heir for him, the consequences of which could be disastrous:

[Should] others fight over the succession and the property, a concubine would not be allowed to concern herself in the matter. Even if overbearing, tyrannical branches of the family were to seize the property for themselves and not appoint an heir for her husband, she would still not be allowed to do anything. All she could do would be to sit and watch her husband's line be cut off and the family property disappear.

Shen Jiaben's conclusion—that the substatute did not make any distinction between a wife and a concubine, and that each, as long as she remained faithful, had the right to receive her husband's property and to establish a successor—was thus consistent with Qing legal practice (Shen Jiaben n.d.: 2204-05).

His response also affirms the importance of widow fidelity as the basis of a concubine's new prerogatives in the Qing. Whereas in the Song a concubine attained limited powers in property and succession matters only through maternity, by the Qing, she had acquired the same set of rights and duties that had once been the sole preserve of a widowed wife. Whether a woman was a wife or a concubine mattered less than whether she was a faithful widow.

Concubines in the Early Republican Period

In the early Republican period, "modern" monogamy replaced widow chastity as the defining principle of the relative positions of concubines and wives. Pronouncing that China's laws were now to uphold the "system of one husband, one wife" (*yifu yiqi zhi*), the Daliyuan ruled that concubinage could no longer be considered a type of marriage, even a lesser one, and that concubines could no longer be considered anything approximating a wife. The relationship between a concubine and her so-called "husband" was to be seen instead as strictly a contractual arrangement between a woman and the family head (*jiazhang*; *DPQ*: 211).

Pursuant to that reconceptualization, the Daliyuan rendered a whole separate set of decisions aimed at defining the rights and obligations of a concubine toward the family head and his larger family network, and their rights and obligations toward her (Bernhardt 1994: 210–11). Those decisions were intended to reverse the Qing trend toward equalizing the prerogatives of wives and concubines. Rather than minimize the differences between the two in the name of widow chastity, the Daliyuan would accentuate them in the name of monogamy.

Concubines and Succession: "Not a Wife"

The Daliyuan made its crucial decision on a concubine's rights in the matter of succession in a Beijing case it heard on appeal in 1914. The litigation had begun in 1912 with a plaint filed at the Capital District Court by Xue Wang Shi, a 57-sui widowed concubine and manager of a prosperous pharmacy. In her plaint, she accused Xue Enlai (28 sui), a secretary in the Bureau of Civil Administration (*Minzhengbu zhushi*), of the unlawful possession of family property. By her account, her late husband, Xue Zengji, had no children by his wife, but had fathered two daughters and a son with her, the concubine. The son had died in infancy in the late 1870's. Sometime in the 1880's, Zengji had brought in one of his grandnephews from Shandong to work as a clerk in his pharmacy, an arrangement that came to an abrupt end when Zengji expelled the grandnephew for selling counterfeit products. But the grandnephew's son, the defendant Xue Enlai, still a young boy, had remained with the Xue family in Beijing. Xue Zengji had died in 1895 and his wife 17 years later, in the spring of 1912. After the wife's death, Xue Wang Shi charged, Xue Enlai, falsely claiming to be Zengji's adopted great-grandson and, as such, successor to his line, stole all of the contracts for the family's nine houses and a large sum of money and refused to return them. Since Xue Enlai was not her husband's successor, she argued, he had no right to any of the family property. Finding her argument and evidence convincing, the Capital District Court ruled in her favor.

Xue Enlai immediately appealed that decision to the Capital Superior Court, which also found for Xue Wang Shi, but for different reasons. It determined on the basis of the available written evidence that Xue Zengji had in fact established Xue Enlai as his successor. Furthermore, it was clear that neither he nor his wife had dismissed him during their lifetimes. The outcome of the case thus depended on whether Xue Wang Shi had the legal right as a concubine to remove Xue Enlai as heir and appoint another in his place (*feiji bieli*).

Through a close analysis of the relevant laws, the Superior Court concluded that she in fact did have that right. It first looked at the substatute on a faithful woman's obligation to receive her husband's property and establish an heir for him. Like Shen Jiaben, the court argued that the "woman" (*furen*) there referred to both wives and concubines. Since other laws clearly distinguished between wives and concubines, it stood to reason that if only wives had been intended, the word "wife" instead of the more inclusive "woman" would have been used. Similarly, the court also noted that the "husband" (*fu*) in the phrase "is to receive her husband's share" (*he cheng fufen*) applied to the husband of a concubine, as well as the husband of a wife. Although the mourning charts referred to a concubine's husband as "family head" (*jiazhu* here, but more commonly *jiazhang*), other laws in the code used the same word, "fu," to mean a concubine's husband. A faithful widowed concubine, no less than a faithful widowed wife, had the right to receive her husband's property and appoint an heir for him.

As for the attendant right to annul an established succession, the Superior Court concluded that the pertinent law—"if the appointed successor [*jizi*] cannot get along with his adoptive parents [*suohou zhi qin*], then they can report the matter to the authorities and appoint another in his place"—also applied to concubines. For support of its position, the court turned to the "Three Fathers, Eight Mothers" (*sanfu bamu*) mourning chart, where children, whether natural or adopted and whether borne by the wife or the concubine, called the latter "concubine mother" (*shumu*).[7] The use of that term, the court reasoned, implied a parent-child (*qinzi*) relationship between a concubine and all of her husband's children. She should therefore be considered an adoptive parent and should have the right to dismiss an established heir and appoint another. On that basis and on evidence Xue Wang Shi presented of Xue Enlai's unsuitability to continue as heir (their long-term acrimonious relationship and his theft of the contracts and money), the Superior Court revoked his succession. That ruling, as we have seen, was wholly in keeping with the legal practice that had evolved during the Qing.

Xue Enlai appealed to the Daliyuan, where he finally found satisfaction. In its 1914 decision, the Daliyuan, insisting on the logic of monogamy, denied Xue Wang Shi the right to appoint or dismiss an heir on her own. It ruled that "woman" (*furen*) applied only to chaste widowed wives. If a concubine wanted to establish an heir for her husband after his death, all she could legally do was to request that a family council (*qinzu huiyi*) be convened to take care of the matter. Unlike a wife, she did not have the exclusive right to select the heir.

Nor did she, like an adoptive parent, have any right to remove an already established heir. The Daliyuan rejected the Superior Court's notion that a concubine, as the "concubine mother" (*shumu*) of the adopted heir, enjoyed a parent-child relationship with him. Referring to the mourning chart of a concubine for her husband (*jiazhang*) and his relatives, the court noted that a clear distinction was made there between the offspring of the legal wife (*diqi*) and the offspring of a concubine. A parent-child relationship existed only between a concubine and her own children and not between a concubine and the children of the wife. Since an adopted heir acquired the status of *dizi*, or son of the husband and his wife, a concubine by definition could not have a parent-child relationship with him. The

---

7. The "Three Fathers, Eight Mothers" chart laid out mourning obligations that were not covered in the regular charts. The other seven mothers were "adoptive mother" (*yangmu*); "main or legal mother" (*dimu*), or what the children of concubines called their father's wife; "stepmother" (*jimu*); "benevolent mother" (*cimu*), a concubine who raised a child of a deceased concubine to adulthood; "remarried mother" (*jiamu*), a mother who remarried after the death of the father; "ousted mother" (*chumu*), a mother who was expelled by the father; and "wet-nurse mother" (*rumu*), a concubine who had served as one's wet-nurse. The three fathers were "co-habiting stepfather" (*tongju jifu*); "non-cohabiting stepfather" (*bu tongju jifu*); and the man whom a widowed stepmother had remarried and with whom the child had lived (*cong jimu jia*). The chart is reproduced in Wu Tan, ca. 1780: 93.

phrase "adoptive parents" in the law thus referred only to a man and his wife. That being the case, the Daliyuan concluded, Xue Wang Shi had no right to dismiss Xue Enlai as heir and was to turn over to him all of the family property, including the pharmacy (Beijing: 65-5-1689-1700; *DPQ*: 292).

Elsewhere, the Daliyuan took up a different question: if a concubine did not possess a widowed wife's exclusive right to select an heir for her husband, how then was an heir to be chosen if a man was survived by a concubine but not his wife? In that case, the Daliyuan specified, the right to select a successor passed to his parents or grandparents (*zhixi zunshu*; lit., direct lineal ascendants). If none of these were still alive, then a family council (*qinshu huiyi*) was to be convened to take charge of the matter. But it did make a certain concession here, at least, in holding that the concubine was to occupy an important position (*zhongyao diwei*) in the council (*DPQ*: 249, 262).

This ruling is of particular interest because it indicates that, determined as the Daliyuan was to maintain a strict status differentiation between wives and concubines in order to promote monogamy, it could not completely ignore the interests of a concubine, who would, after all, have to depend on the chosen heir for her livelihood and most likely would also have to share a residence with him. Negotiating between these two concerns was not easy, however, as can be seen in the court's rulings on the relative weight of a concubine's voice in the family council. On the one hand, it ruled that the concubine had to endorse the family council's selection for it to acquire legal force (*DPQ*: 249, 276). On the other hand, it ruled that the concubine could not obstruct the right of her husband's family to select an heir for him (*DPQ*: 277). In other words, the family council was forbidden to select an heir without the widowed concubine's consent, and she was forbidden to do so without their consent. Should the concubine and other members of the family council fail to reach a consensus, both sides had the right to bring the dispute to court for resolution (*DJQ*: no. 903).

What this meant in practice was that a concubine was permitted to go to court to request the cancellation of a succession that had not gotten her consent. On just that basis, the peasant woman Wu Xu Shi (35 sui), of Shangyu county (Zhejiang), won her appeal to the Daliyuan in 1918. Her husband Wu Kaiseng and his wife had died without any sons to survive them, so his two brothers had met with the lineage head, where Wu Shuimu, a son of one of the brothers, was designated to succeed Kaiseng. The concubine claimed that she had not been present at the family meeting, nor had her consent been gotten afterward. On those grounds, the Daliyuan threw out the lower court decision affirming Wu Shuimu as heir (Daliyuan: 241-3030).

By the same token, a husband's agnatic relatives could go to court to overturn a widowed concubine's designated heir if she had not secured their agreement. Thus, in 1914, the Daliyuan ruled against two women of Dongwan county (Guangdong)—one the deceased man's "concubine mother" and the other his concubine—who had designated a certain lineage nephew as heir. Since neither had the right to appoint a successor for the deceased, the Daliyuan ordered that a family council be convened to decide the matter (Daliyuan: 241-209). Similarly, in 1918, the Daliyuan ruled against the widowed concubine Yang Huang Shi (46 sui), of Guiyang city (Guizhou), for failing to consult a family council and adopting an heir on her own (Daliyuan: 241-3354).

A concubine's removal of an established heir likewise required the consensus of a family council. Perhaps if the aforementioned Xue Wang Shi had not moved unilaterally, she would have succeeded in ridding herself of the troublesome Xue Enlai. In a similar case, Pan Song Shi, a 33-sui widowed bannerwoman of Beijing, was unable to persuade the court to remove her husband's adopted heir, Pan Wenzhi, despite his wasteful spending of the family wealth and his physical abuse of her, simply because she, as a concubine, could not revoke a succession on her own (Beijing: 65-5-1-5). And in 1913, Zhao Li Shi, an aged (89-sui) concubine from Qinghe county (Zhili), lost her suit against her husband's heir for the same reason (*Zhili* 1915, 1: 158–60).

For a concubine to remove an unwanted heir, she first had to convince the members of the family council of the justness of her cause, and if they were amenable, they then had to go to court to request the revocation of the succession. In 1914, another Beijing bannerwoman, Pu Yang Shi, used this method to dismiss the heir her husband had adopted before his death and to appoint another in his place. The heir had two years earlier tied her up and beaten her, a crime for which he was sentenced to some time in prison. In 1919, he brought suit to get reinstated, but in the end, he lost his case, because it was determined that Pu Yang Shi had followed the proper procedures for a concubine to remove an heir (Jingshi: 239-5536).

Through its careful detailing of a concubine's rights in succession, the Daliyuan managed to whittle down a widowed concubine's legal prerogatives. For Shen Jiaben and others of like mind in the Qing, the great divide in succession matters lay not between wives and concubines, but between widows who maintained their chastity and those who did not. For the Daliyuan, what was important was not so much the ideal of chaste widowhood as the "modern" ideal of monogamy. Since a concubine was not a wife, she by definition could not be granted the same set of legal rights and responsibilities.

Combined Succession and Multiple Marriage

The Daliyuan's insistence on making monogamy the standard extended to those instances in popular practice of multiple main wives. We have already discussed the custom of combined or concurrent succession (*jiantiao*), in which an only son could succeed both his father and one or more of his father's brothers. Part and parcel of this practice was multiple marriage, with the son formally marrying two or more wives, one for each branch. The women in this arrangement were often called *pingqi*, "wives of equal standing," to underscore the fact that one did not stand above the other(s) in the hierarchical manner of a wife to a concubine (V. Chiu 1966: 35–36).

The Qing government permitted combined succession in 1775, but was not forced to confront the question of multiple marriage for some decades. Did multiple marriage in such circumstances constitute bigamy, and if so, what should be done about the later wives? The occasion was an inquiry sent in 1814 to the Board of Rites by the Henan Director of Studies (*xuezheng*) about a son's mourning obligations for his father's other wife. A certain She Dusheng of Baofeng county was the heir to two branches of his lineage. For the senior branch, he first married a woman surnamed Zhang and then a woman surnamed Wang, by whom he had a son, Wanquan. For the junior branch, he married a woman surnamed Lei, and when she failed to produce children, acquired a concubine surnamed Du, who bore him a son, Wande. Wanquan was to be the heir to the senior branch, and Wande the heir to the junior branch. The wife of the junior branch, Lei, had recently died. The ritual obligations of Wande, the son of the concubine Du, were not in doubt, the director of studies averred. As in any such situation, a concubine's son was to mourn his father's wife as his "legal mother" (*dimu*). But the obligations of

Wanquan, the other son, toward Lei were not clear. What exactly was his relationship to her, the director asked, and how should he mourn her?

In its response, the Board of Rites condemned She Dusheng's unorthodox marital relationships, as well as the director's apparent acceptance of them. By marrying more than one wife, She Dusheng had committed the crime of bigamy (*erqi bingqu*). Only the first woman he married, Zhang, could be considered his wife; the other two women he took as wives, Wang and Lei, could only be concubines. As for Wanquan's relationship to the deceased Lei, since she was not his legal mother, his birth mother or, being childless herself, his concubine mother, he bore no mourning obligations toward her at all. The same applied to Wande, for, contrary to the director of studies' understanding, Lei was just a concubine and not a legal wife. She therefore could not be Wande's "legal mother." And since she was not his legal mother, his birth mother, or his concubine mother, he too, strictly speaking, had no mourning obligations toward her. But here the Board of Rites made a concession to the multiple succession and Wande's status as the legal successor to the second branch. He was permitted to mourn Lei as his "benevolent mother," *cimu* (lit., a concubine who raised a child of a deceased concubine to adulthood; cited in *Taiwan* 1961, 4: 645–46).

For our purposes, the significant part of the board's response is that, in the eyes of the law, She Dusheng's two later wives, Wang and Lei, were concubines. That ruling represented a revision of the Qing code's statute on male bigamy, which demanded that a later wife be divorced immediately and returned to her natal family (Qing: 103), and became the "established case" (*cheng'an*) for fixing the status of later wives in instances of combined succession (*Xuzeng Xing'an huilan* 1886, 11: 4b–6a; Bao Shichen 1888, 28: 22b–24b; *Taiwan* 1961, 4: 645–46).

Inheriting the Qing's position on the matter, the Daliyuan in the 1910's continued to relegate later wives in combined succession marriages to concubine status (*DPQ*: 218, 234). That posture, when combined with the court's rulings on a concubine's position in succession matters, meant that in law, as opposed to popular practice, the later wife in a multiple marriage did not possess the right to select an heir for the branch into which she had married.

A dispute between a first and a later wife in a peasant family in Cheng'an county (Zhili) in the first years of the Republican period illustrates well the conflict between law and custom. The senior generation of the Li family had had four brothers. The second brother had been adopted out as a boy to a Li family in Shandong province. The eldest brother was sonless, and the third and fourth brothers each had only one son. The only son of the third brother was adopted out to succeed the eldest brother, and the only son, Li Guozhong, of the fourth brother was designated to be the dual heir (*jiantiaozi*) of both his own father and his third uncle. As the successor to two branches, Li Guozhong married two wives, first a woman surnamed Zhang and then a woman surnamed Zhao.

The occasion of the lawsuit was the death of this successor, Li Guozhong, and his first wife's designation of the second (adopted-out) brother's great-great grandson, Li Tongchun, to succeed Guozhong as the two branches' heir. Her unorthodox choice came under fire from two directions. Some of her husband's kinsmen took such strong exception to it that they raided Guozhong's house and manhandled the two widows as they were making funeral preparations. The widow Zhao, also disgruntled with the choice, filed suit against the widow Zhang and Li Tongchun's grandfather, Li Molin, at the Cheng'an county yamen on the grounds that Li Tongchun, though of the same surname, was not of the same lineage (*tongxing bu tongzong*), and that she, as Guozhong's other wife, had the legal right to a say in the matter of succession. The Cheng'an magistrate upheld the widow Zhang's choice of heir (on what basis it is not clear), but at the same time decreed a division of property that gave 25 mu of Li Guozhong's 40 mu of land to the widow Zhang and the heir and the remaining 15 mu to the widow Zhao.

The second wife appealed that decision to the Zhili Superior Court, once again arguing that Zhang's choice was not proper, and that she herself, as one of two wives in a combined succession, had as much right as the other to pick an heir. The Superior Court judges ruled that the widow Zhang's selection did in fact violate the law, not because Li Tongchun was of a different lineage (the law after all permitted same-surname, different-lineage succession), but because he was three generations removed from Li Guozhong instead of just one. But the widow Zhao's victory was a Pyrrhic one at best, for the judges also ruled that, as the second woman married by a dual heir, she had acquired only the legal status of a concubine. The right to select another heir of the proper generation thus lay with the wife, the widow Zhang. Bad as this was from her perspective, we can imagine her chagrin when the judges went on to rebuke the Cheng'an magistrate for giving her 15 mu of land, "as if she had the qualifications [*zige*] of a wife," and ordered that all the land be put under the widow Zhang's control (*Zhili* 1915, 1: 163–68).

In 1924, the Daliyuan moved to narrow the gap between law and local custom. Although it still maintained that the later "wife" in a combined succession marriage held only the legal status of concubine, it granted her the same rights in succession matters as the first wife. If the concubine and her husband failed to produce a son to continue the branch of the family into which she had married, she had the right after his death to receive his share of that branch's property, to select a successor for that branch, and, if the heir was still a minor, to manage the property on his behalf (*DPQ*: 294). This was the only instance, be it noted, in which the Daliyuan accorded a concubine the same succession and property rights as a wife.

Claims on Family Property

In the early Republican period, widowed concubines were explicitly denied the rights of management that widowed wives possessed toward family property. Early Republican law, following imperial law, required that before household division, adult sons (including an adopted heir) get the widowed legal mother's (*dimu*) consent to dispose of family property. If they failed to do so, she could apply to the court to cancel the transaction. In the case of an unusually profligate or inept son or heir, a widow could petition the court to place the property under her sole control (*DPQ*: 751; *DJQ*: nos. 228, 912, 922; Jingshi: 239-7081).

Widowed concubines in the early Republican period did not possess the same rights toward family property vis-à-vis adult sons. In 1913, for instance, the widowed concubine Wang Li Shi of Tianjin lost the suit she instigated against her deceased husband's adopted heir for the wasteful management of the family property (three houses, a grain store, and a meat store). Both the Tianjin District Court and the Zhili Superior Court on appeal ruled that, as a concubine, she had no right to interfere with the heir's actions (*Zhili* 1915, 1: 160–63).

Furthermore, early Republican law, again following imperial law, required adult sons to obtain a widowed wife's consent before dividing up the family property. A widowed concubine did not have the same legal protection. Thus, in 1917, the merchant Zheng Yingwu (28 sui) of Beijing easily won his suit against his father's 51-sui concubine Zheng Yang Shi and her son Zheng Yingcai for the right to divide the family property (Beijing: 65-5-85-91).

Finally, early Republican law granted widowed wives the right to manage family property on behalf of a minor son, whether natural or adopted, including the right to dispose of it to meet living expenses if necessary. The right of widowed concubines to do the same, although not entirely nonexistent, was strictly limited. She could do so only if the husband had designated her to be the property manager in a will or if there was no other possible close relative for the job (*DPQ*: 296).

Nevertheless, a concubine did retain one strong claim in respect to family property: her right to be supported by that property (*DPQ*: 208, 250–53). This claim to maintenance under Daliyuan law, as under imperial law, derived from her membership in the "common living, common budget" group. Her claim was thus not against any person, but rather against the property itself, regardless of who happened to be in charge of it.

For this reason, the obligation to provide for a widowed concubine fell equally on all of her husband's sons, once they had come to control the property. The young merchant Zheng Yingwu's victory in 1917 over his father's concubine, for instance, came at a price. By the Capital District Court's order, he was to bear equal responsibility with his half-brother Zheng Yingcai for the support of Yingcai's mother, Zheng Yang Shi. Each was to give the widowed concubine 20 yuan a month for her living expenses and to contribute 350 taels toward her funeral expenses when she died (Beijing: 65-5-85-91).

Moreover, like a widowed daughter-in-law in early Republican law, a widowed concubine did not necessarily have to reside with the heirs to property in order to receive maintenance from it (*DPQ*: 252). Thus, in a case heard by the Capital Superior Court in 1915, Zhang Sun Shi (35 sui), the widowed concubine of Zhang Yunji, won a judgment against his wife (61 sui) and son for the right to receive a stipend of 10 yuan a month. Even though Zhang Sun Shi no longer shared a residence with the defendants, the court explained, she retained her status as Zhang Yunji's concubine until the day she died or remarried. And that status gave her the right to maintenance from the heirs to the family property. Coresidence was not a prerequisite for maintenance (Jingshi: 239-1884). Similarly, the widowed concubine Tian Cui Shi (26 sui) secured a judgment granting her 200 yuan a year from her deceased husband's wife (60 sui), even though the two were no longer living together (ibid.: 239-3889).

The Daliyuan's rulings on maintenance were just one part of the body of laws it developed to reinforce the status distinction between concubines and wives in the name of monogamy. Yet for all its efforts, the Daliyuan was still caught between two marriage logics—the Qing logic of a concubine as a kind of wife and the new logic of monogamy. However much the court sought to emphasize the differences between wives and concubines, it continued to accord concubines a legal existence, thereby thwarting its own efforts to make monogamy the law of the land. It was up to the GMD lawmakers to take the next step and deny concubines any legal identity at all.

Concubines Under the Republican Civil Code

In deciding what to do with concubinage, the architects of the new civil code faced an impossible dilemma. On the one hand, they espoused the ideals of monogamy and male-female equality, which meant in principle outlawing the custom. Yet on the other hand, they could not completely ignore the fact of the practice's existence and the need to define a concubine's position in the new legal regime. The GMD lawmakers considered as a possible solution creating a separate law (*danxingfa*) on concubines distinct from the civil code itself, just as they had created separate laws on a host of other matters (e.g., land law, corporate law, insurance law). In the end, though, the Central Political Council, the final decision-maker, instructed the Legislative Yuan to reject that option. As it explained in its 1930 "Statement of Opinion on the Preliminary Problems of Family Law": "The system of concubinage is in urgent need of abolition. Although it in fact still exists, the law cannot recognize its existence. The concubine's position need not be provided for in the legal codes or in separate laws" (*Qinshufa xianjue gedian* 1930).

With this decision, the Central Political Council effectively sidestepped the issue altogether. Codified law was not to prohibit the practice of concubinage, but it was not to give it legal recognition either. And in fact the word "concubine" appears nowhere in the civil code or in any other body of codified law in the late Republican period. Concubines had ceased to exist as legal persons with their own special set of rights and responsibilities. They no longer had a legal existence.

Dodging the issue, as it turned out, was no real solution, for by not prohibiting concubines, the law in effect allowed for their continued *social* existence. Women who were concubines were consequently put in a legal limbo, neither recognized nor proscribed. It was left to the Judicial Yuan through its interpretive powers to decide how exactly such women were to fit into the new legal order.

Once "concubine" ceased to be a legally recognized group, the Judicial Yuan had to break the category into its constituent parts. No longer a concubine and of course not a wife, a concubine became in the eyes of the law a daughter, a sister, a mother, a grandmother, and so on, and as such enjoyed the same rights and had the same obligations as any other woman in those roles. The Central Political Council's decision not to accord concubines a legal identity, in the end, made for a great deal of change in a concubine's actual legal rights.

The Judicial Yuan made two important rulings that bore directly on a concubine's property rights. In one, it held that a concubine was legally the mother of her own children. In the other, it held that she was a member of her husband's household. The first ruling had important implications for her right to inherit, and the second important implications for her right to maintenance.[8]

Inheritance

In imperial and early Republican law, as we have seen, a man's wife had full legal authority over the children of a concubine. As their "legal mother" (*dimu*), she had the right to supervise their upbringing, arrange their marriages, manage property on their behalf, act as their legal representative in court, and so on. A concubine's rights to her own children were residual ones at best; she could function legally as a parent to them only after the death of the wife.

This wifely prerogative had no place in the GMD's new legal order. The civil code recognized only two sorts of parent-child relationships, those of blood and formal adoption. Accordingly, the Judicial Yuan ruled that a concubine was the direct lineal ascendant by blood of the children she produced, and they in turn were of course her direct lineal descendants by blood. A wife had absolutely no parental claims on these children (*SJQ*: nos. 237, 585, 1226). A concubine for the first time in Chinese history exercised full rights of motherhood over the children she herself had borne.

As defined by the code, those rights now included the right in certain situations for parents to inherit the property of their children and for grandparents to inherit the property of their grandchildren.

---

8. Since the civil code did not recognize patrilineal succession and since the courts were not to accept such cases for adjudication, a concubine's role in the designation of an heir, just like a wife's, was no longer a legal issue.

Parents, as second-order heirs, had statutory rights to inherit all of the property of an unmarried child who had no descendants, and to a 50-50 split with the surviving spouse in the case of a married child. Grandparents, as fourth-order heirs, were entitled to inherit all of the property of an unmarried grandchild who had no descendants, parents, or siblings, and to a third in the case of a married grandchild (against two-thirds for the spouse).

The redefinition of a concubine's legal relationship with her own descendants meant that she acquired the same statutory inheritance rights as any parent or grandparent (*SJQ*: no. 585). In our group of Beijing inheritance cases, we have an example of a concubine exercising those newfound rights under the law. In 1933, Wang Liang Guozhen (35 sui) filed suit at the Beijing District Court over the 200,000-yuan estate of her consort, Wang Ruxian. Upon his death in 1922, she had assumed management of the household, composed at the time of Wang Liang Guozhen herself and her young son Wang Yuanjun (3 sui); another concubine, Wang Peng Shizhen, and her daughter, Wang Yuanzhao (5 sui); an adopted son of the same surname, Wang Yuanming (14 sui); and an adopted son originally of a different surname, Wang Yuanyi (17 sui).

What precipitated the court battle was the death in 1932 of Concubine Liang's son, Yuanjun. In her plaint, she charged the two adopted sons, now adults, with seizing the family property and failing to provide living expenses for her or for Wang Peng Shizhen and her daughter. She was therefore requesting that the property be divided up among the family members. As for her own particular rights in the matter, she requested that since her son had died unmarried and childless, she should receive his share as provided in the civil code.

The two adopted sons, Yuanming and Yuanyi, argued in their defense that their father's death had predated the implementation of the civil code, so that the old laws should be used to decide the matter. Concubine Liang, therefore, had only the right to request maintenance from them; she did not have the right to inherit any property in her son's stead.

The Beijing District Court rejected their argument. The date of the father's death was important in determining the division of property among his children, but it was the date of her son's death that was important in determining whether Concubine Liang could inherit any of the property. Under the laws in force at the time of Ruxian's death in 1922, Yuanyi, as an adopted son of a different surname, was entitled to some property, though not as much as his brothers, and Wang Yuanzhao was at most entitled only to a dowry. But under the laws in force at the time of her son's death, Concubine Liang was perfectly entitled to inherit his share of the property. The court ruled that 8 percent of the estate was to go to the other concubine for her maintenance, 10 percent to the daughter as her dowry, and 10 percent to the different-surname adopted son, Yuanyi. The remaining 72 percent was to be split equally between the other adopted son, Wang Yuanming, and Concubine Liang. She thus received 72,000 yuan of the 200,000-yuan estate (Beijing: 65-5-261-263).

Maintenance

Explicitly repudiating the Daliyuan's interpretation of concubinage as a special contractual relationship between a woman and the family head (*jiazhang*), the Judicial Yuan went one step further and ruled that a concubine was merely a member of the family head's family. As defined by the civil code, a family (*jia*) was composed of all relatives and nonrelatives who "live together in one household with the object of sharing a life in common permanently" (arts. 1122, 1123). As a family member (*jiashu*), a concubine's relationship with the family head (her husband) was legally no different from other family members' relationships with him (Bernhardt 1994: 211).

This ruling both helped and hurt the concubine. In marriage matters, as I have examined elsewhere, she gained a new measure of freedom in the sense that the dissolution of her relationship with the husband–family head no longer came under the province of divorce law, but instead was governed by the laws on the separation of a family member from the family (Bernhardt 1994: 209–12). Like any other adult family member, she was perfectly free to leave the household whenever she wanted, even against the wishes of the family head (art. 1127). Perhaps even more important, like any other family member, she could not be expelled by him without just cause (art. 1128). In these respects, the ruling decidedly improved a concubine's position under the law.

But now that maintenance had come to be detached from property and attached to people instead, a widowed concubine suffered the same fate as a widowed daughter-in-law. For a concubine, just as for a widowed daughter-in-law, maintenance now depended entirely on cohabitation as a family member (art. 1114). Once she ceased to reside with her husband's family, she automatically forfeited her status as one of its members and, with it, her right to support.

Under the new legal order, the reasons for a widowed concubine's estrangement from her deceased husband's family were immaterial, as a Supreme Court case of 1935 makes clear. Concubine Yan Li Shi's husband, Yan Tingrui of Tianjin, had disappeared and was presumed dead, after which time she continued to live with his wife and son. In her suit against them, she charged them with all manner of abuse and requested the means to live separately. She won her suit at the Tianjin District Court and the Hebei Superior Court, both of which were still operating under the old rights of maintenance, but lost at the Supreme Court. It ruled that if a concubine was not willing to live with her family head's kin, no matter the reasons, she could not claim maintenance from them (*Sifa gongbao* [Nanjing], Dec. 10, 1935: 28–30).

The difference between a widowed concubine's right to maintenance under the old laws and under the new is illustrated well in an earlier case, filed at the Beijing District Court in late 1930. According to the plaintiff, Cui Zhang Shi, her husband Cui Hanchen's first wife (*qianqi*) suffered from mental illness (*shenjingbing*) and was unable to take care of the family. Consequently, in 1927, he had married her in a formal ceremony as his second wife (*erfang qishi*), whereupon she had entered the household, taken charge of the family, and assisted him in his financial affairs. After his death in the summer of 1930, her relationship with his first wife and his children and grandchildren, never good, became intolerable. She had no choice but to leave the Cui household and seek shelter with her natal family. She was now asking as a wife for a share of the family property.

The defendants—Cui Hanchen's first wife, a daughter, and two grandsons—maintained that the plaintiff was just a prostitute with whom Cui Hanchen had had an illicit relationship. She could not even claim to be a concubine, much less a wife, since she had not even lived with Hanchen, but would just steal into the house late at night to spend time with him and then leave by morning. As neither a wife nor a concubine, she had absolutely no claim against them.

The Beijing District Court found that Cui Zhang Shi had in fact lived in the Cui household for several years. Since Cui Hanchen was already married, legally she could be no more than his concubine, regardless of the ceremony that had cemented their relationship. But as a concubine, she was fully entitled to support. It would be best if she could reside with the defendants, the court wrote, but since she found it impossible to do so, they were still obligated to provide for her maintenance. As to the amount, the court determined that Cui Hanchen's estate of 24 houses and 2,900 mu of land was worth 100,000 yuan. Out of that, Cui Zhang Shi was to receive a lump sum settlement of 5,000 yuan, the interest from which would yield the 30 to 40 yuan a month she needed for her living expenses.

The defendants appealed the decision to the Hebei Superior Court. At this level, they changed tack and argued that since the new civil code did not recognize the legal status of concubine, they were obligated to support her only as long as she remained a member of the family. With her departure, she had lost her status as family member and thus her right to maintenance.

Their argument did not prevail. The Hebei Superior Court noted that their understanding of maintenance under the civil code was correct, but pointed out that Cui Zhang Shi had become a concubine in the Cui household before the code took effect. Consequently, the applicable laws on maintenance were the old ones, under which cohabitation was not required. The Superior Court then went on to affirm her right to the 5,000 yuan, as did the Supreme Court on further appeal (Beijing: 65-5-135-138). As we saw earlier, timing could make all the difference in the outcome of a case.

Ironically, under the terms of the code, a concubine who had never lived with her husband's family stood a better legal chance of obtaining maintenance from them after his death than a concubine who had. Nothing in the code prevented a man from having two (or more) households, with a wife and children by her in one and a concubine and children by her in the other. For the legal options available to a concubine in such a situation, let us take the following case.

In 1940, a wife, Ding Zhu Shuying (45 sui), and her three adult children brought suit at the Shanghai First Special District Court against her husband's "mistress" (*pinfu*), Ding Wu Huizhen (44 sui), and her young adopted son. In her plaint, Ding Zhu Shuying explained that after the death of her husband, Ding Congdao, earlier that year, the defendant Wu Huizhen had engaged a lawyer and had placed an announcement in local newspapers claiming that she was his legal wife and that no one else had the right to inherit his property. In the circumstances, the plaintiffs said, they had no choice but to bring suit to foil the defendants' plot to seize the property and to affirm their status as his legal wife and offspring. They claimed that Ding Congdao and Wu Huizhen had just been living together (*pinju*) and that since she was just his mistress, she had no legal status as a family member and was thus not entitled to any property. The same, they argued, held true for the adopted son, for the code specified that an adoption was legally binding only if it had the agreement of both spouses (art. 1074), and the plaintiff Ding Zhu Shuying had obviously not been a party to it.

In her defense, Wu Huizhen, though admitting that she and Ding Congdao had not gone through a formal wedding ceremony, nevertheless insisted that they were husband and wife. They had maintained a household together since 1932; he had provided for all of her expenses; they had adopted a son together; and he had referred to her as his wife in conversations and letters with his friends. Clearly, their intention was to live together as a family, and as his wife and son, they were entitled to inherit his property.

The judge found for the plaintiffs, but added a caveat that left the door open for the defendants. He ruled that as a mistress and not a legally wedded wife, Wu Huizhen had no right to inherit a share of Ding's property,[9] and that the young boy was not Ding's legally adopted son, since he had not been adopted jointly with Ding's wife. Nevertheless, the judge was convinced that both were legally entitled to continued support from Ding's property by reason of article 1123, which stipulated that "persons who are not relatives but who live together in one household with the object of sharing a life in common permanently are deemed to be members of the house." Clearly, Ding Congdao had had such an objective in mind in his relationship with Wu Huizhen, since they had shared a domicile and had "adopted" a son together, albeit illegally. As members of his household, she and the boy had the right to a share of his property, as provided in article 1149 that "[a] person who received maintenance from the deceased continuously during the latter's life-time shall be assigned a certain portion of the deceased's property by the family council." Since Ding had supported Wu Huizhen and the boy during his lifetime, his estate ought to continue that support after his death (Shanghai: 180-1-48). The judge could not bestow a settlement upon them, constrained as he was by legal procedure (Wu Hui-

9. Had Wu Huizhen and Ding Congdao gone through a ritual that conformed to the code's requirements for a legally valid marriage (an open ceremony in the presence of two or more witnesses), she would have been entitled to inherit some of his property. In 1940, the Judicial Yuan ruled that so long as a bigamous marriage was not legally annulled by court order, the woman held the status of wife and had the right to inherit a share of her husband's property equal in value to half of the first wife's share (*SJQ*: no. 1985).

zhen and her son being the defendants and not the plaintiffs in the suit), but his decision might well have paved the way for another suit.

Cases from newspapers show that other concubines who lived in separate households did in fact avail themselves of those two articles to secure maintenance from their deceased husbands' families. In Shanghai in 1932, the concubine Chen Baoqin (29 sui) successfully brought suit against the wife and mother of her deceased husband, Fang Wenxue, securing a maintenance allowance of 200 yuan a month (*Shenbao*, Aug. 30, 1932). Similarly, in 1934, also in Shanghai, Hu Xue Shi, a former prostitute who had lived with the deceased merchant Hu Ganqing in a separate residence, won a judgment against the dead man's son for a maintenance allowance of 100 yuan a month (*Shenbao*, March 19, April 2, 16, 22, 1934). These women secured those favorable judgments not on the basis of their status as concubines, but on the basis of their status as members of their family heads' households.

The civil code's impact on a concubine's rights to property was thus plainly mixed, in certain circumstances granting her rights she had not previously had, but in others denying her rights she had had before. The important point is that whatever rights and duties she had under the civil code came to her not because she was a concubine, since the code did not recognize her as such, but rather because of her roles as a daughter, sister, mother, grandmother, and/or family member. A concubine no longer legally existed as a concubine.

To a very large extent, the code's architects, like the Daliyuan before them, had created a legal fiction for the sake of monogamy. Neither the Daliyuan nor the GMD lawmakers criminalized concubinage, thus sanctioning its continued social existence. Yet at the same time, they both insisted on the principle of "one husband–one wife" as the law of the land. The Daliyuan, bent on reversing the late imperial trend toward according concubines the same rights as wives, assigned to them at every turn different sets of legal rights and responsibilities. In so doing, it created the fiction that "China upholds monogamy, since concubines are not in fact legally wives." The GMD lawmakers took the fiction one step further by writing concubines out of legal existence altogether: "China upholds monogamy, since concubines no longer exist in law." But legal fictions or not, these solutions to the problem of concubinage had very real consequences for a concubine's legal claims to property.

Conclusion

A focus on women in their various roles shows that household division and patrilineal succession were two separate processes and conceptual complexes with different implications for property inheritance. The one governed inheritance when a man had birth sons, and the other when he did not. For women, it made all the difference whether they were women in the presence of men or women in the absence of men. Women's rights in household division did not change in the imperial period; from the Song on, they possessed only a claim to dowry and to maintenance. But their rights in patrilineal succession changed substantially.

The imperial period, as we have seen, was characterized by three distinctly different regimes of patrilineal succession. First, in the Song, women could still inherit by default in the absence of men. Patrilineal succession had not yet become a universal legal requirement. In the early Ming, women's rights underwent a sharp contraction with the adoption of mandatory nephew succession. A daughter could no longer inherit in default of brothers, but had to defer to all of her paternal cousins out to fourth cousins. Similarly, a widow no longer had the right to inherit in default of sons, but was merely to serve as the custodian of the property, holding it intact for the required heir (the lineage nephew most closely related to the deceased), whom she herself was now legally obligated to adopt. In the mid-Qing, finally, a widow's custodial powers expanded greatly with new legislation that permitted her free choice among lineage nephews. In that, the law came to recognize what had been long-standing practice in the late Ming and early Qing: judges had been rewarding widows for their chastity by giving them greater latitude in the selection of an heir.

The group most heavily impacted by these changes in women's rights were the father-husband's agnatic male kin. From no rights of inheritance in the face of a surviving widow or daughter, they came to take precedence in the rigidly fixed system of mandatory nephew succession in the early Ming. Although they continued to retain their rights in the Qing, they lost ground as the code was amended to give widows the exclusive say in which nephew was to inherit.

Past scholarship has not grasped these changes because it did not separate out patrilineal succession from household division, and it did not separate the two because it considered inheritance principally from the perspective of men. In that light, the two processes merely reinforced each other as two sides of the same coin of inheritance by sons. That is the basic view of both Niida Noboru and Shiga Shūzō, arguably the two giants in the field. Both assume a complete congruency between household division and patrilineal succession, and both, as a consequence, assume an essential continuity in inheritance throughout the imperial period.[1] It is only when patrilineal succession is separated out from household division and analyzed on its own terms that we can fully grasp the patterns of change in inheritance in imperial China.

For the Republican period as well, it is essential to see the two as separate systems with different conceptual underpinnings and different consequences. To be sure, changes in one affected the other, but inheritance as a whole could not be completely revamped without overturning the separate logics and processes of both.

The early Republican period was a time of transition. The Qing code and its provisions on inheritance remained in force, adopted by the early Republican authorities as the law of the land. The Dali-yuan therefore operated within the legal frameworks of household division and patrilineal succession. Yet, at the same time, it interpreted the old laws to give widows complete autonomy in the choice of a successor. If by the mid-Qing, a widow no longer had to follow the lineage order in her selection of a nephew as heir, she could now bypass a nephew altogether. The high court's rulings effectively put

---

1. As discussed in Chapter One, Niida and Shiga do address the question of stronger daughter inheritance rights in the Song. But both consider Song law to be unique in this respect (albeit for different reasons), and both otherwise see basic continuity throughout imperial times.

an end to mandatory nephew succession. That was the most important change in inheritance in the Daliyuan period, and it came wholly within the laws on patrilineal succession.

The Guomindang lawmakers were determined to overturn the very logic of the old inheritance regime, not just to reinterpret it. They focused their energies on patrilineal succession, in their view the source of the "feudal" ideas and practices that disenfranchised women. If they dismantled patrilineal succession and replaced it with individual property (as opposed to family property) and gender equality (as opposed to inheritance by sons only), they assumed, they would deal a death blow to the old inheritance regime and women would thereby gain the same rights as men.

What actually happened ran counter to their expectations in several ways. First, by failing to target household division as a separate process, they unwittingly allowed it to continue. Their assumption was that granting women equal inheritance rights would spell the end of sons-only household division. But, in fact, their Western-derived inheritance theories took effect only upon the death of the property owner, with women inheriting equally only postmortem. That in effect gave legal sanction for old household division practices to continue under the rubric of gift-giving during the property owner's lifetime. A father could disinherit his daughters simply by parceling out his property as gifts before his death. As a result, daughters did not gain the inheritance rights the lawmakers had intended for them.

Second, the lawmakers took away the custodial powers that a widow had enjoyed under earlier law. Once her husband died, his estate passed in shares to his heirs as separate individuals, regardless of her wishes. She no longer had the right to adopt an heir as a way to secure her control over his property. To be sure, the lawmakers granted a widowed wife a set portion of her husband's property, but that gain in inheritance came at the cost of her custodial powers over his entire estate. Their elimination of patrilineal succession had an even greater impact on widowed daughters-in-law and widowed concubines, for the loss of custodial rights was not balanced by any gain in inheritance rights to their husbands' property. These issues did not occur to them because they did not consider inheritance from the point of view of women in their different capacities.

The "modern" law of the Guomindang therefore had mixed consequences for women. There was no simple transition from a regime of no property rights for women to a regime of full property rights for women, as the lawmakers intended. Instead, the practices of household division persisted, albeit in a different legal guise. And the custodial powers enjoyed by women under patrilineal succession vanished completely, only to be partially offset by the acquisition of inheritance rights. In the end, women lost even as they gained under the Republican Civil Code.

It might be well to reflect briefly, by way of closing, on the implications of this book for women's history. When I began this study, I was not at all certain whether it would merely tell an untold part of the story of inheritance or whether it would have broader implications for our understanding of late imperial and Republican inheritance in general. Now at the end of the project, I can say that the focus on women led me to an entirely different understanding not only of women's inheritance, but of the very logics and consequences of the two conceptual complexes governing inheritance. The women's story, then, is not just about women, but about rethinking the subject of inheritance as a whole.

References

I have reduced a few of the Chinese works and archival sources with excessively long titles to short form. *Zhili gaodeng shenpanting pandu jiyao*, for example, is cited as simply *Zhili* 1915. The Tang, Song, and Ming imperial legal codes are cited by dynasty name alone (Tang = *Tanglü shuyi*, Song = *Song xingtong*, and Ming = *Minglü jijie fuli*). All references to the Qing code are to Xue Yunsheng's 1905 compilation, as edited and numbered by Huang Tsing-chia. The first number refers to a statute, and the second, if any, to a substatute. The Civil Code of the Republic of China (1930) is cited by article number alone. Other works are abbreviated as follows:

DJQ *Daliyuan jieshili quanwen*
DPQ *Daliyuan panjueli quanshu*
QMJ *Minggong shupan qingmingji*
SJQ *Sifayuan jieshili quanwen*

Allee, Mark A. 1994. *Law and Local Society in Late Imperial China: Northern Taiwan in the Nineteenth Century*. Stanford, Calif.: Stanford University Press.

Bao Shichen 包世臣 [1888]. 1968. *An Wu sizhong* 安吳四種 (Four treatises on governing Wu). Reprint. Taibei: Wenhai chubanshe.

Baodixian dang'an 寶坻縣檔案 (Baodi County Archives). First Historical Archives, Beijing. [Classified under Shuntianfu; cited by juan number and lunar date.]

Barlow, Tani. 1991. "Theorizing Woman: *Funü, Guojia, Jiating* [Chinese Women, Chinese State, Chinese Family]," *Genders*, no. 10 (Spring): 132–60.

Baxian dang'an 巴縣檔案 (Baxian Archives). Sichuan Provincial Archives, Chengdu. [Cited by category number, juan number, and lunar date.]

Beijing difang fayuan 北京地方法院 (Beijing District Court). Beijing Municipal Archives, Beijing. [Cases cited by catalog number.]

Bernhardt, Kathryn. 1996. "A Ming-Qing Transition in Chinese Women's History? The Perspective from Law." In Hershatter et al., pp. 42–58.

———. 1995. "The Inheritance Rights of Daughters: The Song Anomaly?" *Modern China*, 21.3 (July): 269–309.

———. 1994. "Women and the Law: Divorce in the Republican Period." In Bernhardt & Huang 1994b: 187–214.

Bernhardt, Kathryn, and Philip C. C. Huang. 1994a. "Civil Law in Qing and Republican China: The Issues." In Bernhardt & Huang 1994b: 1–12.

———, eds. 1994b. *Civil Law in Qing and Republican China*. Stanford, Calif.: Stanford University Press.

Birge, Bettine. 1995. "Levirate Marriage and the Revival of Widow Chastity in Yüan China," *Asia Major*, 3d series, 7.2: 107–46.

———. 1992. "Women and Property in Sung Dynasty China (960–1279): Neo-Confucianism and Social Change in Chien-chou, Fukien." Ph.D. dissertation, Columbia University.

Buxbaum, David C., ed. 1978. *Chinese Family Law and Social Change in Historical and Comparative Perspective*. Seattle: University of Washington Press.

Cai Xin 蔡新 [n.d.]. 1972. "Jisi shuo" 繼嗣說 (On establishing an heir). In He Changling, 59: 2b–3b.

Carlitz, Katherine. 1997. "Shrines, Governing-Class Identity, and the Cult of Widow Fidelity in Mid-Ming Jiangnan," *Journal of Asian Studies*, 56.3 (Aug.): 612–40.

Chen Peng 陳鵬. 1990. *Zhongguo hunyin shigao* 中國婚姻史稿 (A draft history of marriage in China). Beijing: Zhonghua shuju.

Chen Zhichao 陳智超. 1987. "Songshi yanjiu de zhengui shiliao—Ming keben 'Minggong shupan qingmingji' jieshao" 宋史研究的珍貴史料——明刻本'名公書判清明集' 介紹 (Valuable historical materials for research on Song history: Introduction to the Ming edition of the "Collection of Lucid Decisions by Celebrated Judges"). In *Minggong shupan qingmingji*: 645–86.

Cheng, F. T., tr. [1923]. 1976. *The Chinese Supreme Court Decisions Relating to General Principles of Civil Law, Obligations, and Commercial Law*. Reprint. Arlington, Va.: University Publications of America. [Originally published in Beijing by the Commission on Extraterritoriality.]

Cheng He 程龢 [n.d.]. 1972. *Zhe hong zhao yin* 浙鴻爪印 (Traces of my correspondence [while serving as an official] in Zhejiang). Reprint. Taibei: Wenhai chubanshe.

Chikusa Tatsuo. 1978. "Succession to Ancestral Sacrifices and Adoption of Heirs to the Sacrifices: As Seen from an Inquiry into Customary Institutions in Manchuria." In Buxbaum, pp. 151–75.

The China Law Review.

Chiu, Vermier Y. 1966. *Marriage Laws and Customs of China*. Hong Kong: Chinese University of Hong Kong.

Chow Kai-wing. 1994. *The Rise of Confucian Ritualism in Late Imperial China: Ethics, Classics, and Lineage Discourse.* Stanford, Calif.: Stanford University Press.

Ch'ü T'ung-tsu. 1961. *Law and Society in Traditional China.* Paris: Mouton.

The Civil Code of the Republic of China [1930]. 1976. Reprint. Arlington, Va.: University Publications of America.

Conner, Alison W. 1994. "Lawyers and the Legal Profession During the Republican Period." In Bernhardt & Huang 1994b: 215–48.

Da Ming huidian 大明會典 (Collected statutes of the Great Ming) [1587]. 1964. Reprint. Taibei: Dongnan shubaoshe.

Da Qing xianxing xinglü anyu 大清現行刑律按語 (The Criminal Code of the Great Qing Currently in Use, with commentary). 1909. Ed. Shen Jiaben 沈家本 et al. Beijing: Falüguan.

Dai Zhaojia 戴兆佳 [1721 (date of Preface)]. 1970. *Tiantai zhilüe* 天臺治略 (Policies for governing Tiantai [county]). Reprint. Taibei: Chengwen chubanshe.

Daliyuan 大理院. Second Historical Archives, Nanjing. [Cases cited by catalog number.]

Daliyuan jieshili quanwen 大理院解釋例全文 (Complete texts of Daliyuan interpretations). 1931. Ed. Guo Wei 郭衛. Shanghai: Shanghai faxue bianyishe.

Daliyuan panjueli quanshu 大理院判決例全書 (Complete collection of Daliyuan judgments on important cases) [1933]. 1972. Ed. Guo Wei 郭衛. Reprint. Taibei: Chengwen chubanshe.

Dan-Xin dang'an 淡新檔案 (Danshui Subprefecture and Xinzhu County Archives). Catalogued by Dai Yanhui 戴炎輝. Microfilm copy, UCLA East Asian Library.

Dardess, John W. 1983. *Confucianism and Autocracy: Professional Elites in the Founding of the Ming Dynasty.* Berkeley: University of California Press.

Dawanbao 大晚報 (China evening news). Shanghai.

Deng Yao 鄧瑤 [n.d.]. 1972. "Yu youren lun zhi si gu hou shu" 與友人論姪嗣姑後書 (A letter to a friend on a nephew succeeding a paternal aunt as heir). In Sheng Kang, 67: 53a–54a.

Dong Jiazun 董家遵 [1937]. 1991. "Lidai jiefu lienü de tongji" 歷代節婦烈女的統計 (Statistics on chaste widows and virtuous women in the successive dynasties). Reprint in Gao Hongxing 高洪興 et al., eds., *Funü fengsu kao* 婦女風俗考 (Examination of customs regarding women). Shanghai: Shanghai wenyi chubanshe, pp. 578–84. [Originally published in *Xiandai shixue*, 3.2.]

Dong Pei 董沛. 1884 (date of Preface). *Hui'anzhai biyu* 晦闇齋筆語 (Words from the pen of the Hui'an Studio).

———. 1883 (date of Preface). *Rudong panyu* 汝東判語 (Judgments from east of the Ru River).

———. 1881 (date of Preface). *Wuping zhuiyan* 吳平贅言 (Superfluous words from Wuping).

Ebrey, Patricia Buckley. 1993. *The Inner Quarters: Marriage and the Lives of Chinese Women in the Sung Period.* Berkeley: University of California Press.

————. 1991a. *Confucianism and Family Rituals in Imperial China: A Social History of Writing about Rites.* Princeton, N.J.: Princeton University Press.

————. 1991b. "Shifts in Marriage Finance from the Sixth to the Thirteenth Century." In Watson & Ebrey, pp. 97–132.

————. 1986. "Concubines in Sung China," *Journal of Family History,* 11.1: 1–24.

————. 1984a. "Conceptions of the Family in the Sung Dynasty," *Journal of Asian Studies,* 43.2 (Feb.): 219–45.

————. 1984b. *Family and Property in Sung China: Yuan Ts'ai's Precepts for Social Life.* Princeton, N.J.: Princeton University Press.

Ebrey, Patricia Buckley, and James L. Watson, eds. 1986. *Kinship Organization in Late Imperial China.* Berkeley: University of California Press.

Elvin, Mark. 1984. "Female Virtue and the State in China," *Past and Present,* no. 104 (Aug.): 111–52.

Falü cao'an huibian 法律草案匯編 (Compendium of the draft legal codes). 1973. Taibei: Chengwen chubanshe.

Fan Zengxiang 樊增祥 [1910]. 1971. *Fanshan zhengshu* 樊山政書 (Records of Mr. Fanshan's administration). Reprint. Taibei: Wenhai chubanshe.

———— [1897]. 1978. *Fanshan pipan* 樊山批判 (Mr. Fanshan's judicial decisions). Reprint. Taibei: Wenhai chubanshe.

Farmer, Edward L. 1995. *Zhu Yuanzhang and Early Ming Legislation: The Reordering of Chinese Society Following the Era of Mongol Rule.* Leiden: E. J. Brill.

Fuma Susumu 夫馬進. 1993. "Chūgoku Min-Shin jidai ni okeru kafu no chii to kyōsei saikon no fūshū" 中國明清時代における寡婦の地位と強制再婚の風習 (The position of widows and the custom of forced remarriage in the Ming and Qing periods). In Maekawa Kazuya 前川和也, ed., *Kazoku, setai, kamon: Kōgyōka izen no sekai kara* 家族, 世帶, 家門: 工業化以前の世界から (Family, household, clan: Since the preindustrial world). Kyoto: Minerva shobō, pp. 249–87.

Gao Tingyao 高庭瑤. 1862. *Huanyou jilüe* 宦游紀略 (Brief account of my life as an official).

"Geji shenpanting shiban zhangcheng" 各級審判廳試辦章程 (Provisional regulations for the courts of different levels). [1907]. 1911. In *Xin faling jiyao* 新法令輯要 (Important new laws and regulations). Shanghai: Shangwu yinshuguan.

The German Civil Code. 1907. Tr. and annotated, with a Historical Introduction and Appendixes, by Chung Hui Wang [Wang Chonghui] 王寵惠. London: Stevens & Sons.

Gui Danmeng 桂丹盟 [1863]. 1972. *Huanyou jilüe* 宦游紀略 (Brief account of my life as an official). Reprint. Taibei: Guangwen shuju.

Gujin tushu jicheng 古今圖書集成 (Imperial compendium of books of all ages) [1728]. 1985. Reprint. Beijing: Zhonghua shuju.

Hanley, Susan B., and Arthur P. Wolf, eds. 1985. *Family and Population in East Asian History*. Stanford, Calif.: Stanford University Press.

Harrell, Stevan, ed. 1995. *Chinese Historical Microdemography*. Berkeley: University of California Press.

He Changling 賀長齡, ed. [1826]. 1972. *Huangchao jingshi wenbian* 皇朝經世文編 (Collected essays on statecraft from the reigning dynasty). Reprint. Taibei: Wenhai chubanshe.

Hershatter, Gail, Emily Honig, Jonathan N. Lipman, and Randall Stross, eds. 1996. *Remapping China: Fissures in Historical Terrain*. Stanford, Calif.: Stanford University Press.

Holmgren, Jennifer. 1986. "Observations on Marriage and Inheritance Practices in Early Mongol and Yuan Society, with Particular Reference to the Levirate," *Journal of Asian History*, 20.2: 127–92.

———. 1993. "The Economic Foundations of Virtue: Widow Remarriage in Early and Modern China," *Australian Journal of Chinese Affairs*, no. 13 (Jan.): 1–27.

Hu Jitang 胡季堂 [1773]. 1972. "Qing ding jisi tiaogui shu" 請定繼嗣條規疏 (Explication of my request for the establishment of regulations on succession). In He Changling, 59: 5a–6a.

Hu Xuechun 胡學醇. 1851 (date of Preface). *Wenxin yiyu* 問心一隅 (Examining a corner of my conscience).

Huang, Philip C. C. Forthcoming. *Code, Custom, and Legal Practice in China: The Republic and the Qing Compared*.

———. 1996. *Civil Justice in China: Representation and Practice in the Qing*. Stanford, Calif.: Stanford University Press.

———. 1991. "Civil Justice in Rural China During the Qing and the Republic." Paper presented at the conference on Civil Law in Chinese History, UCLA, Aug. 12–14.

———. 1985. *The Peasant Economy and Social Change in North China*. Stanford, Calif.: Stanford University Press.

Huang Wensu 黃文肅. n.d. *Mianzhai xiansheng Huang Wensu gongwen ji* 勉齋先生黃文肅公文集 (Collected writings of Mr. Mianzhai, Huang Wensu). Appendix to *Minggong shupan qingmingji*: 569–613.

Huang Zhangjian 黃彰健, comp. 1979. *Mingdai lüli huibian* 明代律例匯編 (Compendium of Ming statutes and substatutes). Taibei: Academia Sinica.

Itabashi Shinichi 板橋眞一. 1993. "Sōdai no kozetsu zaisan to joshi no zaisanken o megutte" 宋代の戶絶財産と女子の財産權をめぐて (On extinct household property and female property rights in the Song period). In *Yanagida Setsuko sensei koki kinen: Chūgoku no dentō shakai to kazoku* 柳田節子先生古稀記念: 中國の伝統社會と家族 (In commemoration of Professor Yanagida Setsuko's seventieth birthday: Traditional society and family in China). Tokyo: Kyūko sho-in, pp. 365–82.

Jamieson, George. 1921. *Chinese Family and Commercial Law*. Shanghai: Kelly & Walsh.

Jaschok, Maria. 1988. *Concubines and Bondservants: A Social History*. London: Zed Books.

Ji Dakui 紀大奎 [n.d.]. 1972. "Zongfa lun" 宗法論 (On the descent-line system). In He Changling, 58: 2a–5b.

Jiaxingfu zhi 嘉興府志 (Gazetteer of Jiaxing prefecture). 1879.

Jichengfa xianjue gedian shencha yijian shu 繼承法先決各點審查意見書 (Statement of opinion on the preliminary problems of the inheritance law) [1930]. 1960. In *Zhonghua minguo fazhi ziliao huibian* 中華民國法制資料匯編 (Compendium of source materials on the legal system of the Republic of China). Taibei: Sifa xingzhengbu, no. 3: 19–24.

Jing Junjian 經君健. 1994. "Legislation Related to the Civil Economy in the Qing Dynasty." Tr. Matthew Sommer. In Bernhardt & Huang 1994b: 42–84.

———. 1993. *Qingdai shehui de jianmin dengji* 清代社會的賤民等級 (The status of "mean" people in Qing society). Hangzhou: Zhejiang renmin chubanshe.

Jingshi gaodeng shenpanting 京師高等審判廳 (Capital [Jingshi] Superior Court). Second Historical Archives, Nanjing. [Cases cited by catalog number.]

Kuai Demo 蒯德模. 1874 (date of Preface). *Wuzhong pandu* 吳中判牘 (Judgments rendered while serving in Wu).

Langlois, John D., Jr. 1981. "Political Thought in Chin-hua Under Mongol Rule." In Langlois, ed., *China Under Mongol Rule*. Princeton: Princeton University Press, pp. 137–85.

"Law Governing the Application of the Book of Inheritance of the Civil Code." 1930. In *The Civil Code of the Republic of China*.

Lee, Bernice June. 1975. "The Change in the Legal Status of Chinese Women in Civil Matters from Traditional Law to the Republican Civil Code." Ph.D. dissertation, University of Sydney.

Lee, James, and Cameron Campbell. 1997. *Fate and Fortune in Rural China: Social Organization and Population Behavior in Liaoning, 1774–1873*. Cambridge, Eng.: Cambridge University Press.

Lee, James, Cameron Campbell, and Lawrence Anthony. 1995. "A Century of Mortality in Rural Liaoning, 1774–1873." In Harrell, pp. 163–82.

Li Chenyu 李陳玉. 1636. *Tuisitang ji* 退思堂集 (Writings from Tuisi Hall).

Li Jia 李佳. 1904 (date of Preface). *Boyuan suozhi* 柏垣瑣志 (A trifling record of my service as a judicial commissioner).

Li Jun 李鈞. 1833. *Panyu lu cun* 判語錄存 (My surviving judgments).

Li Qing 李清 [n.d.; late Ming]. 1989. *Zheyu xinyu* 折獄新語 (New words on deciding lawsuits). Ed. Huadong zhengfa xueyuan falü guji zhengli yanjiusuo 華東政法學院法律古籍整理研究所. Jilin: Jilin chubanshe.

Li Tao 李燾 [n.d.]. 1974. *Xu zizhi tongjian changbian* 續資治通鑒長編 (Expanded version of the "Comprehensive Mirror of Aid in Governance"). Reprint. Taibei: Shijie shuju.

Li Xin 李新. n.d. *Kua'ao ji* 跨鰲集 (The writings of Mr. Kua'ao).

Li Yu 李漁. 1667 (date of Preface). *Zizhi xinshu* 資治新書 (A new book to assist in governance).

Li Zhifang 李之芳. 1654. *Ji ting cao* 棘聽草 (My service as a judge).

Liang Zhangju 梁章鉅 [1875]. 1969. *Tui'an suibi* 退菴隨筆 (Miscellaneous jottings of Mr. Tui'an). Reprint. Taibei: Wenhai chubanshe.

Liu Jihua 劉紀華 [1934]. 1991. "Zhongguo zhenjie guannian de lishi yanbian" 中國貞節觀念的歷史演變 (The historical evolution of the concept of chastity in China). In Gao Hongxing 高洪興 et al., eds., *Funü fengsu kao* 婦女風俗考 (Examination of customs regarding women). Shanghai: Shanghai wenyi chubanshe, pp. 515–44. [Originally published in *Shehui xuejie*, vol. 8.]

Liu Kezhuang 劉克莊. n.d. *Houcun xiansheng da quanji* 後村先生大全集 (Complete collected writings of Mr. Houcun). Sibu congkan ed.

Liu Langquan 劉朗泉. 1931. "Woguo nüzi qude caichan jichengquan de jingguo" 我國女子取得財產繼承權的經過 (The process by which daughters in our country acquired property inheritance rights), *Funü zazhi*, 17.3 (March): 13–21.

Liu Ruyu 劉如玉 [1860 (date of Preface)]. 1972. *Qinshentang zizhi guanshu ou cun* 勤慎堂自治官書偶存 (Remnants of the official documents on governance of Qinshen Hall). Reprint. Taibei: Wenhai chubanshe.

Liu Ts'ui-jung (Liu Cuirong) 劉翠溶. 1995. "A Comparison of Lineage Populations in South China, ca. 1300–1900." In Harrell, pp. 94–120.

———. 1985. "The Demography of Two Chinese Clans in Hsiao-shan, Chekiang, 1650–1850." In Hanley & Wolf, pp. 13–61.

———. 1983. "Ming Qing renkou zhi zengzhi yu qianyi" 明清人口之增殖與遷移 (Population growth and migration in the Ming and Qing). In Hsu Cho-yun, Mao Han-kuang, and Liu Ts'ui-jung, eds., *Zhongguo shehui jingji shi yantaohui lunwenji* 中國社會經濟史研討會論文集 (Collection of papers from the conference on Chinese socioeconomic history). Taibei: Center for Chinese Studies.

Liufa quanshu 六法全書 (Complete text of the six codes). 1932. Shanghai: Shanghai faxue bianyishe.

Lu Chongxing 盧崇興. 1739 (date of Preface). *Shou He riji* 守禾日記 (A diary of my service in Jiaxing).

Lu Jianzeng 盧見曾 [1725 (date of Preface)]. 1876. *Yajiang xinzheng* 雅江新政 (Reforming government in the Ya River region [Sichuan]). Reprint. Chengdu: Huiyuantang.

Lu Weiqi 陸維祺. 1893. *Xue zhi ou cun* 學治偶存 (Remnants of learning and governance).

Lu Xinyuan 陸心源 [n.d.]. 1967. *Songshi yi* 宋史翼 (Supplement to the "History of the Song"). Reprint. Taibei: Wenhai chubanshe.

Lu Ying 逯英. 1746 (date of Preface). *Cheng qiu lu* 誠求錄 (A record of a sincere quest).

Luo Ding 羅鼎 [1933]. 1946. *Minfa jicheng lun* 民法繼承論 (On inheritance in the Civil Code). Reprint. Shanghai: Huiwentang xinji shuju.

Ma Duanlin 馬端臨 [1324]. 1963. *Wenxian tongkao* 文獻通考 (Comprehensive examination of documents). Reprint. Taibei: Xinxing shuju.

Macauley, Melissa. 1988. *Social Power and Legal Culture: Litigation Masters in Late Imperial China*. Stanford, Calif.: Stanford University Press.

Mann, Susan. 1997. *Precious Records: Women in China's Long Eighteenth Century*. Stanford, Calif.: Stanford University Press.

———. 1991. "Grooming a Daughter for Marriage: Brides and Wives in the Mid-Ch'ing Period." In Watson & Ebrey, pp. 204–30.

———. 1987. "Widows in the Kinship, Class, and Community Structures of Qing Dynasty China," *Journal of Asian Studies*, 46.1 (Feb.): 37–56.

McKnight, Brian E. 1992. *Law and Order in Sung China*. Cambridge, Eng.: Cambridge University Press.

———. 1987. "From Statute to Precedent: An Introduction to Sung Law and Its Transformation." In McKnight, ed., *Law and the State in Traditional East Asia: Six Studies on the Sources of East Asian Law*. Honolulu: University of Hawaii Press, pp. 111–31.

———. 1971. *Village and Bureaucracy in Southern Sung China*. Chicago: University of Chicago Press.

Meijer, Marinus Johan [1950]. 1976. *The Introduction of Modern Criminal Law in China*. Reprint. Arlington, Va.: University Publications of America.

Minggong shupan qingmingji 名公書判清明集 (Collection of lucid decisions by celebrated judges) [Song]. 1987. Reprint. Beijing: Zhonghua shuju.

Minguo Hangzhoufu zhi 民國杭州府志 (Republican gazetteer of Hangzhou prefecture) [1916]. 1993. Reprint. Shanghai: Shanghai shudian.

Minglü jijie fuli 明律集解附例 (The Ming code with collected commentaries and appended substatutes) [1898]. 1969. Reprint. Taibei: Chengwen chubanshe.

Nagata Mie 永田三枝. 1991. "Nansōki ni okeru josei no zaisanken ni tsuite" 南宋期における女性の財產權について (Female property rights in the Southern Song period), *Hokudai shigaku*, no. 31 (Aug.): 1–15.

Nakada Kaoru 中田薫 [1943]. 1971. "Tō Sō jidai no kazoku kyōsansei" 唐宋時代の家族共產制 (The communal property system of the family in the Tang and Song periods). In Nakada, *Hōseishi ronshū* 法制史論集 (Collected essays on legal history). Reprint. Tokyo: Iwanami shoten, pp. 1295–1360.

Niida Noboru 仁井田陞. 1964. *Chūgoku hōseishi kenkyū: hō to kanshū, hō to dōtoku* 中國法制史研究: 法と慣習, 法と道德 (A study of Chinese legal history: law and custom, law and morality). Tokyo: Tokyo University Press.

———. 1962. *Chūgoku hōseishi kenkyū: dorei nōdo hō, kazoku sonraku hō* 中國法制史研究: 奴隸農奴法, 家族村落法. (A study of Chinese legal history: law of slave and serf, law of family and village). Tokyo: Tokyo University Press.

———. 1942. *Shina mibunhō shi* 支那身分法史 (A history of status law in China). Tokyo: Tōhō bunka gakuin.

————. [1937]. 1967. *Tō Sō hōritsu bunsho no kenkyū* 唐宋法律文書の研究 (A study of the legal documents of the Tang and the Song). Tokyo: Daian.

————, comp. [1933]. 1964. *Tōrei shūi* 唐令拾遺 (A collection of neglected Tang edicts). Tokyo: Tokyo University Press.

————, ed. 1952–58. *Chūgoku nōson kankō chōsa* 中國農村慣行調査 (Investigations of customary practices in rural China). 6 vols. Tokyo: Iwanami.

Nüzi jichengquan xiangjie 女子繼承權詳解 (Detailed explanation of the inheritance rights of daughters) [n.d.]. Shanghai: Shanghai zhongyang shudian.

Pan Shaocan 潘杓燦. 1688 (date of Preface). *Weixin bian* 未信編 (Compilation of the unbelievable).

Pan Weihe 潘維和. 1982. *Zhongguo lici minlü cao'an jiaoshi* 中國歷次民律草案校釋 (Collation and explanation of the successive drafts of the Civil Code of China). Taibei: Hanlin chubanshe.

Panqiao Yeren [pseud.] 盤嶠野人. 1835. *Juguan guaguo lu* 居官寡過錄 (A record of acquitting oneself well as an official).

Qin Huitian 秦蕙田 [n.d.]. 1972. "Bian xiaozong bu lihou" 辨小宗不立後 (Distinguishing [the circumstances under which] heirs are not to be appointed to lesser descent lines). In He Changling, 59: 1b–2a.

Qinding libu zeli 欽定禮部則例 (Imperially endorsed edition of the regulations of the Board of Rites) [1845]. 1966. Reprint. Taibei: Chengwen chubanshe.

Qing huidian shili 清會典事例 (Collected statutes of the Qing, with substatutes based on precedent) [1899]. 1991. Reprint. Beijing: Zhonghua shuju.

Qingyuan tiaofa shilei 慶元條法事類 (Laws of the Qingyuan period) [1203]. 1990. Ed. Xue Yunsheng 薛允升. Reprint. Beijing: Zhongguo shudian.

Qinshufa xianjue gedian shencha yijian shu 親屬法先決各點審查意見書 (Statement of opinion on the preliminary problems of family law) [1930]. 1960. In *Zhonghua minguo fazhi ziliao huibian* 中華民國法制資料匯編 (Compendium of source materials on the legal system of the Republic of China). Taibei: Sifa xingzhengbu, no. 3, pp. 11–18.

Qufu shifan xueyuan lishixi 曲阜師范學院歷史系, ed. 1980– . *Qufu Kongfu dang'an shiliao xuanbian* 曲阜孔府檔案史料選編 (Selection of historical materials from the Kong archives in Qufu). 3 vols. to date. Shandong: Qilu shushe.

Shanghai diyi tequ difang fayuan 上海第一特區地方法院 (Shanghai First Special District Court). Shanghai Municipal Archives, Shanghai. [Cases cited by catalog number.]

Shanxi tongzhi 山西通志 (Comprehensive gazetteer of Shanxi) [1892]. 1990. Reprint. Beijing: Zhonghua shuju.

Shen Jiaben 沈家本 [n.d.]. 1985. *Lidai xingfa kao* 歷代刑法考 (Examination of the penal law of the successive dynasties). Reprint. Beijing: Zhonghua shuju.

Shen ke Yuan dianzhang 沈刻元典章 (Mr. Shen's edition of the "Compendium of Yuan Laws") [1908]. 1985. Reprint. Beijing: Zhongguo shudian.

Shen Yanqing 沈衍慶 [1862]. 1969. *Huaiqing yigao* 槐卿遺稿 (The writings of Huaiqing, posthumously collected). Reprint. Taibei: Wenhai chubanshe.

Shenbao 申報 (Shun pao). Shanghai.

Shenbao nianjian 申報年鑒 (Annual almanac of the *Shun pao*). 1933. Shanghai: Shenbao nianjian she.

Sheng Kang 盛康, ed. [1897]. 1972. *Huangchao jingshi wenbian xubian* 皇朝經世文編續編 (Collected essays on statecraft from the reigning dynasty, continued). Reprint. Taibei: Wenhai chubanshe.

Shibao 時報 (The eastern times). Shanghai.

Shibao 實報 (The truth post). Beijing.

Shiga Shūzō 滋賀秀三. 1978. "Family Property and the Law of Inheritance in Traditional China." In Buxbaum, pp. 109–50.

———. 1967. *Chūgoku kazokuhō no genri* 中國家族法の原理 (Principles of Chinese family law). Tokyo: Sōbunsha.

———. 1953–55. "Chūgoku kazokuhō hokō" 中國家族法補考 (Supplementary studies on Chinese family law), *Kokka gakkai zasshi*. 4 parts. Part 1, 67.5–6 (Nov. 1953): 1–31; part 2, 67.9–10 (Aug. 1954): 54–83; part 3, 67.11–12 (Oct. 1954): 89–123; part 4, 68.7–8 (March 1955): 33–57.

Shishi xinbao 時事新報 (The China times). Shanghai.

Sichuansheng dang'anguan 四川省檔案館, ed. 1991. *Qingdai Baxian dang'an huibian: Qianlong juan* 清代巴縣檔案匯編: 乾隆卷 (Compendium of materials from the Baxian archives of the Qing period: the Qianlong volume). Beijing: Dang'an chubanshe.

Sifa gongbao 司法公報 (Judicial gazette). Nanjing.

Sifayuan jieshili quanwen 司法院解釋例全文 (Complete texts of Judicial Yuan interpretations). 1946. Ed. Guo Wei 郭衛. Shanghai: Shanghai faxue bianyishe.

Smith, Paul J. 1991. *Taxing Heaven's Storehouse: Horses, Bureaucrats, and the Destruction of the Sichuan Tea Industry, 1074–1224*. Cambridge, Mass.: Council on East Asian Studies, Harvard University.

Sommer, Matthew H. 1996. "The Uses of Chastity: Sex, Law, and the Property of Widows in Qing China," *Late Imperial China* 17.2 (Dec.): 77–130.

———. 1994. "Sex, Law, and Society in Late Imperial China." Ph.D. dissertation, University of California, Los Angeles.

Song huiyao jigao 宋會要輯稿 (Amalgamated edition of "Collected Song Documents"). 1964. Ed. Yang Jialuo 楊家駱. Taibei: Shijie shuju, 1964.

Song xingtong 宋刑統 (The Song penal code) [963]. 1984. Ed. Wu Yiru 吳翊如. Reprint. Beijing: Zhonghua shuju.

Songshi 宋史 (History of the Song) [n.d.]. 1977. Reprint. Beijing: Zhonghua shuju.

Sun Dinglie 孫鼎烈. 1904. *Sixizhai jueshi* 四西齋決事 (Decisions from the Sixi Studio).

Taga Akigorō 多賀秋五郎. 1960. *Sōfu no kenkyū* 宗譜の研究 (Research on lineage genealogies). Tokyo: Tōyō bunko.

Taihu limin fu wenjian 太湖理民府文件 (Documents on governing the people in Taihu). Tokyo: Microfilm Service Center, 1990.

Taiwan sifa renshi bian 臺灣私法人事編 (The civil affairs chapters of "Taiwan Private Law"), vol. 4. 1961. Ed. Taiwan yinhang jingji yanjiushi 臺灣銀行經濟研究室. Taibei: Taiwan yinhang. [This is a Chinese translation of parts of the 1910 Japanese work *Taiwan shihō* 臺灣私法 (Taiwan private law).]

Takahashi Yoshirō 高橋芳郎. 1995. "Oya o nakushita musumetachi: Nansōki no iwayuru joshi zaisanken ni tsuite" 親を亡くした女たち――南宋期のいわゆる女子財產權について (Orphaned daughters—The property rights of daughters in the Southern Song), *Tōhoku daigaku Tōyō shi ronshū*, 6 (Jan.): 343–72.

Tang huiyao 唐會要 (Collected Tang documents) [n.d.]. 1991. Reprint. Shanghai: Shanghai guji chubanshe.

Tanglü shuyi 唐律疏議 (Commentary on the Tang code) [n.d.]. 1983. Ed. Liu Junwen 劉俊文. Reprint. Beijing: Zhonghua shuju.

Telford, Ted A. 1995. "Fertility and Population Growth in the Lineages of Tongcheng County, 1520–1661." In Harrell, pp. 48–93.

T'ien Ju-k'ang. 1988. *Male Anxiety and Female Chastity: A Comparative Study of Chinese Ethical Values in Ming-Ch'ing Times*. Leiden: E. J. Brill.

Van der Valk, Marc [1939]. 1969. *An Outline of Modern Chinese Family Law*. Beijing: Henri Vetch. Reprint. Taibei: Chengwen Publishing Co.

Wakefield, David. 1998. *Fenjia: Household Division and Inheritance in Qing and Republican China*. Honolulu: University of Hawaii Press.

Wakeman, Frederic, Jr. 1985. *The Great Enterprise: The Manchu Reconstruction of Imperial Order in Seventeenth-Century China*. 2 vols. Berkeley, Calif.: University of California Press.

Waltner, Ann. 1990. *Getting an Heir: Adoption and the Construction of Kinship in Late Imperial China*. Honolulu: University of Hawaii Press.

Wang Huizu 汪輝祖 [1889]. 1970. *Wang Longzhuang yishu* 汪龍莊遺書 (The writings of Wang Longzhuang, posthumously collected). Reprint. Taibei: Huawen shuju.

——— [1796]. n.d. *Bingta menghen lu* 病榻夢痕錄 (Traces of dreams from a sickbed). Reprint. Taibei: Guangwen shuju.

Wang Wan 汪琬 [n.d.]. 1972. "Zhi hou jie" 置後解 (Explanation of the establishment of an heir). In He Changling, 59: 1a–1b.

Watson, Rubie S. 1991. "Wives, Concubines, and Maids: Servitude and Kinship in the Hong Kong Region, 1900–1940." In Watson & Ebrey, pp. 231–55.

Watson, Rubie S., and Patricia Buckley Ebrey, eds. 1991. *Marriage and Inequality in Chinese Society*. Berkeley: University of California Press.

Wei Tianan 魏天安. 1988. "Songdai 'hujue tiaoguan' kao" 宋代 '戶絕條貫' 考 (Examination of "Regulations on Extinct Households" of the Song period), *Zhongguo jingji shi yanjiu*, no. 3 (March): 31–38.

Wu Guangyao 吳光耀. 1903 (date of Preface). *Xiushan gongdu* 秀山公牘 (Official documents from [my service as magistrate of] Xiushan county).

Wu Hong 吳宏. 1721 (date of Preface). *Zhishang jinglun* 紙上經綸 (Idle speculations on statecraft).

Wu Kuntian 吳昆田 [n.d.]. 1972. "Jisi yili wenda" 繼嗣義例問答 (Questions and answers on establishing heirs). In Sheng Kang, 67: 16a–19a.

Wu Ruikai 伍瑞鍇. 1930. "Lun nüzi caichan jichengquan wenti" 論女子財產繼承權問題 (On the question of the property inheritance rights of daughters), *Funü zazhi*, 16.2 (Feb.): 23–28.

Wu Tan 吳壇 [ca. 1780]. 1992. *Da Qing lüli tongkao jiaozhu* 大清律例通考校注 (Thorough examination of the Qing Code, collated and annotated). Ed. Ma Jianshi 馬建石 and Yang Yutang 楊育棠. Reprint. Beijing: Zhongguo zhengfa daxue chubanshe.

Wujiangxian zhi 吳江縣志 (Gazetteer of Wujiang county) [1747]. 1991. Reprint. Nanjing: Jiangsu guji chubanshe.

Xing Tie 邢鐵. 1992. "Songdai de caichan yizhu jicheng wenti" 宋代的財產遺囑繼承問題 (On the inheritance of property through wills during the Song period), *Lishi yanjiu*, no. 6 (June): 54–66.

Xing'an huilan 刑案匯覽 (Conspectus of penal cases) [1886]. 1968. Reprint. Taibei: Wenhai chubanshe.

Xingtai falü 刑臺法律 (Laws of the judicial bench) [Ming]. 1990. Reprint. Beijing: Zhongguo shudian.

Xinke fabi tianyou 新刻法筆天油 (New edition of "Essentials of Legal Writing"). Qing.

Xinzeng xing'an huilan 新增刑案匯覽 (New supplement to the "Conspectus of Penal Cases") [1886]. 1968. Appendix to *Xing'an huilan*.

Xu Baiqi 徐百齊. 1935. *Minfa jicheng* 民法繼承 (Inheritance in the Civil Code). Shanghai: Shangwu yinshuguan.

Xu Dixin 許滌新 and Wu Chengming 吳承明, eds. 1990. *Zhongguo ziben zhuyi fazhan shi* 中國資本主義發展史 (The history of the development of Chinese capitalism). Vol. 2: *Jiu minzhu zhuyi geming shiqi de Zhongguo ziben zhuyi* 舊民主主義革命時期的中國資本主義 (Chinese capitalism during the period of the old democratic revolution). Beijing: Renmin chubanshe.

Xu Shilin 徐士林. 1906. *Xu Yufeng zhongcheng kanyu* 徐雨峰中丞勘語 (The judgments of Vice Censor-in-Chief Xu Yufeng). Wujin: Li Shi shengyilou.

Xu Xiaoqun. 1997. "The Fate of Judicial Independence in Republican China, 1912–1937," *China Quarterly*, no. 149 (March): 1–28.

Xu zizhi tongjian 續資治通鑑 (Continuation of the "Comprehensive Mirror of Aid in Governance") [n.d.]. 1958. Ed. Bi Yuan 畢沅 et al. Reprint. Beijing: Guji chubanshe.

Xue Yunsheng 薛允升 [1905]. 1970. *Duli cunyi* 讀例存疑 (Doubts remaining after perusing the substatutes). Ed. Huang Tsing-chia [Huang Jingjia] 黃靜嘉. Reprint. Taibei: Chinese Materials and Research Aids Service Center.

Xuzeng xing'an huilan 續增刑案匯覽 (Supplement to the "Conspectus of Penal Cases") [1886]. 1968. Appendix to *Xing'an huilan*.

Yanagida Setsuko 柳田節子. 1995. *Sō Gen shakai keizaishi kenkyū* 宋元社會經濟史研究 (Research on the social and economic history of the Song and the Yuan). Tokyo: Sōbunsha.

———. 1993. "Sōdai no joko" 宋代の女戸 (Female-headed households in the Song period). In *Yanagida Setsuko sensei koki kinen: Chūgoku no dentō shakai to kazoku* 柳田節子先生古稀記念: 中國の伝統社會と家族 (In commemoration of Professor Yanagida Setsuko's seventieth birthday: Traditional society and family in China). Tokyo: Kyūko sho-in, pp. 89–105.

———. 1990. "Sōdai joshi no zaisanken" 宋代女子の財産權 (Female property rights in the Song period), *Hōsei shigaku*, no. 42 (March): 1–14.

———. 1989. "Nansōki kasan bunkatsu ni okeru joshōbun ni tsuite" 南宋代家産分割における女承分について (Female property rights in the division of family property during the Song period). In Kinugawa Tsuyoshi 衣川強, ed., *Ryū Shiken hakushi shōsu kinen Sōshi kenkyū ronshū* 劉子健博士頌壽紀念宋史研究論集 (Collected studies on Song history dedicated to Professor James T. C. Liu in celebration of his seventieth birthday). Tokyo: Dohōsha, pp. 51–62.

Yang Yifan 楊一凡. 1992. *Hongwu falü dianji kaozheng* 洪武法律典籍考證 (Textual research on legal records from the Hongwu reign). Beijing: Falü chubanshe.

Yuan Li 袁俐. 1991. "Songdai nüxing caichanquan shulun" 宋代女性財產權述論 (Detailed account of female property rights in the Song period). In Bao Jialin 鮑家麟, ed., *Zhongguo funü shi lunji xuji* 中國婦女史論集續集 (Collected essays on Chinese women's history, continued). Taibei: Daoxiang chubanshe, pp. 173–213. [Originally published in 1988 in *Songshi yanjiu jikan* 宋史研究集刊 (Collected articles on research on Song history). Hangzhou: Zhejiangsheng shelian tansuo zazhi.]

Zhang Kentang 張肯堂 [1634 (date of Preface)]. 1970. *Xunci* 螢辭 (Words of deep cultivation). Reprint. Taibei: Xuesheng shuju.

Zhang Wuwei 張五緯. 1812 (date of Preface). *Jiang qiu gong ji lu* 講求共濟錄 (A record of striving for the common good).

Zhang Xubai 張虛白. 1930. *Nüzi caichan jichengquan xiangjie* 女子財產繼承權詳解 (Detailed explanation of the property inheritance rights of daughters). Shanghai: Shanghai fazheng xueshe.

Zhang Zhentao 張甄陶 [n.d.]. 1972. "Shi yi min zheng jisi yanyu" 示邑民爭繼祀讞語 (A judgment on a succession dispute to instruct the people of the county). In He Changling, 59: 6b–8b.

Zhao Fengjie 趙鳳喈. 1928. *Zhongguo funü zai falüshang zhi diwei* 中國婦女在法律上之地位 (The legal status of Chinese women). Shanghai: Shangwu yinshuguan.

Zhao Yashu 趙雅書. 1969. *Songdai de tianfu zhidu yu tianfu shouru zhuangkuang* 宋代的田賦制度與田賦收入狀況 (The land tax system and land tax revenue in the Song period). Taibei: Jinghua yinshuguan.

Zhili gaodeng shenpanting pandu jiyao 直隸高等審判廳判牘集要 (Important judgments of the Zhili Superior Court). 1915. 4 vols. Tianjin: Shangwu yinshuguan Tianjin yinshuaju.

Zhong Tizhi 鍾體志. 1890. *Chaisang yonglu* 柴桑傭錄 (A record of my employment in the land of firewood and mulberry). N.p.: Zaoxuetang.

Zhu Jiayuan 朱家源. 1983. "Liang Song shehui jingji guanxi de bianhua yu nongmin jieji" 兩宋社會經濟關系的變化與農民階級 (The transformation of socioeconomic relations and the peasant class in the Song). In Zhuang Zhao 莊昭, ed., *Song shi lunji* 宋史論集 (Collected essays on Song history). N.p.: Zhongzhou shuhuashe, pp. 244–84.

Zhu Shi 朱軾 [n.d.]. 1972. "Zupu jiehuo" 族譜解惑 (Dispelling doubts about lineage genealogies). In He Changling, 58: 16a–17a.

Zongfan tiaoli 宗藩條例 (Regulations on the imperial clan) [1565]. 1994. In Liu Hainian 劉海年 and Yang Yifan 楊一凡, eds., *Zhongguo zhenxi falü dianji jicheng* 中國珍稀法律典籍集成 (Compendium of valuable legal records). Part 2, vol. 1: *Mingdai tiaoli* 明代條例 (Ming regulations). Beijing: Kexue chubanshe, pp. 509–602.

Zuigao fayuan jieshili quanwen 最高法院解釋例全文 (Complete texts of Supreme Court interpretations). 1946. Ed. Guo Wei 郭衛. Shanghai: Shanghai faxue bianyishe.

Zuigao fayuan panli huibian 最高法院判例匯編 (Compendium of Supreme Court decisions). 1929–37. Ed. Shanghai faxue bianyishe 上海法學編譯社. 28 vols. Shanghai: Huiwentang xinji shuju.

Character List

Well-known places, figures, terms, institutions, and individual litigants are not included in this list. Characters for the published works and archives cited are given in the References, p. 201.

aiji	愛繼	bufen nannü	不分男女
aiji zhi ren	愛繼之人	buqu	部曲
anchashi	按察使		
Anci xian	安次縣	Cai Fulin	蔡福林
Anqing fu	安慶府	Cai Hang	蔡杭
		caichan	財產
ban	半	caichan bing ting wei zhu	財產幷聽爲主
baochang	報償		
Baodi xian	寶坻縣	caichan jicheng kaishi	財產繼承開始
Baofeng xian	寶豐縣	caichanquan	財產權
baojia	保甲	caituan faren	財團法人
baozheng	保正	Caizhengbu	財政部
Baxian	巴縣	Changzhou xian	長洲縣
beiyou	卑幼	chanye	產業
benshen de jiefang	本身的解放	cheng	承
benzhi	本支	Cheng Jiong	程迥
bieju	別居	cheng'an	成案
bingji	併繼	Cheng'an xian	成安縣
bingli	併立	chengchan	承產
bo	撥	chengfen	承分
Boping xian	博平縣	chengfen zhi ren	承分之人
bu tongju jifu	不同居繼父	chengguan	承管

chengji	承繼	dang	黨
chengjia	承家	dangshiren	當事人
chengjiquan	承繼權	Danshui ting	淡水廳
chengshou	承受	danxingfa	單行法
chengtiao	承祧	daomai	盜賣
chengzong	承宗	Daxing xian	大興縣
chi	笞	dazong	大宗
chi ling ge shi	敕令格式	di	嫡
chongde baogong	崇德報功	di shu you bie,	嫡庶有別, 義則一
Chongren xian	崇仁縣	yi ze yi	
chuixian	垂涎	diaoqie miedi,	刁妾滅嫡,
chuji (adopted out)	出繼	shanzhu jiazheng	擅主家政
chuji ([court of] first instance)	初級	dibao	地保
chujia	出嫁	dimu	嫡母
chumu	出母	dingfa	定法
cifang	次房	diqi	嫡妻
cimu	慈母	dizi	嫡子
cinü	次女	Dongguang xian	東光縣
ciqi	次妻	Dongwan xian	東莞縣
cixu	次序	Dongxiang xian	東鄉縣
cizi	次子	Dongyang xian	東陽縣
cong jimu jia	從繼母嫁	duodi zhuji	奪嫡逐繼
congyi er zhong	從一而終	duoqizhi	多妻制
cunmingzhe quan	存命者權		
		en	恩
Da Qing	大清	enyi	恩義
Da Qing minshi susonglü cao'an	大清民事訴訟律草案	erfang	二房
		erfang qishi	二房妻室
Da Qing xianxing xinglü	大清現行刑律	ernü	兒女
		ernü fenchan	兒女分產
Da Qing xingshi susonglü cao'an	大清刑事訴訟律草案	ernü ge he de nan zhi ban	兒女各合得男之半
dagong	大功	erqi bingqu	二妻并娶
dahu	大戶	erzi	兒子
Dai Gengxin	戴耕莘	eyi	惡意
daibi yizhu	代筆遺囑		
daibiren	代筆人	fa	法
Dalisi	大理寺	fa li bi sheng	法立弊生
danding	單丁	Fagongtang	法公堂

Falü bianzuan guan	法律編纂館	fushupin	附屬品
Fan Yingling	范應鈴	fuyang	撫養
fang	房	fuzheng	扶正
Fang Dazong	方大琮	Fuzhou fu	撫州府
fangzhi jiansong	防止健訟	fuzi yiti	父子一體
Fazhiju	法制局		
fei jijue zhi dao	非繼絕之道	gaishi	改適
feiji bieli	廢繼別立	gaozheng	告爭
feili	非理	ge cheng ge ye	各承各業
fen	分	gei	給
fen dawang	糞大王	geren sichan	個人私產
fenbie caichanzhi	分別財產制	geren ziyou chufen	個人自由處分
fencai yiju	分財異居	gongchan	公產
fendan	分單	gongkai	公開
fenge yichan	分割遺產	gongtong caichanzhi	共同財產制
fengei	分給	gongtong gongyou	共同共有
fengjue	封爵	gongtong gongzuo	共同工作
fenjia	分家	gongtong shenghuo	共同生活
fenjiadan	分家單	gongxian	貢獻
fu (husband)	夫	gongyou caichan	共有財產
fu (married woman)	婦	gongyouzhe	共有者
fu cheng fufen	婦承夫分	guan (1,000 copper cash)	貫
fu cheng fuye	婦承夫業	guan (official)	官
fu si cong zi	夫死從子	Guangping fu	廣平府
fu wang cong qi	夫亡從妻	Guangzhou fu	廣州府
fu wang qi zai,	夫亡妻在,	guanhu	官戶
cong qi qi	從其妻	guantian	官田
fumu	父母	guaqi	寡妻
funü	婦女	guaqiqie	寡妻妾
funü yundong jueyi an	婦女運動決議案	guinü	閨女
fuqi caichanzhi	夫妻財產制	Guiyang xian	貴陽縣
fuqi yiti	夫妻一體	guizong	歸宗
fuquan	夫權	guofang	過房
furen	婦人	guofang zhi ren	過房之人
furen fu wang wuzi	婦人夫亡無子	guofen zhi ganshe	過分之干涉
shouzhizhe	守志者	guomin geming	國民革命
furen wuzi	婦人無子	guomin guoti	國民國體
fusai ittai	夫妻一體	Guomin zhengfu sifa	國民政府司法
fushi ittai	父子一體	xingzheng weiyuanhui	行政委員會

Haining zhou	海寧州	jiazhu	家主
Haiyan xian	海鹽縣	jiazi	嫁資
haomin	豪民	jiazu gongchanzhi	家族共產制
he cheng fufen	合承夫分	jichan	祭產
Hebei gaodeng fayuan	河北高等法院	jicheng	繼承
diyi fenyuan	第一分院	jicheng caichan	繼承財產
Henan fu	河南府	jicheng yichan	繼承遺產
Hu Ying	胡穎	jicheng zongtiao	繼承宗祧
Huaide xian	懷德縣	jichengbian	繼承編
hujue	戶絕	jichengquan	繼承權
hujueren	戶絕人	jichengren	繼承人
hunqin	婚親	jidan	繼單
		jidi	基地
ji furenzhe bubi zheng	繼婦人者不必爭	jiefu	節婦
ji ren hou	繼人後	jieshi	解釋
ji shengzhe	繼生者	jiezhi ziben	節制資本
ji sizhe	繼死者	jijue	繼絕
jia	家	jijue zisun zhi de	繼絕子孫止得
jiachan	家產	caichan sifen zhi yi	財產四分之一
jiachan wei qing,	家產爲輕,	jimu	繼母
lunli wei zhong	倫理爲重	jingbiao	旌表
jiamai	嫁賣	Jingshi difang	京師地方審判廳
jiamu	嫁母	shenpanting	
jian	賤	Jinhua fu	金華府
Ji'an fu	吉安府	jinqin	近親
Jian'an xian	建安縣	jinqin zunzhang	近親尊長
jianbing zhi jia	兼併之家	jinshi	進士
Jianchang xian	建昌縣	jishang rou	丌上肉
jianghu	匠戶	jishi	繼室
jianmin	賤民	jishu	繼書
jiantiao	兼祧	jizi	繼子
jiantiaozi	兼祧子	jizong	繼宗
Jianyang xian	建陽縣	juehu	絕戶
Jiashan xian	嘉善縣	juekisha	受益者
jiashu	家屬	junfen	均分
jiawu tongyi yu	家務統一於一尊	junhu	軍戶
yizun			
Jiaxing xian	嘉興縣	kazoku kyōsansei	家族共產制
jiazhang	家長	keguan shishi	客觀事實

kehu (serf-tenant)	客戶	mingji zhi ren	命繼之人
kehu (tax household)	課戶	Minlü cao'an	民律草案
koufentian	口分田	Minshi susong fa	民事訴訟法
Kuaiji xian	會稽縣	Minshi susong tiaoli	民事訴訟條例
kyōyūsha	共有者	Minzhengbu zhushi	民政部主事
laojihu	老疾戶	Nanchang shi	南昌市
li (customary practice)	例	nannü pingdeng	男女平等
li (profit)	利	nanzi	男子
li (rites)	禮	naosang zhengji	鬧喪爭繼
li buxia shuren,	禮不下庶人,	neiqin	內親
xing bushang daifu	刑不上大夫	neizhu	內助
Li Jingfang	李經方 (芳)	Ningbo fu	寧波府
Li Weiqing	李惟清	Ningdu xian	寧都縣
liang	良	nü	女
liangmin	良民	nubi	奴婢
lianhe caichanzhi	聯合財產制	nühu	女戶
lidi	立嫡	nüxing	女性
lidi weifa	立嫡違法	nüxu buying zhongfen	女婿不應中分
liefu	烈婦	qijia caichan	妻家財產
liji	立繼	nüzi	女子
Lin'an xian	臨安縣		
ling	令	pangxi xieqin	旁系血親
Linhai xian	臨海縣	panjueli	判決例
Linjiang fu	臨江府	peiou	配偶
linsheng	廩生	pi	批
lisi	立嗣	pici	批詞
Liu Ji	劉基	pincai	聘財
Longxing fu	隆興府	pinfu	姘婦
Luoyang xian	洛陽縣	ping zuzhang	憑族長
lütiao	律條	Pinghu xian	平湖縣
		pingqi	平妻
Ma Fuqi	馬福祺	pingzheng	憑證
Manting Zengsun	幔亭曾孫	pinju	姘居
min fumu	民父母	Poyang xian	鄱陽縣
Minfa qicao	民法起草委員會		
weiyuanhui		qi (wife)	妻
mingfen	名分	qi (breath)	氣
mingji	命繼	qi shoujie zhi wuhou	其守節之無後

qian Qing	前清
Qian Qing xianxing lü	前清現行律
qiangxing fagui	强行法規
qiangzhi guiding	强制規定
qiangzhi zhixing	强制執行
qianqi	前妻
Qianshan xian	潛山縣
Qiantang xian	錢塘縣
qichu	七出
Qidong xian	啓東縣
qie	妾
Qinghe xian	清河縣
Qingjiang xian	清江縣
qinnü	親女
qinshu huiyi	親屬會議
qinshubian	親屬編
qinshufa	親屬法
qinzi	親子
qinzu	親族
qinzu huiyi	親族會議
qiqin	妻親
Qizhou	蘄州
quan Hu jiansong zhi kui	全滬健訟之魁
quanli	權利
Qufu xian	曲阜縣
Renhe xian	仁和縣
ruguan	入官
rumu	乳母
Runzhou	潤州
ruo yi tajun junfen zhi li chu zhi, ernü yu yangzi ge he shou qi ban	若以他郡均分之例處之, 二女與養子各合受其半
san buqu	三不去
san buzheng	三不爭
sancong	三從
Sanfasi	三法寺
sanfu bamu	三父八母
sanyu	三玉
shan	擅
Shanghai dier tequ difang fayuan	上海第二特區地方法院
Shanghai gonggong zujie linshi fayuan	上海公共租界臨時法院
Shangqiu xian	商邱縣
Shangyu xian	上虞縣
Shaoxing fu	紹興府
Shaoyang xian	邵陽縣
She Dusheng	佘篤生
(She) Wande	(佘) 萬德
(She) Wanquan	(佘) 萬全
shenfen	身分
Sheng Xuanhuai	盛宣懷
shengmu	生母
shengyuan	生員
shenhou liji	身後立繼
shenjingbing	神經病
shenshou jiu da, kaikou jiu ma	伸手就打, 開口就罵
shi	氏
shifeng	食封
shinü	使女
shiyetian	世業田
shiyong	使用
shiyong shouyiquan	使用受益權
shouyizhe	受益者
shouzhi	守志
shumu	庶母
shun shuangfu zhi xin	順孀婦之心
Shuntian fu	順天府
si	嗣
sichan	私產
siguan	寺觀
siji	私繼
sili	私立

sima	緦麻	tongyi caichanzhi	統一財產制
sizhe mu wei ming	死者目未瞑	tongyiquan	同意權
sizi	嗣子	tongzong	同宗
Song Lian	宋濂	tuhao lieshen	土豪劣紳
Songming xian	嵩明縣		
Sun Xunchu	孫詢芻	waiqin	外親
suohou zhi qin	所後之親	wangnan	亡男
suoji fumu	所繼父母	weichi qinshu guanxi	維持親屬關系
suosheng fumu	所生父母	weisuo	衛所
suoyouquan	所有權	wu suogui	無所歸
		wufu	無服
Taihe xian	泰和縣	wuguo jiuli	吾國舊例
Taihu ting	太湖廳	wuhouzhe wei hujue	無後者爲戶絕
Taiping xian	太平縣	Wujiang xian	吳江縣
Taixing	泰興	wuqi	無期
tajun	他郡	wuquan	物權
Tang liudian	唐六典	wusheng	武生
tangduan	堂斷	Wuxian	吳縣
tangxiong	堂兄		
tangzhi	堂侄	xi	媳
taotian	逃田	Xi'an fu	西安府
teliufen	特留分	xiancheng	縣丞
teyou caichan	特有財產	Xiangshan xian	象山縣
tezhao	特詔	Xiangtan xian	湘潭縣
tianzhai	田宅	xiangyu	鄉愚
tiao	條	Xianning xian	咸寧縣
tiaoling	條令	xianwei	縣尉
tidian xingyu gongshi	提點刑獄公事	xianxi	嫌隙
tiju changping	提舉常平	Xianxing lü	現行律
ting	聽	xiaogong	小功
tingsang zuzang	停喪阻葬	Xiaojie zhengchan	小姐爭產
Tongcheng xian	通城縣	xiaozong	小宗
tongju	同居	xieqin	血親
tongju gongcai	同居共財	Xin xinglü	新刑律
tongju jifu	同居繼父	Xinchang xian	新昌縣
tongpan	通判	Xingfa	刑法
Tongxian	通縣	Xingshi susong fa	刑事訴訟法
tongxing	同姓	Xingshi susong tiaoli	刑事訴訟條例
tongxing bu tongzong	同姓不同宗	Xinzhu xian	新竹縣

xiongdi	兄弟	yizhu	遺囑
xishi	細事	yizi	義子
Xiuding falü guan	修訂法律館	Yongnian xian	永年縣
Xiushan xian	秀山縣	yu (desire)	欲
Xiuzheng minshi susong fa	修正民事訴訟法	yu (give)	與
		yuehu	樂戶
Xiuzheng xingfa	修正刑法	yueji	越繼
Xiuzheng xingshi susong fa	修正刑事訴訟法	Yuhang xian	餘杭縣
		Yuzhai yizhuang	愚齋義莊
xu (must)	須		
xu (permit)	許	zai fa	在法
Xue Baorun	薛寶潤	zai fa, fumu yi wang,	在法, 父母已亡,
xuezheng	學政	ernü fenchan, nü	兒女分產, 女
xuming daiji	虛名待繼	he de nan zhi ban	合得男之半
		zaishinü	在室女
yangmu	養母	zaishinü yi zi cheng	在室女依子承
yangzi	養子	fu fen fa gei ban	父分法給半
yi	義	zaitang	在堂
yi quan zhenfu zhi zhi	以全貞婦之志	zangai	殘骸
yichan	遺產	zejiquan	擇繼權
yichan jicheng	遺產繼承	zengyu	贈與
yichan jichengren	遺產繼承人	zengyu ziju	贈與字據
yichan zhi chengshou	遺產之承受	zesiquan	擇嗣權
yifu	義父	zexian zeai	擇賢擇愛
yifu yiqi zhi	一夫一妻制	zhai	債
yifu zhi nan	遺腹之男	zhancui	斬衰
yiji	議繼	Zhang Siwei	張四維
Yijia nüzi zhuisu	已嫁女子追溯	Zhang Yong (Guaiya)	張詠 (乖崖)
jicheng caichan	繼承財產	zhangfang	長房
shixing xize	施行細則	zhangqi	杖期
yiju	異居	zhangshang zhu	掌上珠
Yili	儀禮	Zhanxing xin xinglü	暫行新刑律
yili	議立	zhaojie jiaofu	召接腳夫
yin	蔭	zhaotiao	照條
yingfenren	應分人	zhengchan	爭產
yingji	應繼	zhengdao	正道
yingji zhi ren	應繼之人	zhengshi	正室
yingjifen	應繼分	zhixi xieqin	直系血親
Yizheng xian	儀徵縣	zhixi zunshu	直系尊屬

zhixi zunzhang	直系尊長	ziyou zhi chan	自有之產
zhong nan qing nü	重男輕女	zong	宗
zhong zunzhang	眾尊長	zong zunzhang	宗尊長
zhong'an	重案	zongtiao	宗祧
Zhongyang zhengzhi huiyi	中央政治會議	zongtiao jicheng	宗祧繼承
		zongze	總則
zhongyao diwei	重要地位	zonmeishaken	存命者權
zhu	主	zu xiongdi	族兄弟
zhuanquan	專權	zuanji	鑽繼
zhuguan zhi yisi	主觀之意思	Zuigao fayuan	最高法院
zhushi	主事	zuji	阻繼
zi cheng fu fen	子承父分	zulian qiangji	阻殮强繼
zicui	齊衰	zunzhang	尊長
zicui zhangqi	齊衰杖期	zuren	族人
zige	資格	zuye	祖業
zisun	子孫	zuzhi	族侄

Index

Library of Congress Cataloging-in-Publication Data

Bernhardt, Kathryn.
  Women and property in China : 960–1949 / Kathryn Bernhardt.
    p.   cm. — (Law, society, and culture in China)
  Includes bibliographical references and index.
  ISBN 0-8047-3526-3 (cloth : alk. paper)
    1. Inheritance and succession—China—History.   2. Women—Legal
status, laws, etc.—China—History.   3. Right of property—China—
History.   I. Title.   II. Series.
KNN778.B47   1999
346.5105′2—dc21   99-27947

♾ This book is printed on acid-free, archival-quality paper.

Original printing 1999

Last figure below indicates year of this printing:

08   07   06   05   04   03   02   01   00   99

Typeset in Trump Mediaeval by TypeWorks, Tucson, Arizona.